Michael Collins is a qualified chartered management accountant and is a member of the Chartered Institute of Management Accountants (CIMA). He is also a technician member of the Irish Taxation Institute. He has a diploma in economics and is an accredited trainer.

Michael Collins has considerable financial and commercial experience gained in a variety of industry sectors. For over two decades he has worked in various roles in finance, from ledger clerk to financial controller to partner in an accounting practice. In addition, he has many years' experience of providing finance training to a broad range of clients. He has also lectured in business management and accounting.

Do-It-Yourself
Bookkeeping
for Small Businesses

Michael Collins

ROBINSON

ROBINSON

First published in Great Britain in 2015 by Robinson

A CIP catalogue record for this book is available from the British Library.

ISBN 978-1-84528-588-3 (paperback)
ISBN: 978-1-84528-589-0 (ebook)

Typeset in Great Britain by Ian Hughes, Mousemat design Limited
Illustrations by Jerry Goldie, jerrygoldiegraphicdesign.co.uk
Printed and bound in Great Britain by CPI Group (UK) Ltd., Croydon, CR0 4YY

Robinson
is an imprint of
Constable & Robinson Ltd
100 Victoria Embankment
London EC4Y 0DY

An Hachette UK Company
www.hachette.co.uk

www.constablerobinson.com

Dedicated to business people
who require a simple bookkeeping system
to maintain their financial records.

Contents

List of Illustrations

Acknowledgements

I'd like to acknowledge that I wrote this book with the support of some very helpful people, thank you all:

To Karolina-Anna Siedlik, for her machine-like efficiency, insatiable appetite for reviewing material, and supplying reference documents by the truckload!
To Annie Collins, the ultimate silent partner.
To Joanna Collins for her pertinacious encouragement.
To John Love for his advice on the technical aspects of writing.
To Brian Heerey for the use of his critical eye.
To AJE for supplying pertinent reference material.
To Emma Sherry for assistance way beyond the call of duty.
To Giles Lewis for his help dealing with publishing formalities.
To Nikki Read for her prompt and helpful replies to my queries.

To anyone else I forgot to mention, thank you.

Introduction

This book describes a practical and easy-to-implement bookkeeping system. It is not necessary to have any knowledge of finance, accounting or bookkeeping in order to use the Do-It-Yourself Bookkeeping system, and it will enable you to actually do bookkeeping yourself.

DIY Bookkeeping uses flowcharts to illustrate the system. The flowcharts should be used as an anchor from which you can build your knowledge sequentially. There are six primary flowcharts that summarize the entire DIY Bookkeeping system.

Figure 0.1
Flowchart 1 – DIY Bookkeeping System Overview

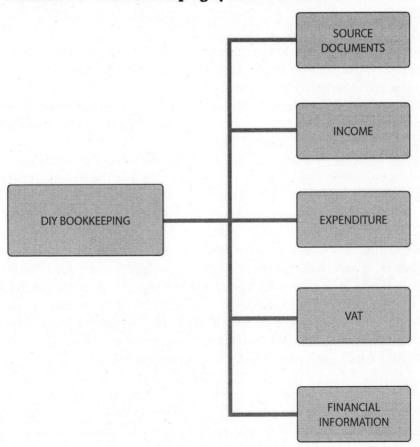

The first flowchart, noted above, identifies the components of the system. The DIY Bookkeeping system begins with processing source documents, such as sales and purchase invoices. The financial transactions identified on the source documents are then categorized as income or expenditure transactions and are recorded accordingly. If the business is VAT (value added tax) registered, then VAT needs to be processed as part of the bookkeeping system. When all financial transactions are recorded for a period, it is possible to create financial information based on the records contained in the DIY Bookkeeping system.

Flowchart 2 illustrates that source documents can be grouped by type for filing and processing purposes. Source documents are documents that record the activities of a business, which can be financial or non-financial. Source documents are the foundation upon which the financial records of a business are built. The source documents flowchart illustrates a non-exhaustive list of the type of documents that can be used to capture financial data concerning the financial transactions of a business. The data contained in the source documents can be used to record financial transactions in the DIY Bookkeeping system, validate the accuracy of the financial records and exercise control over the business.

Flowchart 3 shows that source documents are used to identify the financial transactions that need to be recorded in the DIY Bookkeeping system. These financial transactions are identified as either income transactions or expenditure transactions. Income financial transactions can be further categorized as sales income or non-sales income, while expenditure financial transactions can be further categorized by the type of expenditure.

The financial transactions are then recorded into the daybooks of the business according to transaction type. Daybooks are simply lists of financial transactions, grouped by type. Daybooks are a reference to the traditional method of recording transactions into a physical book, containing rows and columns for analysis, on a daily basis. The term 'doing the books' refers to updating the daybooks of a business to record the financial transactions. Daybooks record basic information relating to transactions; for example, the date, monetary value, the source of the income or recipient of the expenditure.

Income is recorded in the sales daybook or the bank receipts book. The expenditure of a business is recorded in any of the following books, as determined by the type of expenditure: purchases daybook, petty cash book, bank payments book, credit card book, payroll records book.

Flowchart 4 illustrates that a business can either be registered for VAT or not registered for VAT. The DIY Bookkeeping system can be used for both non-VAT-registered businesses and VAT-registered businesses. If a business is registered for

Figure 0.2
Flowchart 2 – Source Documents

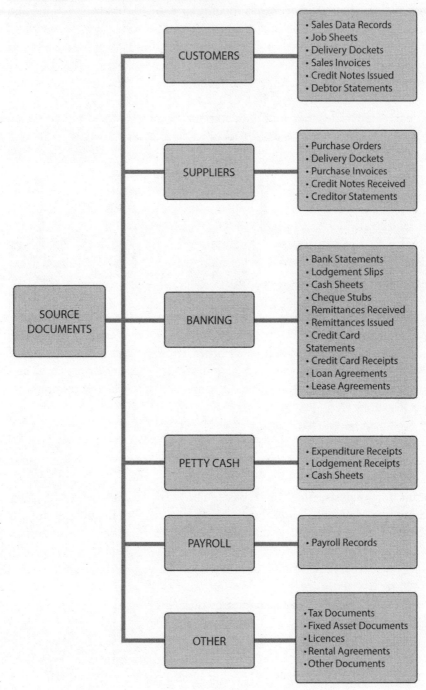

SOURCE DOCUMENTS

CUSTOMERS
- Sales Data Records
- Job Sheets
- Delivery Dockets
- Sales Invoices
- Credit Notes Issued
- Debtor Statements

SUPPLIERS
- Purchase Orders
- Delivery Dockets
- Purchase Invoices
- Credit Notes Received
- Creditor Statements

BANKING
- Bank Statements
- Lodgement Slips
- Cash Sheets
- Cheque Stubs
- Remittances Received
- Remittances Issued
- Credit Card Statements
- Credit Card Receipts
- Loan Agreements
- Lease Agreements

PETTY CASH
- Expenditure Receipts
- Lodgement Receipts
- Cash Sheets

PAYROLL
- Payroll Records

OTHER
- Tax Documents
- Fixed Asset Documents
- Licences
- Rental Agreements
- Other Documents

Figure 0.3 Flowchart 3 – Income and Expenditure

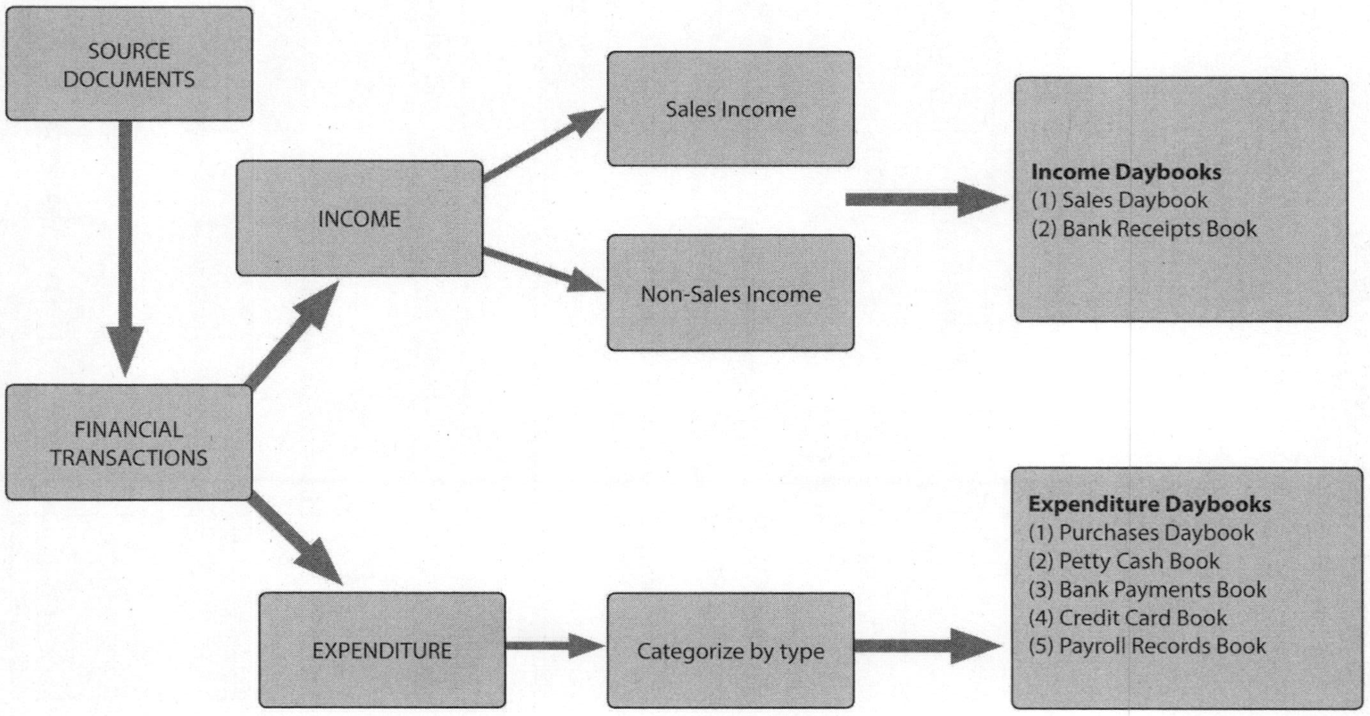

SOURCE DOCUMENTS

FINANCIAL TRANSACTIONS

INCOME

Sales Income

Non-Sales Income

Income Daybooks

(1) Sales Daybook
(2) Bank Receipts Book

EXPENDITURE

Categorize by type

Expenditure Daybooks

(1) Purchases Daybook
(2) Petty Cash Book
(3) Bank Payments Book
(4) Credit Card Book
(5) Payroll Records Book

Figure 0.4
Flowchart 4 – Value Added Tax (VAT)

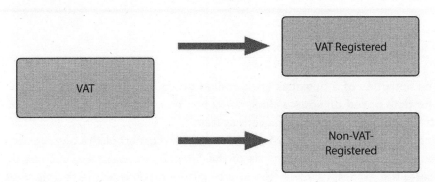

VAT, the bookkeeping system needs to record the VAT element of financial transactions separately, in the relevant daybook. The DIY Bookkeeping system separately identifies VAT for VAT-registered businesses in three daybooks:

• **Sales daybook**
• **Purchases daybook**
• **Petty cash book**

Flowchart 5 shows that financial information can be created at two levels. The DIY Bookkeeping system captures data concerning the financial transactions of a business in the daybooks and this raw data can be used to create financial information. The financial information generated can be at level 1 or level 2. Level 1 financial information relates to key financial figures (KFFs) concerning assets, liabilities, income and expenditure. Level 2 financial information relates to financial statements, i.e., the profit and loss account and balance sheet.

Figure 0.5
Flowchart 5 – Financial Information

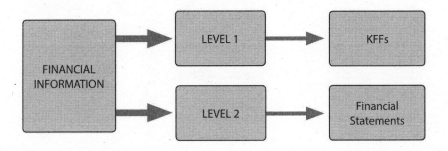

Summary

Flowchart 6 illustrates the components of the DIY Bookkeeping system and the related aspects of each component.

DIY Bookkeeping system summary

- The activities of a business are detailed on source documents
- The data noted on source documents can be used to record the financial transactions in the bookkeeping system
- The financial transactions of a business are recorded in the appropriate daybook. Daybooks list details of the financial transactions, such as the date, the monetary value, the source of the income or the recipient of the expenditure
- If a business is VAT registered, the bookkeeping system needs to identify VAT due or VAT reclaimable
- Financial information can be generated from the financial data recorded in the bookkeeping system
- DIY Bookkeeping is a system that can accommodate all of the above

Figure 0.6 Flowchart 6 –
DIY Bookkeeping System Summary

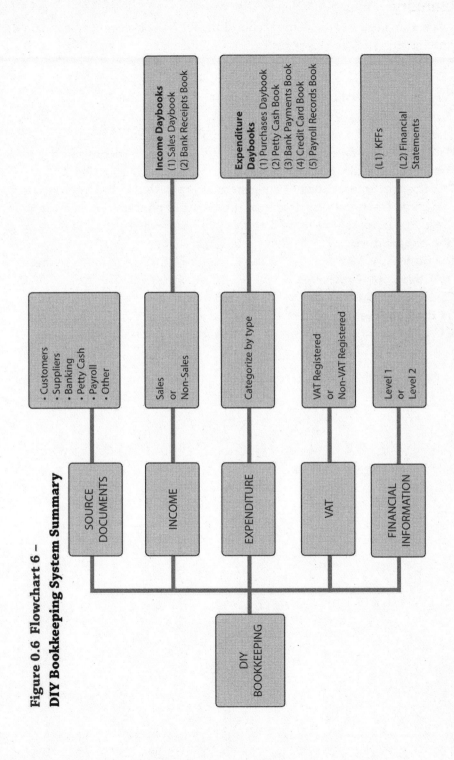

Bookkeeping – overview

CHAPTER 1

How to get the most out of this book

Do-It-Yourself Bookkeeping is a system that can be adapted to virtually any given business. You can choose the level of knowledge you want to acquire regarding the DIY Bookkeeping system. In order to get the most out of this book:

1. Read the introduction as this will give you a clear overview of the DIY Bookkeeping system
2. Decide what level of bookkeeping skill you want to acquire, from level one to level six

> **LEVEL 1**
> Develop a clear understanding of the bookkeeping process
> **READ SECTION 1**

Skill level one will make you aware of the barriers associated with developing an understanding of bookkeeping and how to overcome such barriers. In addition, you will develop a clear overview of bookkeeping as a system and a process.

> **LEVEL 2**
> Learn how to create, process and file source documents
> **READ SECTIONS 1 and 2**

Skill level two will develop your ability to create, process and file source documents so as to maintain control over the business paperwork. As a result of having paperwork filed and processed correctly you will have two options:

(a) Use the source documents to record the financial transactions in the bookkeeping system yourself.
(b) Give the filed and processed paperwork to a third party, such as a bookkeeper or accountant, to record the financial transactions in the bookkeeping system.

> **LEVEL 3**
> Learn how to record income financial transactions
> **READ SECTIONS 1, 2 and 3**

Skill level three will develop your ability to record income financial transactions in the bookkeeping system. The recording of income financial transactions involves the ability to distinguish between sales income and other sources of monetary receipts into a business.

LEVEL 4
Learn how to record expenditure financial transactions
READ SECTIONS 1, 2 and 4

Skill level four will develop your ability to record expenditure financial transactions in the bookkeeping system. The recording of expenditure financial transactions involves the ability to record expenditure according to the method of payment and also the ability to categorize expenditure to aid analysis.

LEVEL 5
Processing Value Added Tax (VAT)
READ SECTIONS 1, 2, 3, 4 and 5

Skill level five will develop your ability to process VAT in order to ascertain VAT due for payment or VAT to be reclaimed.

LEVEL 6
Creating financial information
READ SECTIONS 1, 2, 3, 4, 5 and 6

Skill level six will develop your ability to create financial information from the bookkeeping records.

CHAPTER 2

How to overcome learning barriers associated with bookkeeping

Prior to delving into the detail concerning how to operate a DIY Bookkeeping system, it can be of considerable benefit to reflect on issues that often impede understanding and motivation when dealing with the subject matter. Furthermore, by addressing issues such as incentives, fear of learning, fear of terminology, fear of numbers and fear of complexity at the outset of your studies, you can arm yourself with the necessary knowledge to overcome these obstacles.

IDENTIFYING YOUR INCENTIVES

In order for you to make the effort to learn about bookkeeping there must be an incentive to do so. If you do not have an incentive, you will most likely not put in the effort required to acquire the level of knowledge needed. You need to identify what your incentive is. For example, understanding bookkeeping will:

- Enhance your ability to run your business successfully
- Reduce the accounting costs of your business
- Reduce stress when running your business
- Enhance your ability to identify profit opportunities
- Enhance your ability to identify loss-making activities
- Enable you to control your business better
- Enable you to obtain the best service from your accountant
- Enable you to plan for the future of your business
- Enhance your ability to make more money from your business
- Enhance your ability to survive recessions
- Help you progress in your business education
- Help you contribute more to the organization in which you work
- Increase your promotion prospects
- Give you a greater insight into the organization in which you work
- Improve your employment prospects
- Improve your ability to set up your own business

If none of the above is an incentive for you, it is necessary for you to consider what will act as an incentive. Without at least one incentive, you are unlikely to succeed in your studies of the subject. When you have identified the incentives that will motivate you, remind yourself of them when you run into difficulties. Your incentives will be your motivator to complete the course of study you have started.

> **MICRO TASK**
> Identify THREE incentives you have that will motivate you to learn how to operate a bookkeeping system.

FEAR OF LEARNING

Some people find learning a new subject off-putting. It may be due to any of the following:
- **They do not like to get out of their comfort zone**
- **They fear failure if they cannot develop an understanding of the subject**
- **They lack confidence and do not want to appear foolish**

The way to overcome the fear of learning something new is to focus on the benefits of succeeding. Start with a positive mindset, seek help from others and remind yourself of the incentives you identified at the beginning of the process.

Learning is an active process so it is necessary to engage, read, review, reflect and answer questions. By engaging in learning activities it makes the process of learning more enjoyable, productive and interesting.

FEAR OF TERMINOLOGY

It is easy to be put off a subject when it is shrouded in jargon. However, the problem of bookkeeping jargon can be overcome if the most common terminologies are identified and explained in simple terms. To assist in this endeavour this book clearly explains essential terminology and encourages the reader to relate the terminology to their own business. Furthermore, when dealing with people who degenerate into jargon-laden explanations, it is important to request that they explain terms that you do not understand. Often the case will be that prolific users of jargon are unable to explain financial records in plain language and use jargon to hide this inability. It is important that you do not allow such people to avoid their responsibility to communicate with you clearly.

FEAR OF NUMBERS

A phobia is an irrational fear of something. Many people who are not comfortable dealing with numbers can develop a phobia towards bookkeeping, as they assume bookkeeping is all about numbers. To a point they are correct. However, numbers are just a tool used in bookkeeping to represent a business and the activity in which it is engaged.

In order to overcome a phobia about numbers, and by extension bookkeeping, it is necessary to break down the subject matter into its most basic components. It takes effort to set aside preconceived notions and concentrate the mind on a new subject. However, the reward is worth the effort.

In order to gain an understanding of the fundamentals of bookkeeping it is necessary to study simple examples. If a computer shop that is not VAT registered spends £5,000 to buy several computers from a computer manufacturer to resell to its customers, it will need to make a record of the transaction. The financial transaction could be shown by way of a flowchart as per Figure 2.1.

Figure 2.1
Financial Transaction Flowchart

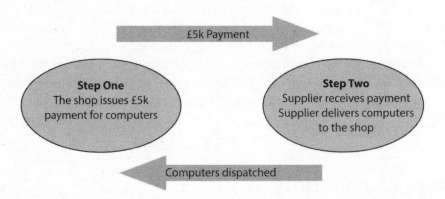

Obviously when many transactions need to be recorded to reflect the trading activities of a business, flowcharts or images would not be viable. However, it is helpful for those who are new to the subject of bookkeeping to use images to visualize what lies behind the numbers recorded in the accounts of a business.

If the purchase of the computers was recorded using conventional bookkeeping it would affect a number of records. The first record to be affected would be the bank payments book. The entry would be triggered by the issuing of the payment to the supplier. The bank payments book records all payment transactions affecting the bank account. The £5,000 payment would be noted as in Figure 2.2:

Figure 2.2
Bank Payments Book

BANK PAYMENTS BOOK		
DATE	Details	Amount
01 July 2014	Computer Manufacturer	£5k

The next record to be affected would be the purchases daybook, a record that deals with purchases made by the business. The entry would be triggered by the receipt of the goods with the purchase invoice. The £5,000 purchase would be noted as in Figure 2.3.

Figure 2.3
Purchases Daybook

PURCHASES DAYBOOK		
DATE	Details	Amount
01 July 2014	Computer Manufacturer	£5k

If you were shown the above financial records without an explanation, it may not be immediately clear what transaction has taken place. The explanation is simplified when the transaction is considered in image form as per Figure 2.1 above. Money leaves the retail business and is given to the computer manufacturer, and in return the retailer receives a consignment of computers.

Whenever presented with a financial transaction, consider what actually lies behind the numbers. Can you visualize what is being detailed? If you can do this, you are in a better position to see the big picture. If the financial transaction relates to a business that has a premises worth £1m, can you see where the premises is located? If a financial transaction relates to a business holding stock to the value of £50,000, where is this stock located: in a shop, in a warehouse? Numbers are less scary when you visualize what they represent.

FEAR OF COMPLEXITY

Bookkeeping for the non-initiated may appear to be complicated, as it is a system that follows certain rules. However once the rules are clearly explained and you attempt to apply them, bookkeeping becomes straightforward.

In the main, bookkeeping is concerned with maintaining records of the financial transactions of a business. In general, a business buys and sells products and/or services and in addition holds assets and liabilities at any given time. Assets are things that a business owns, such as a motor vehicle, and liabilities are debts owed by the business to third parties, such as a loan from a bank.

The information concerning the activities of the business is obtained from source documents, for example sales invoices issued to customers, purchase invoices received from suppliers, bank statements received from banks or creditor statements received from suppliers. All these documents need to be systematically filed in order to create a solid foundation for bookkeeping.

In summary, bookkeeping merely records financial transactions of a business relating to income, expenditure, assets and liabilities, and the information relating to the transactions is generally identified from source documents.

CHAPTER 3

How to understand bookkeeping

Figure 3.1
Simple Finance Model

Bookkeeping at its most basic is a system used to record the financial transactions of a business. The simple finance model above illustrates that a business receives money in and issues money out. Bookkeeping records financial transactions relating to the movement of money in and out of a business. Therefore to understand bookkeeping it is only a matter of having a clear understanding of how to record the financial transactions generated by:

- **Money received or due to be received by a business**
- **Money paid or due to be paid by a business**

BOOKKEEPING EXPLAINED

'Bookkeeping' refers to the traditional method of recording the financial transactions of a business into a book or books. The books used traditionally were hardback books, and more modern hardback books can be recognized by their distinctive red cover and pages set out in rows and columns to aid analysis. These books are often referred to as daybooks, as financial transactions were entered on a daily basis. They record basic information relating to financial transactions, for example the date, the monetary value, the source of the income or recipient of the expenditure.

The financial transactions recorded in the books of a business are ascertained from source documents such as sales invoices, purchase invoices, bank statements, credit card statements, creditors' statements, petty cash vouchers, etc. Integral to robust bookkeeping is a system that facilitates the proper filing and processing of source documents.

With advances in technology the financial transactions of a business can now be maintained on software that replicates the manual bookkeeping system. Software, for example spreadsheets, can easily be configured to set up soft-copy 'books' that record financial transactions.

Specialist accounting software can also be used to record the financial transactions of a business. Such software has the added benefit of other functions that help considerably with the financial management of a business.

In addition, there are a variety of software applications that deal with specific aspects of bookkeeping, for example phone apps, that may be worth considering as part of your bookkeeping system. It is possible to use a hybrid of the aforementioned systems to create a bookkeeping system. This could result in some of the financial records being paper based, some being spreadsheet software based and some being accounting software based.

There are two types of bookkeeping systems:
- **Single-entry bookkeeping**
- **Double-entry bookkeeping**

Both of the above bookkeeping systems literally state the type of bookkeeping involved.

- **Single-entry bookkeeping is a system where each financial transaction of a business is recorded once in the records of a business**
- **Double-entry bookkeeping is a system where each financial transaction of a business is recorded twice in the records of a business, once as a debit and once as a credit**

DIY BOOKKEEPING OVERVIEW

Figure 3.2 identifies the components of the system. The DIY Bookkeeping system starts with processing source documents, such as sales and purchase invoices. The financial transactions identified on the source documents can then be categorized as income or expenditure transactions and are recorded accordingly. If the business is VAT registered, then VAT needs to be processed as part of the bookkeeping system. When all financial transactions are recorded for a period, it is possible to create financial information based on the records contained in the DIY Bookkeeping system.

DIY Bookkeeping uses single-entry bookkeeping to record the financial transactions of a business in the daybooks.

Figure 3.2

Flowchart 1 – DIY Bookkeeping System Overview

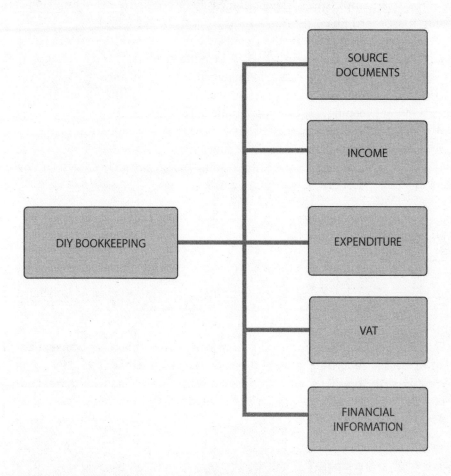

DIY BOOKKEEPING – SOURCE DOCUMENTS

The starting point of the DIY Bookkeeping system is the source documents of the business. Source documents are generated by a business, for instance, sales data records, cash sheets or sales invoices. Alternatively, source documents can be received by a business from third parties, for example purchase invoices or bank statements. Source documents record the activities of a business. The activities recorded can be financial or non-financial. Source documents are the foundation upon which the financial records of a business are built.

The flowchart Figure 3.3 illustrates a non-exhaustive list of the type of documents that can be used to capture financial data. The data contained in the source documents can be used to record financial transactions in the bookkeeping system, validate the accuracy of the financial records and exercise control over the business. Each different type of source document noted in the

Figure 3.3
Flowchart 2 – Source Documents

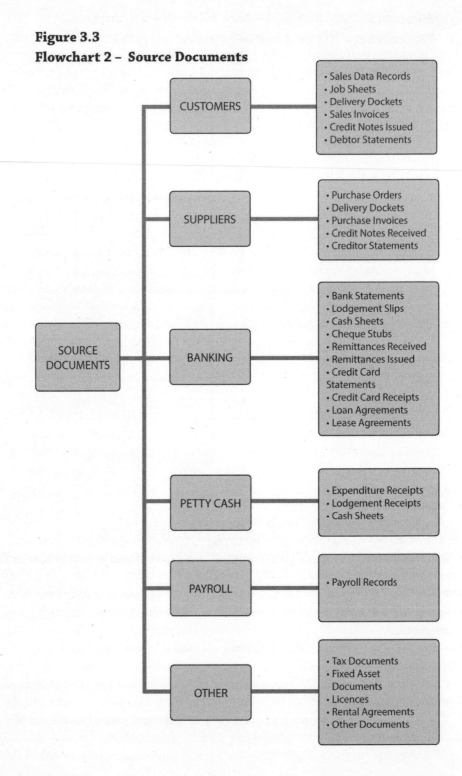

source documents flowchart will be dealt with in detail in chapter 6.

One of the major obstacles to maintaining an effective bookkeeping system is an inability to maintain proper control over source documents. Source documents need to be filed consistently and regularly to avoid backlogs. Source documents need to be filed according to document type. Each business will generate and receive different types of source documents, depending on the type of business they are engaged in.

DIY BOOKKEEPING – SYSTEM EXPLAINED

The relevant source documents are used to identify financial transactions that need to be recorded in the DIY Bookkeeping system. Figure 3.4 illustrates that financial transactions are identified as income transactions or expenditure transactions. Income financial transactions can then be categorized as sales income or non-sales income. Expenditure financial transactions can then be categorized according to expenditure type. The financial transactions can then be recorded into the daybooks of the business according to transaction type. Daybooks are lists of financial transactions, grouped by type of transaction.

Income is recorded in the sales daybook or the bank receipts book. All expenditure of a business is recorded into any of the following books: purchases daybook, petty cash book, bank payments book, credit card book, payroll records book.

DIY Bookkeeping creates lists in daybooks of financial transactions relating to income and expenditure. Using the daybook lists, it is possible to calculate value added tax (VAT) liabilities or refunds and also to generate financial information to manage a business.

DIY Bookkeeping is a system that:
- **Illustrates how to create internal source documents**
- **Illustrates how to process and systematically file source documents**
- **Records financial transactions identified on internal and external source documents**
- **Identifies if the financial transaction relates to income or expenditure**
- **Compiles separate lists of income and expenditure transactions in daybooks**
- **Analyses the daybook lists of income and expenditure into sub-categories**
- **Calculates VAT liabilities or refunds based on the daybook lists of income and expenditure**
- **Creates financial information based on the daybook lists of income and expenditure**

Figure 3.4 Flowchart 3 – Income And Expenditure

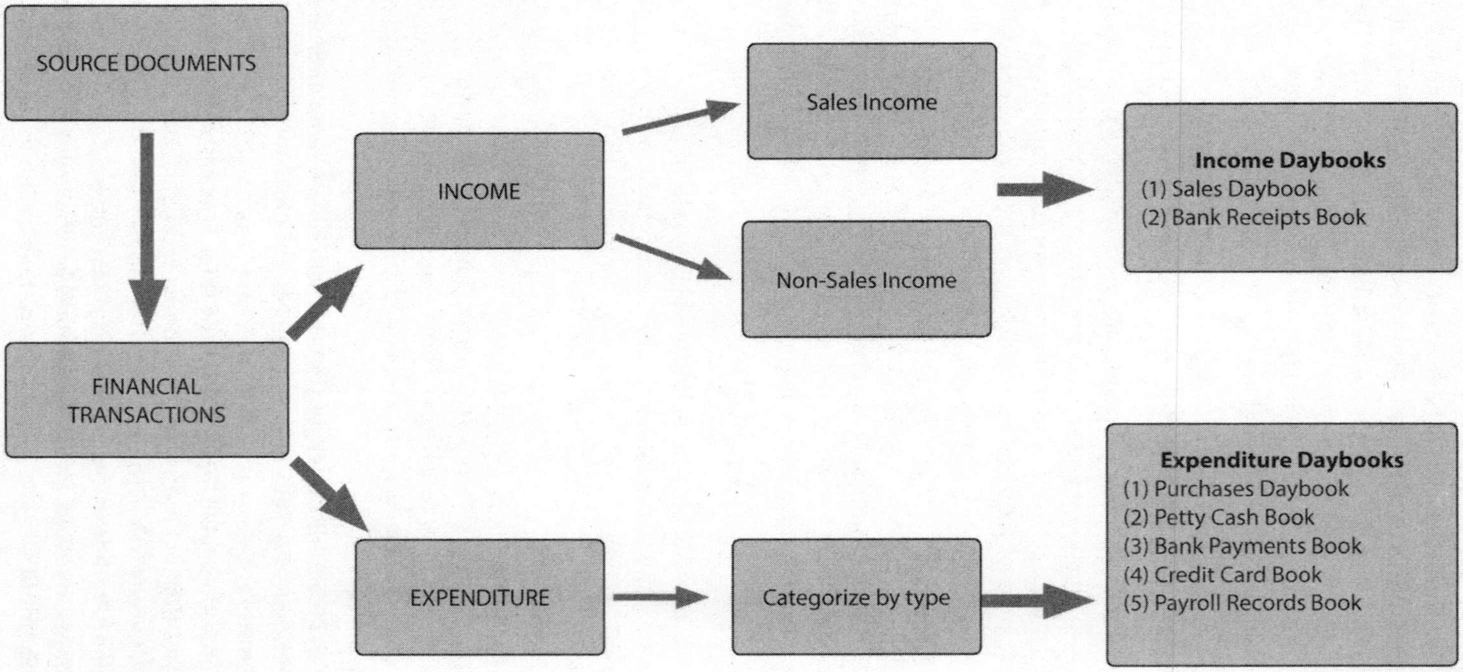

SOURCE DOCUMENTS

FINANCIAL TRANSACTIONS

INCOME

EXPENDITURE

Sales Income

Non-Sales Income

Categorize by type

Income Daybooks
(1) Sales Daybook
(2) Bank Receipts Book

Expenditure Daybooks
(1) Purchases Daybook
(2) Petty Cash Book
(3) Bank Payments Book
(4) Credit Card Book
(5) Payroll Records Book

DIY BOOKKEEPING – INCOME

DIY Bookkeeping is a system that records the financial transactions of a business into two separate categories, income and expenditure. Income and expenditure are then further analysed into sub-categories. Therefore it is vitally important to have a clear understanding of the types of transactions that fall into each category and sub-category.

Income

A business can receive monies in from various sources. The DIY Bookkeeping system refers to 'monies in' as income. Income can originate from two sources (see Figure 3.5):

Figure 3.5
Income

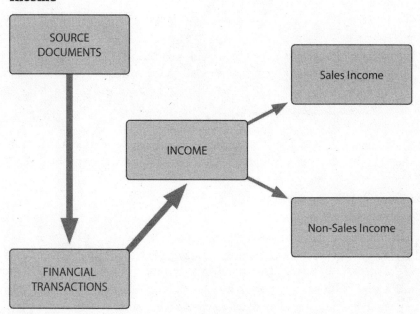

- Sales income is generated by the sale of products and/or services to customers. For example, a business sells a chair it has made to a customer, then the monies relating to this sale is sales income for the business. The source document for this type of sales income would be a sales invoice
- Non-sales income refers to monies NOT relating to the sale of products or services to customers, such as monies invested in the business by the owners or a loan from a financial institution. The source document for monies invested into the business by the owners would be the bank lodgement slip identifying the details of the investment

Figure 3.6
Income – Daybooks

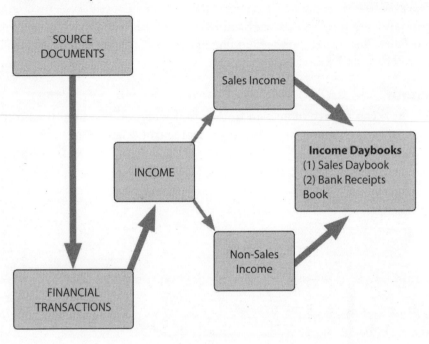

When the income has been categorized as either sales income or non-sales income, then it can be recorded into either of the following daybooks (see Figure 3.6):

- **Sales daybook**
- **Bank receipts book**

Sales daybook

This is a record of all sales generated in a certain period, e.g., a day, a week, a month, a year. The sales daybook lists all sales invoices generated in a period, noting such details as: invoice date, customer name, invoice number, gross monetary value and VAT (if VAT was charged). The sales daybook would also list the details of credit notes issued to customers.

Bank receipts book

This is a record of all monies received from customers to pay for the supply of services and/or products and any other monies received. The bank receipts book will record such details as: the date the money was received, the name of the customer who has paid or the source of the receipt, and the amount of money received.

DIY BOOKKEEPING – EXPENDITURE

Expenditure

Figure 3.7
Expenditure

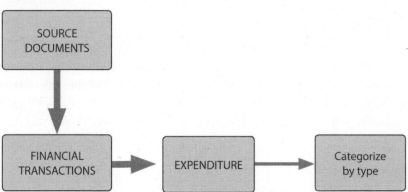

Expenditure is grouped together according to type. For example, in a month several payments issued from a bank account to pay suppliers for goods and services can be grouped by type, i.e., supplier payments, and noted in the bank payments book as purchases daybook payments. See Figure 3.8.

Figure 3.8
Expenditure – Daybooks

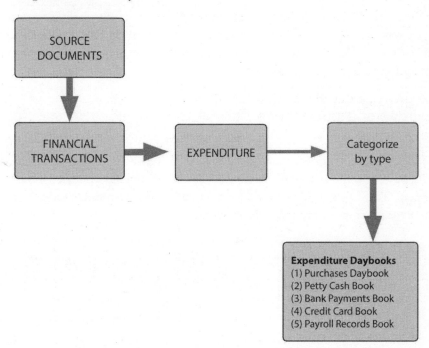

Expenditure is recorded into the following books:
- **Purchases daybook**
- **Petty cash book**
- **Bank payments book**
- **Credit card book**
- **Payroll records book**

Purchases daybook

This is a list of all the services and goods purchased by a business for a given period: a day, a week, a month, a year. The purchases daybook lists all purchase invoices received by the business in a period, noting such details as invoice date, supplier name, invoice number, gross monetary value and VAT, if applicable. The purchases daybook would also list the details of credit notes received from suppliers.

Petty cash book

This is a record of all miscellaneous low-value cash purchases. The details recorded would be the date of the transaction, the value of the transaction and a brief description of the transaction. Miscellaneous cash purchases would be minor expenditure such as the purchase of postage stamps. The petty cash book is also used to record the details of cash lodgements received to fund miscellaneous expenditure.

Bank payments book

This is a record of all payments issued to suppliers for goods or services and any other payments issued from the bank account. The bank payments book records such details as the date of the payment, the name of the supplier/payee being paid and the value of the payment.

Credit card book

This a record of all payments issued to suppliers for goods or services that have been paid with a credit card. This book is similar to the bank payments book. The credit card book needs to record details of transactions, including the date of the payment, the name of the supplier/payee being paid and the value of the payment. The credit card book is also used to record payments made to reduce the balance owing on the credit card account.

Payroll records book

This records details of wages for a given period and identifies such details as net pay per staff member and taxes relating to the payroll.

DIY BOOKKEEPING – VALUE ADDED TAX (VAT)

Figure 3.9
Flowchart 4 – Value Added Tax (VAT)

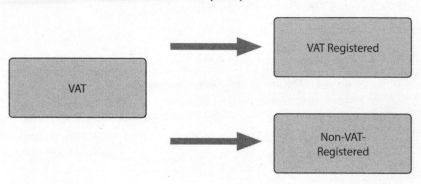

The VAT flowchart, Figure 3.9, illustrates that a business can either be registered for VAT or not registered for VAT. If a business is registered for VAT the bookkeeping system needs to record the VAT element of financial transactions separately. The DIY Bookkeeping system can be used for non-VAT-registered businesses and VAT-registered businesses.

VAT registered

If a business is registered for VAT it must maintain records of sales VAT and purchase VAT in order to calculate if a VAT payment is due to be made or if a VAT refund is due to be reclaimed. The DIY Bookkeeping system separately identifies the VAT element of transactions, in the following daybooks:
• **Sales daybook**
• **Purchases daybook**
• **Petty cash book**

Non-VAT registered

If your business is not required to register for VAT then it will simplify the bookkeeping records that need to be maintained. It will not be necessary to separately identify the VAT element of financial transactions.

DIY BOOKKEEPING – FINANCIAL INFORMATION

Figure 3.10
Flowchart 5 – Financial Information

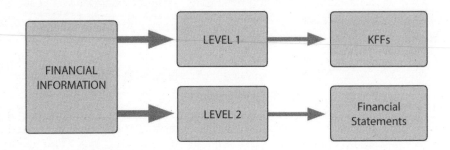

The financial information flowchart, Figure 3.10, illustrates that financial information can be created at two levels. The DIY Bookkeeping system captures data concerning the financial transactions of a business from source documents and this raw data can be used to create financial information. Level 1 financial information relates to key financial figures (KFFs) concerning assets, liabilities, income and expenditure. Assets of a business are resources used by the business. Examples of assets include machinery, motor vehicles or monies owed by third parties to the business, for example monies due from customers. Liabilities of a business are debts due to third parties by the business, for example monies owed to suppliers or banks.

Level 2 financial information relates to financial statements, i.e., the profit and loss account and balance sheet. A profit and loss account details all the sales income for a period less all the expenditure for a period, to identify if a profit or loss has been generated. A balance sheet is a list of assets and liabilities at a particular date.

BOOKKEEPING: SYSTEM IMPLEMENTATION OPTIONS AND ISSUES

In essence, there are three main options to choose from when deciding which type of bookkeeping system to use to record the financial transactions of your business:

- Paper based
- Spreadsheet software based
- Accounting software based

Paper-based systems versus software-based systems

There are advantages and disadvantages associated with both paper-based systems and software-based systems. The choice between each type of system is not mutually exclusive; it is possible to use a paper-based system in conjunction with a software-based system.

You may favour a paper-based system if you have an IT phobia. You may favour a software-based system if you have a high-volume business and require a system that allows for faster processing. You may start off with a paper-based system and then migrate to a software-based system as your business expands.

In order to facilitate your decision-making process, consider the following factors when reviewing which type of system is most appropriate for your business:

Volume of transactions

A low-volume business can be adequately controlled using a paper-based system. A high-volume business is more suited to software-based systems.

Costs

Paper-based systems are cheap to set up and maintain, although it would be important to consider the time spent processing, as this is also a cost to your business. Software-based systems can be relatively inexpensive due to the volume of software providers in the marketplace. Some software packages are even available for free, although their functionality may be restricted.

IT skills level

You need to establish if you have adequate IT knowledge to allow you to set up and run a software-based system. If not, you can learn the basics to get you started. You need to identify the amount of time required for you to increase your IT knowledge levels, as this is also a cost to your business.

Image

You need to be mindful of the image you portray to your customers and suppliers. If you are using a paper-based system, will this make your business look antiquated? Handwritten paperwork does not look as professional as computer-generated documents.

MICRO TASK
Can you explain the following terms?
- Income
- Sales income
- Non-sales income
- Expenditure
See key definitions at the end of this chapter for answers.

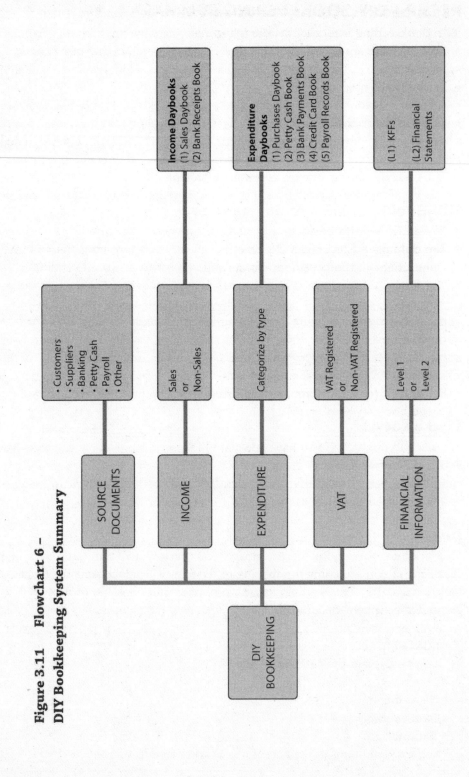

**Figure 3.11   Flowchart 6 –
DIY Bookkeeping System Summary**

DIY
BOOKKEEPING

SOURCE
DOCUMENTS

• Customers
• Suppliers
• Banking
• Petty Cash
• Payroll
• Other

INCOME

Sales
or
Non-Sales

Income Daybooks
(1) Sales Daybook
(2) Bank Receipts Book

EXPENDITURE

Categorize by type

**Expenditure
Daybooks**
(1) Purchases Daybook
(2) Petty Cash Book
(3) Bank Payments Book
(4) Credit Card Book
(5) Payroll Records Book

VAT

VAT Registered
or
Non-VAT Registered

FINANCIAL
INFORMATION

Level 1
or
Level 2

(L1) KFFs

(L2) Financial
Statements

RECAP – DIY BOOKKEEPING SUMMARY

DIY Bookkeeping is focused on the following:
- **Source documents**
- **Income**
- **Expenditure**
- **VAT**
- **Financial information**

Figure 3.11, above, illustrates the components of the DIY Bookkeeping system and the related aspects of each component.

DIY Bookkeeping system summary

- **The activities of a business are detailed on source documents**
- **The data noted on source documents can be used to record the financial transactions in the bookkeeping system**
- **The financial transactions of a business are recorded in the appropriate daybook. Daybooks list details of the financial transactions, such as the date, the monetary value, the source of the income or recipient of the expenditure**
- **If a business is VAT registered, the bookkeeping system needs to identify VAT due or VAT reclaimable**
- **Financial information can be generated from the financial data recorded in the bookkeeping system**
- **DIY Bookkeeping is a system that can accommodate all of the above**

Key DIY Bookkeeping definitions

Income – money actually received or money due to be received, relating to sales income or non-sales income.

Sales income – income relating to the sale of products and/or services.

Non-sales income – income not relating to the sale of products and/or services.

Expenditure – payments actually issued, such as a payment issued from a bank account or expenditure incurred, such as the receipt of a purchase invoice recorded in the purchases daybook.

SECTION 2

Source documents

CHAPTER 4

How to create source documents – sales invoices/receipts

Figure 4.1
Sales Invoices/Receipts

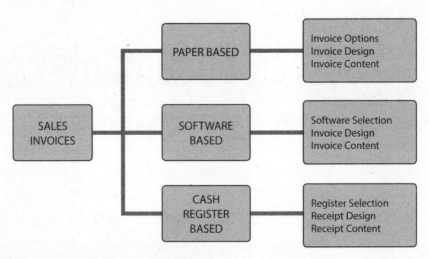

SALES INVOICES – OVERVIEW

A sales invoice is a document that records the details of services rendered and/or goods supplied to a customer. The sales invoice details the monetary amount due from the customer for services rendered and/or goods supplied.

The first decision you need to make in relation to sales invoices is how they will be generated. Will the sales invoice be produced on a manual paper-based system or a software-based system?

The advantages and disadvantages of each system are detailed below:

Paper-based system

Advantages:

- Cheap
- Easy to use
- Easy to set up

Disadvantages:
- **Can be time consuming when sales volume increases**
- **Can create an unprofessional image with customers**
- **Can lead to calculation mistakes**

Software-based system

Advantages:
- **Relatively cheap**
- **Easy to use if familiar with basic software**
- **Easy to set up if familiar with basic software**
- **Looks more professional**

Disadvantages:
- **Need to maintain back-ups**
- **Need to purchase software**
- **Need to learn how to use software if you have not used it previously**

SALES INVOICES – PAPER BASED

The options available for recording sales invoices using a paper-based system are as follows:

Option 1 – use a standard pre-printed invoice book (available at most stationery shops). Pre-printed invoice books come in a variety of designs and formats. They can be single page, duplicate or triplicate. Therefore you need to decide which is the most appropriate for your business.

The most common choice is to opt for a duplicate invoice book with the invoices pre-numbered. This allows you to give a copy invoice to your customer and retain a duplicate of the invoice in the book.

These types of invoice books normally have sufficient scope to record all relevant details of any given sale of a product or service. Details that would need to be noted include:
- **Name and address of your business**
- **Customer name and address**
- **Details of services rendered or quantity and description of goods supplied**
- **Unit price, total price, price excluding VAT or price including VAT, depending on whether your business is VAT registered or not**

The drawback of this type of invoicing is that you need to handwrite the details of your business and of the customer in the book each time an invoice is issued. In addition, you also need to handwrite the details of the sale and manually calculate the value of the sale.

It may be the case that you choose to start with a paper-based invoicing system in the beginning, with the intention of progressing to a software-based invoice system in the future.

Option 2 – design an invoice template and order a bespoke printed invoice book from a printer.

If you would like to use a paper-based invoice system that is tailored to your exact requirements, then you can design an invoice template and order it from a professional printer. This will enable you to have the exact layout you want and allow you to have your company details pre-printed on the sales invoices. Additional details can also be noted, like your VAT number (if VAT registered), contact details and website address.

SALES INVOICES – SOFTWARE BASED

Software selection
The options available for recording sales invoices using a software-based system are as follows:
- **Option 1 – word processing software**
- **Option 2 – spreadsheet software**
- **Option 3 – phone app software**
- **Option 4 – accounting software**

Option 1 – word processing software
Word processing software will allow you to create a re-usable invoice template that will hold basic information, avoiding the need to re-input details; for example, contact details and the business VAT number if VAT registered.

Option 2 – spreadsheet software
Spreadsheet software will allow you to create a re-usable invoice template that will hold basic information, avoiding the need to re-input details, such as contact details and the business VAT number if VAT registered. In addition, spreadsheet software will enable calculations to be processed quickly and accurately.

Option 3 – phone app software
Mobile phone applications – there are a number of mobile phone apps available, with varying degrees of sophistication, allowing you to produce invoices on your phone and forward these to your customers.

Option 4 – accounting software
Accounting software will allow you to create an invoice template that will hold basic

information, avoiding the need to re-input details; such as contact details and the business VAT number if VAT registered. In addition, accounting software will enable calculations to be processed quickly and accurately. Furthermore, accounting software will enable customer details to be retained on file so a record of all sales transactions can be maintained. There is a wide variety of accounting software packages available to choose from. In order to select the most appropriate accounting software package, you need to establish your budget and your requirements.

Making a choice from the options noted above depends on several factors, including:
- Cost of software and the budget you have available
- IT skills you possess
- Volume of transactions
- Information requirements of your business

SALES INVOICES – CONTENT

Invoice content

The information that should be detailed on your invoices comprises two elements:
1. Essential content – this is the bare minimum that you should detail on your invoice, noting details of your business, your customer's details, a description of the sale and the monetary value of the transaction
2. Optional content – this can include additional detail to communicate supplementary information that may facilitate payment or further business with the customer

Invoice content – if your business is NOT registered for VAT

Detailed below is a non-exhaustive list for you to consider in relation to your invoices:

Essential content
- Name of your business
- Address of your business
- Contact details of your business: phone, email, website
- Customer name and address
- Date of invoice
- Sequential invoice number
- Details of services rendered or goods supplied
- Fee for services rendered or price of goods supplied
- Total amount due from customer

Optional content
- Payment terms
- Retention of title condition advising ownership of goods does not pass until payment has been received in full
- Details of discount if payment is made prior to credit terms
- Bank details to allow your customer to issue payment directly to your business bank account
- Terms of trading – detailing the terms and conditions relating to sales transactions
- Details of any special offers your business is currently promoting

Invoice content – if your business is registered for VAT

Detailed below is a non-exhaustive list for you to consider in relation to your invoices:

Essential content
- Name of your business
- Address of your business
- Contact details of your business: phone, email, website
- VAT registration number of your business
- Customer name and address
- Date and tax point of invoice
- Description of the supply of services and/or product(s)
- Sequential invoice number
- Value of services rendered or goods supplied excluding VAT
- VAT rates charged
- Total value of VAT relating to the supply of services or goods supplied
- Total value of services rendered or price for goods supplied including VAT

Optional content
- Payment terms
- Retention of title condition advising ownership of goods does not pass until payment has been received in full
- Details of discount if payment is made prior to credit terms
- Bank details to allow your customer to issue payment directly to your business bank account
- Terms of trading – detailing the terms and conditions relating to sales transactions
- Details of any special offers your business is currently promoting

SALES INVOICES – DESIGN

Design issues you need to consider concerning sales invoices relate to:

Contact details – you need to ensure that your business contact details are clearly and prominently displayed on the invoice.

Document title – you need to ensure that the word 'invoice' is prominently displayed on the document, to ensure there is no confusion concerning the document. The word invoice should be displayed in large typeface.

The colour of the paper – it may help to use an unusual colour to make your invoices stand out from the crowd. Your choice of paper colour may be limited if you use duplicate invoice books.

Logos – if you have a business logo you should have it printed on your invoice to promote your brand.

Paper quality – you need to select paper that is of sufficient quality and not flimsy to handle.

Page size – you need to choose the size of the invoice paper from a variety of options; for example, A4, A5 or anything in between.

Invoice numbering – you may not want to start your first invoice number with the number '1' as this would indicate to customers that your business is a new start-up. You could choose to issue your first invoice at '1001', which would create the impression that your business has issued over a thousand invoices.

Font size/style – you need to have the font size/style set to ensure it is easy to read and pleasing to the eye. If using paper-based duplicate books, ensure your handwriting is clearly legible.

Font colour – you need to choose a font colour that is clear, clean and crisp, making it easy to read the text.

Sales invoices – examples

Figure 4.2 IT Consultancy Services – Example Invoice – Word Processing Software

IT CONSULTANCY SERVICES

Silicon House, Unit 445, Main Street, Big City, Post Code
Phone 00 44 20 1234 1234
VAT No. 1234 56789
E mail: info@itconsultancyservices445.com
www.itconsultancyservices445.com

INVOICE

CLIENT
Sunbeam
Suite 9
River Road
Corporate Park
Post Code

INVOICE NO: 1001

DATE: 01/02/13

CUSTOMER REF: SUNRIV

DETAILS	Net	VAT 20%	Amount
Fees for services rendered:			
February 2013 8 hours x £ 50	£400.00	£80.00	£480.00

TOTAL DUE   £480.00

TERMS: 30 days from date of invoice

PAYMENT:
Account Name   IT Consultancy Services
Account Number   45632145
Sort Code   25-35-80

Figure 4.3 IT Consulting Services – example invoice – spreadsheet software

IT Consultancy Services

Silicon House, Unit 445, Main Street, Big City, Post Code
Phone 00 44 20 1234 1234
Email: info@itconsultancyservices445.com
www.itconsultancyservices445.com

INVOICE

CLIENT		INVOICE NO:	1001
Sunbeam			
Suite 9		DATE:	01/02/2013
River Road			
Corporate Park		CUSTOMER REF:	SUNRIV
Post Code			

DETAILS	Amount
Fees for services rendered:	
February 2013 8 hours x £50	£400.00
TOTAL DUE	£400.00

TERMS: 30 days from date of invoice

PAYMENT:

Account Name	IT Consultancy Services
Account Number	45632145
Sort Code	25-35-80

SALES RECEIPTS – CASH REGISTERS

If your business is retail based, a cash register will accommodate sales record keeping and produce receipts to be given to your customers. There are many options available when selecting a cash register. The choice will depend on funds available and functionality required.

A basic till will cost you less initially but may involve more work overall when producing information for sales analysis and VAT recording. A sophisticated till will cost more initially but should reduce work overall when producing information for sales analysis and VAT recording.

SALES RECEIPTS – DESIGN

The options available to you concerning the layout and design of receipts to be issued to the customer will depend on the cash register you purchase. Some cash registers are very basic and do not allow for any alterations to the layout and design of receipts. More sophisticated cash registers can offer options to alter the layout and design of receipts.

SALES RECEIPTS – CONTENT

The information that should be detailed on your sales receipts comprises two elements:

1. Essential content – this is the bare minimum that you should detail on your receipts
2. Optional content – this can include additional supplementary information

Receipt content – if your business is NOT registered for VAT

Detailed below is a non-exhaustive list for you to consider in relation to your sales receipts:

Essential content
- Name of your business
- Address of your business
- Contact details of your business: phone, email, website
- Date of the supply/transaction
- Details of services rendered and/or goods supplied
- Fee for services rendered/goods supplied
- Total amount due from customer

Optional content
- Details of special offers

- Discount deals
- Advertisements

Receipt content – VAT-registered business

Detailed below is a non-exhaustive list of contents to be considered in relation to VAT receipts for a supply that does not exceed £250:
- Name of your business
- Address of your business
- VAT registration number of your business
- Contact details of your business: phone, email
- Date of receipt, tax point
- Description of the supply of services and/or products
- VAT rates charged
- Total fee for services rendered or price for goods supplied including VAT

Optional content
- Details of special offers
- Discount deals
- Advertisements

> MICRO TASK
> - Compare the contents of your invoices/receipts to the invoice/receipts contents listed above
> - Establish if you need to include additional content on your invoices
> - Consider if you need to make any changes to the design of your invoices/receipts based on the above.

CHAPTER 5

How to create source documents – cash sheets

Figure 5.1
Cash Sheets

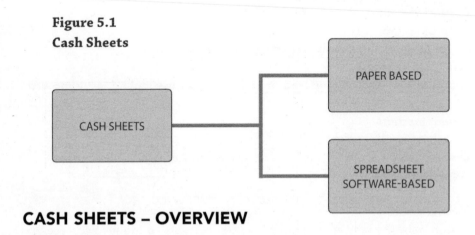

CASH SHEETS – OVERVIEW

A cash sheet is a document used by a business that generates cash sales, such as a retail business. A cash sheet has three main functions:

1. It creates a control check on cash generated from cash sales
2. It identifies and records cash expenditure from cash sales
3. It identifies cash transferred from cash sales to petty cash

A cash sheet records cash sales receipts less cash expenditure, and cash lodgements banked. It also details information such as the date of cash sales receipts and the details of any cash spent from these cash sales receipts. The total of all cash sales receipts less all cash expenditure from these cash sales receipts for a given period, say a day or a week, should equal the value of cash lodged into the business bank account.

Depending on the type of business you are running, you can record cash expenditure from cash sales in a variety of ways:

- You can record cash payments from cash sales manually; i.e., maintaining a handwritten list of all cash payments from cash sales on paper-based cash sheets for a given period
- You can use basic software; for example, a spreadsheet-based cash sheet, to record lists of cash payments from cash sales for a given period

The layout and detail contained on a cash sheet will differ from business to business due to the different circumstances that can exist.

CASH SHEETS – ILLUSTRATION FOR A NON-VAT-REGISTERED BUSINESS

A cash sheet can be handwritten or computer generated on a spreadsheet. A cash sheet normally details a period of a week.
Figure 5.2 details the following:

Figure 5.2
Cash Sheet Example Paper Based No VAT

CASH SHEET										
Week Beginning										
1	2	3	4	5	6	7	8	9	10	11
	Total Sales As per Z report	Sales Non Cash	Sales Cash	Less Wages	Less Drawings	Less Other	Total Deductions T/F to Petty Cash	Net Cash	Cash lodged lodged at bank	Cash lodgement date
Monday										
Tuesday										
Wednesday										
Thursday										
Friday										
Saturday										
Sunday										
Total										

Column 1
The days of the week are listed.

Column 2
Total sales as per the Z report are to be noted for each day of the week in this column. The Z report is a basic report generated by the till/cash register that identifies all the sales for a given day. The sales figure from the Z report normally includes all sales, i.e., cash sales and debit/credit card sales.

Column 3
Non-cash sales are recorded in this column. Non-cash sales are sales paid by customers using debit/credit cards.

Column 4
Cash sales only are recorded in this column. Cash sales only are sales paid by customers using actual cash.

Column 5
Payments of staff wages from cash sales are noted in this column.

Column 6
Monies withdrawn for personal use from cash sales by the owner(s) of a business are known as drawings. Drawings from cash sales are recorded in this column.

Column 7
Cash sales spent on any other item not falling into any of the aforementioned categories are recorded in this column.

Column 8
The total of all deductions from cash sales, i.e., wages, drawings and other, are noted in this column. This total is referred to as total deductions transferred to petty cash. The effect of this is as follows:
- **The total of all deductions is a receipt of monies into petty cash from cash sales**
- **The total of all deductions is an expense from petty cash as per the detail noted; i.e., payment of wages, payment of drawings and payment of any other items**

Column 9
Net cash is the sales cash only figure noted in column 4 less column 8; i.e., the total of deductions transferred to petty cash.

Column 10
Cash lodged at bank is the total of monies lodged at the bank on any given day. The figure in this column can be monies for a single day of net cash or a combination of days.

Column 11
This column is used to record the actual date that cash is lodged into the bank.

CASH SHEETS – ILLUSTRATION FOR A VAT-REGISTERED BUSINESS

Similarly, in Figure 5.3 the columns detail the following:

Column 1
The days of the week are listed.

Column 2
This column records the value of sales excluding VAT.

Figure 5.3
Cash Sheet Example Paper Based – VAT

CASH SHEET													
Week Beginning													
1	2	3	4	5	6	7	8	9	10	11	12	13	14
	Sales Ex VAT	VAT Amount Rate 1	VAT Amount Rate 2	Total Sales As per Z report	Sales Non Cash	Sales Cash	Less Wages	Less Drawings	Less Other	Total Deductions T/F to Petty Cash	Net Cash	Cash lodged at bank	Cash lodgement date
Monday													
Tuesday													
Wednesday													
Thursday													
Friday													
Saturday													
Sunday													

Column 3

This column records the value of sales VAT relating to goods/services at a particular VAT rate, for example 20%.

Column 4

This column records the value of sales VAT relating to goods/services at a particular VAT rate, for example 0%.

> **NOTE: Sales VAT columns need to be inserted as appropriate, depending on the products and services being sold.**

Column 5

Total sales as per the Z report are to be noted for each day of the week. The Z report is a basic report generated by the till/cash register that identifies all the sales for a given day. The sales figure from the Z report normally includes all sales; i.e., cash sales and debit/credit card sales.

Column 6

Non-cash sales are recorded in this column. Non-cash sales are sales paid by customers using debit/credit cards.

Column 7

Cash sales only are recorded in this column. Cash sales only are sales paid by customers using actual cash.

Column 8
Payments of staff wages from cash sales are noted in this column.

Column 9
Monies withdrawn for personal use from cash sales by the owner(s) of a business are known as drawings. Drawings from cash sales are recorded in this column.

Column 10
Cash sales spent on any other item not falling into any of the aforementioned categories are recorded in this column.

Column 11
The total of all deductions from cash sales; i.e., wages, drawings and other, are noted in this column. This total is referred to as total deductions transferred to petty cash. The effect of this is as follows:
- **The total of all deductions is a receipt of monies into petty cash from cash sales**
- **The total of all deductions is an expense from petty cash as per the detail noted; i.e., payment of wages, payment of drawings and payment of any other items**

Column 12
Net cash is the sales cash only figure noted in column 7 less column 11; i.e., the total of deductions transferred to petty cash.

Column 13
Cash lodged at bank is the total of monies lodged at the bank on any given day. The figure in this column can be monies for a single day of net cash or a combination of days.

Column 14
This column is used to record the actual date that cash is lodged into the bank.

CASH SHEETS – HOW TO SET UP A PAPER-BASED CASH SHEET
What do you need to set up a paper-based cash sheet?
1. **A lever arch folder to file Z reports (i.e., cash register daily sales reports printouts)**
2. **An accounts analysis notepad to record cash sales receipts, cash expenditure and bank lodgements**

Set-up

- The spine of the lever arch folder should be clearly marked as 'Cash Sales' and also the financial year should be noted on the spine, e.g., 'Year 2014', so it is clearly visible
- This folder should be subdivided into twelve months for the financial year, e.g., January to December
- The accounts analysis notepad being used as a cash sheet should have the appropriate headings noted
- The headings noted in the columns of the cash sheet will depend on the circumstances of the business, relating to items like VAT or the type of cash expenditure incurred
- Standard column headings relevant to all businesses would be as follows:
  - Day/date of transaction
  - Total sales figure for each day as per Z report from cash register
  - Sales non-cash – the value of the sales that was paid by credit cards, debit cards, etc.
  - Sales cash – the value of sales that was paid by physical cash
  - Expenditure categories, for example wages, i.e., monies taken from cash sales to pay staff in cash; drawings, i.e., monies taken by the owner(s) of the business for private use; and other, a heading to capture all cash expenditure that does not fit into any other category
  - Total deductions transferred to petty cash, i.e., monies taken from cash sales to pay for items like wages, drawings, other
  - Net cash – the amount of cash remaining when cash expenditure has been deducted from cash sales
  - Cash lodged at bank – the amount of actual cash lodged at the bank
  - Cash lodgement date – the actual date the cash was lodged at the bank
  - Specific column headings based on the circumstances of a business would be as follows: sales excluding VAT amount; VAT amounts subdivided into specific VAT rates

CASH SHEETS – HOW TO SET UP A SPREADSHEET SOFTWARE-BASED CASH SHEET

What do you need to set up a spreadsheet software-based cash sheet?

1. A lever arch folder to file Z reports (i.e. cash register daily sales reports printouts)
2. A computer
3. Spreadsheet software installed on computer

Set-up

- The spine of the lever arch folder should be clearly marked as 'Cash Sales' and also the financial year should be noted on the spine, e.g., 'Year 2014', so it is clearly visible
- This folder should be subdivided into twelve months for the financial year, e.g., January to December
- A new spreadsheet file should be set up to be used as a cash sheet and should have the appropriate headings noted in columns
- The headings noted in the columns of the cash sheet will depend on the circumstances of the business, relating to items such as VAT or the type of cash expenditure incurred
- Standard column headings relevant to all businesses would be as follows:
  ‣ Day/date of transaction
  ‣ Total sales figure for each day as per Z report from cash register
  ‣ Sales non-cash – the value of the sales that was paid by credit cards, debit cards, etc.
  ‣ Sales cash – the value of sales that was paid by physical cash
  ‣ Expenditure categories, for example wages, i.e., monies taken from cash sales to pay staff wages in cash; drawings, i.e., monies taken by the owner(s) of the business for private use; and other, a heading to capture all cash expenditure that does not fit into any other category
  ‣ Total deductions transferred to petty cash, i.e., monies taken from cash sales to pay for items like wages, drawings, other
  ‣ Net cash – the amount of cash remaining when cash expenditure has been deducted from cash sales
  ‣ Cash lodged at bank – the amount of actual cash lodged at the bank
  ‣ Cash lodgement date – the actual date the cash was lodged at the bank
  ‣ Specific column headings based on the circumstances of a business would be as follows: sales excluding VAT amount; VAT amounts subdivided into specific VAT rates

CASH SHEETS – HOW TO OPERATE A CASH SHEET

The process to operate a cash sheet using a paper-based system or a spreadsheet system is virtually the same. The only difference is the paper-based system involves handwriting the entries onto paper and the spreadsheet system involves keying entries into a computer.

Step 1 – Run Z report

At the close of business each day, a Z report should be printed from the cash register. The end-of-day Z report will detail the total sales for the day. It will also detail the composition of the sales for the day; i.e., how sales were paid for by customers, for example cash, credit card, debit card, etc.

Step 2 – Input details

The total daily sales figure should be entered onto the cash sheet in the column headed 'Total Sales as per Z report'. If the business is VAT registered then details of the sales excluding VAT and the amount of VAT charged at different rates will need to be entered.

The value of sales paid by non-cash means (credit card, debit card, etc.) should be entered into the cash sheet in the column headed 'Sales Non-Cash'.

The value of sales paid by cash should be entered into the cash sheet in the column headed 'Sales Cash'.

Step 3 – File Z report

After details of sales have been entered onto the cash sheet as described above, the Z report should be marked with the letter 'E' with a circle around it in red ink, to identify that the sales details have been recorded on the cash sheet. The Z report should then be filed in the 'cash sales' lever arch file for the relevant period.

Step 4 – Record expenditure as required

If no money is taken from cash sales, then the cash sales should be lodged at the bank. This will mean that the 'Sales Cash' column on the cash sheet will equal the 'Net Cash' column.

If money has been taken from cash sales, then the details must be recorded on the cash sheet.

If cash has been taken from cash sales to pay for wages, then the value of the cash taken should be recorded in the column 'Less Wages'.

If cash has been taken from cash sales by the owner(s) of the business for private use, then the value of the cash taken should be recorded in the column 'Less Drawings'.

If cash has been taken from cash sales to pay for any other outlay not relating to drawings or wages, then it should be recorded in the column 'Less Other'.

The total of all monies taken from cash sales for such items as wages, drawings, other, should be totalled and the figure should be inserted into the column 'Total Deductions Transferred to Petty Cash'.

NOTE: The value of monies entered into the 'Total Deductions Transferred to Petty Cash' column on the cash sheet also needs to be recorded in the petty cash book as follows:

• As a receipt of cash paid into petty cash, i.e., monies available to spend

• As expenditure recorded as per the cash sheet, detailing how the money was spent, for example wages, drawings, other

---

Step 5 – Record details of cash lodgement(s)

When a cash lodgement is made at the bank the actual amount of cash lodged should be recorded on the cash sheet on the day/date it was lodged.

CASH SHEETS – ILLUSTRATIVE EXAMPLE, NO VAT

This illustrative example is applicable to both a paper-based cash sheet system and a spreadsheet software-based cash sheet system.

Simon operates as a sole trader barber, with one part-time staff member. He also sells hair-related products. The business is not registered for VAT and operates from a city centre shop. During any given week he will sell products and services to his customers.

During a week in March the following activities took place:

1. Monday: the shop was closed
2. Tuesday: total sales as per the Z report from the till were £240, of which £40 was paid by credit cards/debit cards; the balance of £200 was paid by cash. Simon took £50 cash from cash sales receipts for his own private use
3. Wednesday: total sales as per the Z report from the till were £320, of which £50 was paid by credit cards/debit cards; the balance of £270 was paid by cash. Simon paid £25 to the window cleaner for services rendered
4. Thursday: total sales as per the Z report from the till were £240, of which £60 was paid by credit cards/debit cards; the balance of £180 was paid by cash. Simon gave £40 as a donation to a local charity
5. Friday: total sales as per the Z report from the till were £640, of which £30 was paid by credit cards/debit cards; the balance of £610 was paid by cash. Simon took £150 cash from cash sales receipts for his own private use. Simon also paid £75 wages to his staff member out of cash sales
6. Saturday: total sales as per the Z report from the till were £720, of which £70 was paid by credit cards/debit cards; the balance of £650 was paid by cash. Simon paid £75 to his employee as wages. Simon went to the bank and lodged the net cash sales receipts of £1,495
7. Sunday: the shop was closed

Simon needs to record each of the above transactions on the cash sheet. At the close of business each day Simon will print off a copy of the Z report from the cash register. Simon will enter in the amount for total sales for each day and the value of sales that was paid by credit cards/debit cards and the value of sales paid by cash. Furthermore, Simon will record the details of all cash expenditure incurred each day and note this in the appropriate column. At the end of the week when Simon lodges cash at the bank, the total of the 'Net Cash' column should equal the value of the cash lodged at the bank.

When Simon has entered in the sales details from the Z reports he will write the letter 'E' with a circle around it in red ink on the Z report and file the Z report in the cash sales lever arch folder.

The payment of £25 to the window cleaner will be recorded in the 'Less Other' column of the cash sheet. The donation of £40 will also be recorded in the 'Less Other' column of the cash sheet.

After the entries have been made the paper-based cash sheet will be as shown in Figure 5.4.

Figure 5.4
Spreadsheet Example Cash Sheet Paper Based

Week Beginning		17-Mar-14								
	Total Sales As per Z report	Sales Non Cash	Sales Cash	Less Wages	Less Drawings	Less Other	Total Deductions T/F to Petty Cash	Net Cash	Cash lodged at bank	Cash lodgement date
Monday	closed									
Tuesday	240	40	200		50		50	150		
Wednesday	320	50	270			25	25	245		
Thursday	240	60	180			40	40	140		
Friday	640	30	610	75	150		225	385		
Saturday	720	70	650	75			75	575	1,495	22-Mar-14
Sunday	closed									
	2,160	250	1,910	150	200	65	415	1,495	1,495	

After the entries have been made the spreadsheet software-based cash sheet will be as shown in Figure 5.5.

Figure 5.5

Spreadsheet Example Cash Sheet Software Based

CASH SHEET										
Week Beginning			17-Mar-14							
	Total Sales As per Z report	Sales Non Cash	Sales Cash	Less Wages	Less Drawings	Less Other	Total Deductions T/F to Petty Cash	Net Cash	Cash lodged at bank	Cash lodgement date
Monday	closed									
Tuesday	240	40	200		50		50	150		
Wednesday	320	50	270			25	25	245		
Thursday	240	60	180			40	40	140		
Friday	640	30	610	75	150		225	385		
Saturday	720	70	650	75			75	575	1,495	22-Mar-14
Sunday	closed									
	2,160	250	1,910	150	200	65	415	1,495	1,495	

Review of transactions recorded on the cash sheet:
- All transactions are recorded on the day that the actual transaction took place.
- Total sales as per the Z report are subdivided into sales non-cash and sales cash
- Any expenditure from cash sales are recorded in the relevant column
- Based on the transactions recorded in the cash sheet Simon can identify that his business generated £2,160 of sales, of which £250 was paid by credit/debit card and £1,910 was paid in cash

The £1,910 of cash sales was accounted for as follows:
- £150 was paid out in wages
- £200 was taken as drawings
- £25 was paid to the window cleaner
- £40 was given as a donation to a local charity
- £1,495 was lodged into the bank account at the end of the week

CASH SHEETS – ILLUSTRATIVE EXAMPLE WITH VAT

This illustrative example is applicable to both a paper-based cash sheet system and a spreadsheet software-based cash sheet system.

Simon operates as a sole trader barber with one part-time staff member. He also sells hair-related products. The business is registered for VAT and operates from a city centre shop. During any given week he will sell products and services to his customers.

During a week in April the following activities took place:

1. **Monday: the shop was closed**
2. **Tuesday: total sales as per the Z report from the till were £288, of which £72 was paid by credit cards/debit cards; the balance of £216 was paid by cash. Simon paid £25 with cash from cash sales to pay the window cleaner**
3. **Wednesday: total sales as per the Z report from the till were £384, of which £96 was paid by credit cards/debit cards; the balance of £288 was paid by cash. Simon took £200 for his own personal use from cash sales**
4. **Thursday: total sales as per the Z report from the till were £288, of which £72 was paid by credit cards/debit cards; the balance of £216 was paid by cash. Simon took £150 for his own personal use from cash sales**
5. **Friday: total sales as per the Z report from the till were £768, of which £192 was paid by credit cards/debit cards; the balance of £576 was paid by cash. Simon paid £95 wages to his employee with cash from cash sales receipts**
6. **Saturday: total sales as per the Z report from the till were £864, of which £216 was paid by credit cards/debit cards; the balance of £648 was paid by cash. Simon paid £95 to his employee as wages from cash sales. Simon gave £50 to his employee as a loan to be repaid at the end of the following month. Simon went to the bank and lodged the net cash sales receipts of £1,329**
7. **Sunday: the shop was closed**

> **MICRO TASK**
> Can you produce the cash sheet for Simon based on the information above?
> - **Set up the cash sheet using the appropriate headings**
> - **Slot in the figures as per the information noted above**
> - **Compare your cash sheet to the cash sheet for Simon noted below.**

Simon needs to record each of the above transactions on the cash sheet. At the close of business each day Simon will print off a copy of the Z report from the cash register. Simon will enter in the amount for total sales for each day and the value of sales that was paid by credit cards/debit cards and the value of sales paid by cash. Simon will also detail the VAT applicable to sales and the total value of sales excluding VAT.

Furthermore, Simon will record the details of all cash expenditure incurred each day and note the same in the appropriate column. At the end of the week when Simon lodges cash at the bank the total of the 'Net Cash' column should equal the value of the cash lodged at the bank.

When Simon has entered in the sales details from the Z reports he will write the letter 'E' with a circle around it in red ink on the Z report and file the Z report in the cash sales lever arch folder.

The payment of £25 to the window cleaner will be recorded in the 'Less Other' column of the cash sheet. The monies given to the staff member of £50 was also noted in the 'Less Other' column.

After the entries have been made the paper-based cash sheet will be as shown in Figure 5.6.

Figure 5.6
Spreadsheet Example Cash Sheet Paper Based VAT

Week Beginning			14-Apr-14									
	Sales Ex VAT	VAT Amt Rate 1	Total Sales As per Z report	Sales Non Cash	Sales Cash	Less Wages	Less Drawings	Less Other	Total Deductions T/F to Petty Cash	Net Cash	Cash lodged at bank	Cash lodgement date
		20%										
Monday	closed									0	0	
Tuesday	240.00	48.00	288	72	216			25	25	191		
Wednesday	320.00	64.00	384	96	288		200		200	88		
Thursday	240.00	48.00	288	72	216		150		150	66		
Friday	640.00	128.00	768	192	576	95			95	481		
Saturday	720.00	144.00	864	216	648	95		50	145	503	1,329	19-Apr-14
Sunday	closed									0	0	
	2,160.00	432.00	2,592	648	1,944	190	350	75	615	1,329	1,329	

After the entries have been made the spreadsheet software-based cash sheet will be as shown in Figure 5.7.

Review of transactions recorded on the cash sheet:
- All transactions are recorded on the day that the actual transaction took place
- Sales are recorded excluding VAT and including VAT
- VAT on sales is recorded as per the rate applicable
- Total sales as per the Z report are shown at gross value, i.e., sales including VAT
- Any expenditure from cash sales is recorded in the relevant column

Based on the transactions recorded in the cash sheet Simon can identify that his business generated £2,592 of sales including VAT, of which £648 was paid by credit/debit card and £1,944 was paid in cash.

The £1,944 of cash sales including VAT was accounted for as follows:
- £190 was paid out in wages
- £350 was taken as drawings
- £25 was paid to the window cleaner
- £50 was given as a short-term loan to a staff member
- £1,329 was lodged into the bank account at the end of the week

Figure 5.7 Spreadsheet example cash sheet software based VAT

Week Beginning | 14-Apr-14

	Sales Ex VAT	VAT Amt Rate 1	Total Sales As per Z report	Sales Non Cash	Sales Cash	Less Wages	Less Drawings	Less Other	Total Deductions T/F to Petty Cash	Net Cash	Cash lodged at bank	Cash lodgemt date
		20%										
Monday	closed		closed						0	0		
Tuesday	240.00	48.00	288	72	216			25	25	191		
Wednesday	320.00	64.00	384	96	288		200		200	88		
Thursday	240.00	48.00	288	72	216		150		150	66		
Friday	640.00	128.00	768	192	576	95			95	481		
Saturday	720.00	144.00	864	216	648	95		50	145	503	1,329	19-Apr-14
Sunday	closed		closed						0	0		
	2,160.00	432.00	2,592	648	1,944	190	350	75	615	1,329	1,329	

CHAPTER 6

How to organize, process and file source documents

SOURCE DOCUMENTS – OVERVIEW

The most frequent problem associated with bookkeeping is an inability to maintain control over source documents. It is easy to become overwhelmed by the sheer variety and volume of paperwork associated with running a business. Once control over the source document paperwork is lost, the bookkeeping of the business breaks down. Therefore it is vitally important to have a clear understanding of source documents.

Source documents are documents that record the activities of a business. The activities recorded can be financial or non-financial.

Source documents can be produced internally by a business; for example:

- **A delivery docket to record quantities of goods supplied**
- **A sales invoice to record the monetary value of services rendered and/or goods supplied to a customer**

Source documents can also be received by a business from third parties; for example:

- **A purchase invoice detailing the value of goods or services obtained from a supplier**
- **A bank statement detailing banking transactions for a period**

The source documents flowchart illustrates a non-exhaustive list of the types of source documents that can be used to capture data relating to the financial and non-financial activities of a business. The data contained in the source documents can be used to record the financial transactions in the bookkeeping system, validate the accuracy of financial records and exercise control over the business.

Each business will generate and receive a variety of source documents. The source documents affecting a business will depend on the activities of the business. The source documents flowchart shows a detailed array of source documents that any given business may be exposed to. On first review it may appear that there is an overwhelming variety of documents to deal with. However, careful study of the source document flowchart will reveal that the source documents can be grouped together as follows:

Figure 6.1

Flowchart 2 – Source Documents

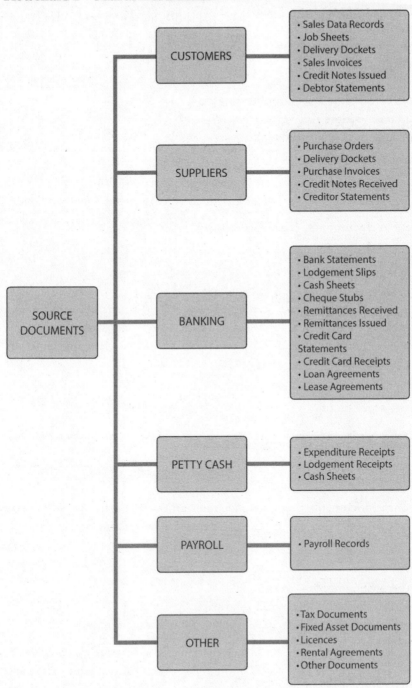

1. Source documents – customer-related
- sales data records
- job sheets
- delivery dockets (goods out)
- sales invoices
- credit notes (issued)
- debtor statements

2. Source documents – supplier-related
- purchase orders
- delivery dockets (goods in)
- purchase invoices
- credit notes (received)
- creditor statements

3. Source documents – banking-related
- bank statements
- lodgement slips
- cash sheets
- cheque stubs/counterfoil
- remittances received
- remittances issued
- credit card statements
- credit card receipts
- loan agreements
- lease agreements

4. Source documents – petty cash-related
- expenditure receipts
- lodgement receipts
- cash sheets

5. Source documents – payroll-related
- all payroll-related paperwork

6. Source documents – other
- tax documents (non-payroll-related)
- fixed-assets documents (e.g., motor vehicle documents)
- licences
- rental agreements
- other documents

Now that it has been established that it is possible to group source documents into six separate categories, it is necessary to clarify the information contained on each type of source document.

SOURCE DOCUMENTS – EXPLAINED

Category 1 source documents – customer-related

Sales data record
A sales data record is used to record basic sales data in a systematic manner, so that the information can be transferred to a sales invoice at the end of a given period. The basic sales data can relate to a service business or a product-based business.

Example – service-based business sales data record: a sole trader, such as a graphic designer, may note his/her time in a diary each day for work done for each particular client. At the end of the month he/she can total up the hours worked for each client noted in the diary in order to produce sales invoices for clients. The diary is a sales data record.

Example – product-based business sales data record: a business selling chairs may record the details of all chairs sold in a given period in a goods outwards book. Each time a chair is sold, it is noted in the goods outwards book, with the details of the customer. At the end of the month all the chairs sold to each customer are totalled up and noted on sales invoices to be issued to the relevant customers. The goods outwards book is a sales data record.

Job sheet
A document that details the labour and/or material costs relating to a job performed for a customer.

Delivery docket – goods out
A document that details the type and quantity of goods delivered to a customer. It is normal practice for the recipient of the goods to sign a copy of the delivery docket. A copy of the signed delivery docket should be retained by both the customer and the supplier of the goods, in case any queries arise concerning the delivery of goods.

Sales invoice
A document that details the monetary value and a description of the supply of a service rendered and/or products supplied to a customer.

Credit note – issued

A document that details the monetary value of a refund to a customer.

Debtor statement

A document that lists the sales invoices issued to a customer that are still unpaid at the date of the debtor statement.

Category 2 source documents – supplier-related

Purchase order

A document that instructs a supplier to provide certain goods or services at a given price and time. It can be used as a control check when the related purchase invoice is received. The value noted on the purchase order should match the value charged on the purchase invoice; if not, it should be queried.

Delivery docket – goods in

A document that details the type and quantity of goods delivered from a supplier. It is normal practice for the recipient of the goods to sign a copy of the delivery docket. A copy of the signed delivery docket should be retained by the supplier and also the customer, so that the quantities noted on the delivery docket can be matched against the related purchase invoice when it is received.

Purchase invoice

This is a document that details the monetary value and a description of goods and/or services supplied to a business.

Credit note – received

A document that details the monetary value of a refund from a supplier.

Creditor statement

A document issued by a supplier to a customer, listing unpaid invoices at a given date, usually at the end of a month.

Category 3 source documents – banking-related

Bank statement

This is a document that details the banking transactions of a business for a given period. It will detail the value of monies received into the bank account and the value of monies paid out of the bank account.

Lodgement slip

A lodgement slip is a document or docket that details the value and composition of a lodgement into a bank account. It may be the case that more than one cheque is lodged at a time, so the details of each cheque need to be recorded on the lodgement slip counterfoil.

Cash sheet

A cash sheet is a document that can be used to trace the composition of cash lodgements to the bank. See chapter 5.

Cheque stub/counterfoil

This is a document that details the value of a cheque issued, the date the cheque was issued and details of the payee. It may also include supplier invoice numbers or a payment reference.

Remittance received

This is a document received from customers paying a business. The document details the sales invoices that a customer is paying.

Remittance issued

This is a document issued by a business when paying a supplier or creditor. The document details the purchase invoices that the business is paying a supplier or details the debt to which the payment relates.

Credit card statement

This is a document that details credit card payment transactions for a given period. It will detail the value of all payments issued and also show monies received to pay against the balance due on the credit card.

Credit card receipt

A receipt obtained when payment is issued by credit card.

Loan agreement

This is a document that will detail the terms and conditions of a loan advanced.

Lease agreement

This is a document that will detail the terms and conditions of a lease agreement.

Category 4 source documents – petty cash-related

Petty cash – expenditure receipts

An expenditure receipt is a receipt obtained when a payment is made from petty cash to validate the expenditure.

Petty cash – lodgement receipts

When money is allocated to petty cash a lodgement receipt will detail the value of money placed into petty cash, the source of the cash and the date of the transaction.

Petty cash – cash sheet

A cash sheet is a document that can be used to trace the composition of cash lodgements into petty cash that originate from cash sales. It can also be used to identify the details of how such money was spent. See chapter 5.

Category 5 source documents – payroll-related

Payroll records

All documents relating to the payroll and staff, including payroll reports showing staff pay and tax deductions and also all tax-related forms.

Category 6 source documents – other

Tax documents

All documents relating to taxes other than payroll-related taxes (see payroll records).

Fixed asset

Any document that refers to a fixed asset, for example a motor vehicle, computer equipment or a premises.

Licence

A document authorizing or permitting a certain type of activity, for example a licence to sell alcohol.

Rental agreement

A document detailing the terms and conditions relating to the rental of a premises.

Other

This a general catch-all category for documents that do not fall into any of the other categories described.

SOURCE DOCUMENTS – FILING

Source documents are the foundation upon which the financial records of a business are built. In order to ensure source documents are processed systematically it is necessary to have a robust filing system in place. The number of files needed to file source documents depends on the volume of activity.

Micro business – source document filing

A micro business may be able to file the entire paperwork for a trading period in one lever arch file. If only one file is required it needs to be subdivided into the relevant sections. As previously noted it is possible to identify six categories of source documents as follows:

- **Customer**
- **Supplier**
- **Banking**
- **Petty cash**
- **Payroll**
- **Other**

A micro business could insert six subject dividers into a lever arch file to group the paperwork according to type noted above. If the micro business did not have staff then it could ignore the entire section relating to payroll.

Small business – source document filing

A basic filing system for a small business that buys and sells goods and/or services could also have six categories of source documents. It may be necessary for such a business to have more than six lever arch files to facilitate the effective processing and management of source documents as follows:

File 1: Sales data records

This file should contain any records relating to sales invoicing. The records normally contain information relating to the supply of goods and/or services that will be invoiced at a later date. The sales data records merely capture data relating to the supply of goods and/or services supplied to customers.

Sales data records may be entries in a diary noting time spent on work carried out for particular customers during a given month. If sales data is captured using this method it is not necessary to create a file, as the information is held in the diary itself.

File 2: Job sheets

This file should contain copies of job sheets. Job sheets can be filed either numerically or alphabetically.

File 3: Delivery dockets

This file should contain copies of the delivery dockets that customers have signed verifying receipt of goods supplied. The delivery dockets can be filed either numerically or alphabetically.

File 4: Sales invoice file – unpaid

This file should contain unpaid sales invoices either filed in numerical order or in alphabetical order. This file of unpaid invoices identifies all monies due to the business and can be used to aid debt collection.

When a sales invoice is paid by a customer the sales invoice should be marked as paid, with the date and method of payment also noted on the sales invoice. The paid sales invoice then needs to be re-filed in the sales invoice paid file, see below.

File 5: Sales invoice file – paid

This file should contain paid sales invoices filed in numerical order. Any 'missing' invoices should be contained in the sales invoice unpaid file.

File 6: Purchase invoices – unpaid

This file should contain unpaid purchase invoices filed in alphabetical order. The file of unpaid purchase invoices identifies all monies due by the business to its trade suppliers. When a supplier invoice is paid, it should be marked 'paid', with the date and method of payment also noted on the purchase invoice. The paid supplier invoice should then be re-filed in the 'Purchase Invoices Paid' file, see below.

File 7: Purchase invoices – paid

This file should contain paid purchase invoices filed alphabetically.

File 8: Debtor statements

This file should contain copies of debtor statements issued to customers. Debtor statements list the invoices owing by a customer at a particular point in time, usually the end of a month. It can be decided not to create a debtor statement file if debtor statements are computer generated and copies are held on computer.

File 9: Banking

This file should be divided into sub-sections as necessary.

Bank statements – this section of the banking file should contain bank statements filed in date order, most recent statement filed on top.

Lodgement slips – this section of the banking file can be used to file lodgement slips. If the business has a lodgement book to record deposits into the bank account it may not be necessary to include this section in the banking file, as all the information will be contained in the lodgement book.

Cheque stubs – this section of the banking file can be used to file cheque stubs. When a chequebook is fully used and all cheques have been issued the cheque stubs can be filed in the banking file in a separate pocket folder in the file.

Remittances received – this section of the banking file can be used to file customer remittances received, filed in alphabetical order, most recent remittance on top.

Remittances issued – this section of the banking file can be used to file supplier remittances issued, filed in alphabetical order, most recent remittance on top.

Credit card statements – this section of the banking file can be used to file credit card statements, filed in date order, most recent on top.

Credit card receipts – this section of the banking file can be used to file receipts obtained when a payment is issued by credit card. It can be helpful to file credit card receipts in a separate plastic wallet folder within this section of the file.

Loan agreements – this section of the banking file can be used to file details of loan agreements entered into.

Lease agreements – this section of the banking file can be used to file details of lease agreements entered into.

File 10 – Petty cash
This file should be sub-divided into two sections as follows:

Section 1: Petty cash lodgements – this section of the file should contain paperwork recording the source of any monies lodged into petty cash.
Section 2: Petty cash receipts – this section of the file should contain receipts obtained when petty cash monies are used to pay for goods and/or services. It can be helpful to file the petty cash receipts in a separate plastic wallet folder in this section of the file.

File 11: Payroll
This file should contain all information and reports relating to payroll.

File 12: Other
This file should contain all paperwork that does not fall into any of the files noted above. It would include paperwork such as tax documents, fixed-assets documents, licences, rental agreements.

MICRO TASK
- Review your current paperwork system
- Establish if you have your paperwork filed in the most appropriate manner
- Consider if you should open new files as suggested above.

Income – how to record income transactions

CHAPTER 7

How to record income transactions – overview

INCOME

Income transactions are identified from source documents. Income into a business, for the purposes of DIY Bookkeeping, can be identified as follows:

- **Sales income – monies from customers relating to the sale of products and/or services**
- **Non-sales income – monies from third parties NOT relating to the sale of products and/or services**

SALES DAYBOOK

A sales daybook is a list of all sales invoices issued for a given period, e.g., a day, a week, a month or a year. A sales daybook will detail the date on which invoices were issued, the name of the customer to whom the invoice was issued and the monetary details relating to the supply of products and/or services.

A sales daybook for a cash-based business, such as a retail shop, is a list of all monies received for a given period, e.g., a day, a week, a month or a year. A sales daybook for a retail business will necessitate the use of a cash register to ensure sales are recorded accurately. A basic report that can be generated from a cash register to identify sales for a period is known as a Z report. The Z report merely lists the sales for a period.

A sales daybook for a VAT-registered business needs to record VAT details. A sales daybook can be paper based or software based and the decision on which is best for your business needs to be considered.

BANK RECEIPTS BOOK

The bank receipts book details payments from customers and other receipts from third parties. The payments from customers may be in cash or by other payment means, for example, cheques, credit cards or electronic funds transfers (EFTs). If a business is supplying services and/or goods on credit, it will be particularly important to maintain accurate details of remittances from customers, to ensure monies owed to the business can be allocated to the relevant customers.

The data to identify bank receipts will be obtained from source documents, such as lodgement slips, remittances received and bank statements.

A bank receipts book can be paper based or software based and the decision on which is best for your business needs to be considered.

Figure 7.1
Income Overview

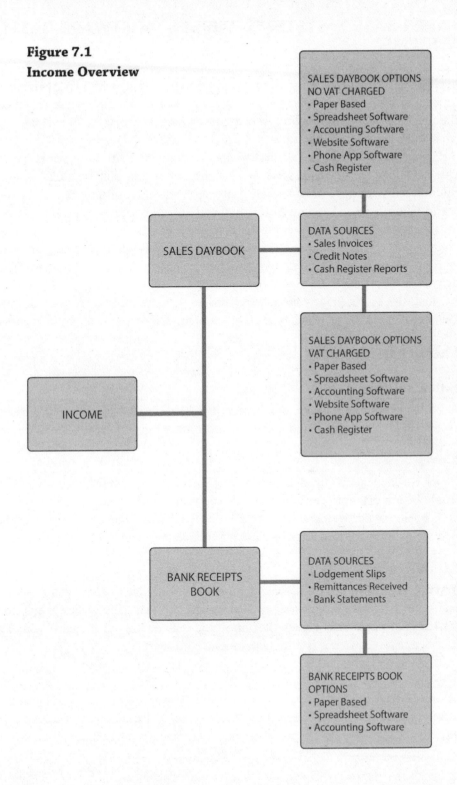

PAPER-BASED SYSTEMS VERSUS SOFTWARE-BASED SYSTEMS

Creating a system to record income/sales transactions involves choosing between a paper-based system, a software-based system or a hybrid system utilizing aspects of both. It is necessary to select the most appropriate system based on the needs of your business and in order to do so it is necessary to evaluate the pros and cons of each system.

There are advantages and disadvantages associated with both paper-based systems and software-based systems. The choice between each type of system is not mutually exclusive. It is possible to use a paper-based system in conjunction with a software-based system. You may favour a paper-based system if you have an IT phobia or you may favour a software-based system if you have a high-volume business and require a system that allows for faster processing. You may start off with a paper-based system and then migrate to a software-based system as your business expands.

In order to facilitate your decision-making process, consider the following factors when evaluating which type of system is most appropriate for your business:

Factors to consider

Sales volume

A low sales volume business can be adequately controlled using a paper-based system. A high sales volume business is more suited to software-based systems.

Costs

Paper-based systems are relatively cheap to set up and maintain, although it would be important to consider the time spent processing as this is also a cost to your business. Software-based systems can be relatively inexpensive due to the volume of software providers in the marketplace.

IT skills level

You need to consider if you have adequate IT knowledge to allow you to set up and run a software-based system. If not, you can learn the basics to get you started. You need to consider the time required for you to increase your IT knowledge levels, as this is also a cost to your business.

Image

You need to consider the image you portray to your customers. If you are using a paper-based system, will this make your business look antiquated? Handwritten paperwork does not look as professional as computer-generated documents.

CHAPTER 8

How to record income transactions in a sales daybook

SALES DAYBOOK — OVERVIEW

A sales daybook (see Figure 8.1) is a record that lists sales transactions for a given period, e.g., a day, a week, a month or a year. It is referred to as a sales book because traditionally it was a paper notebook with rows and columns used to record sales. It is referred to as a sales daybook because the book was traditionally updated on a daily basis. Effectively the content of a sales daybook is merely a list of sales invoices issued to customers for a given period. If credit notes are issued to customers, then the value of sales noted in the sales daybook is reduced by the value of the credit notes.

The sales daybook for a non-VAT-registered business (see Figure 8.2) records basic details of all sales for a period including:
- **The date of the sale**
- **The name of the customer**
- **The invoice number that relates to the sale**
- **The monetary value of the sale**

The sales daybook for a non-VAT-registered retail business records basic details of all sales for a period including:
- **The date of the sale(s)**
- **The monetary value of the sale(s)**

The sales daybook for a VAT-registered business (see Figure 8.3) records basic details of all sales for a period including:
- **The date of the sale**
- **The name of the customer**
- **The invoice number that relates to the sale**
- **The monetary value of the sale including VAT – gross amount**
- **The monetary value of VAT only and the rate of VAT charged**
- **The monetary value of the sale excluding VAT – net amount**

Figure 8.1 Sales Daybook

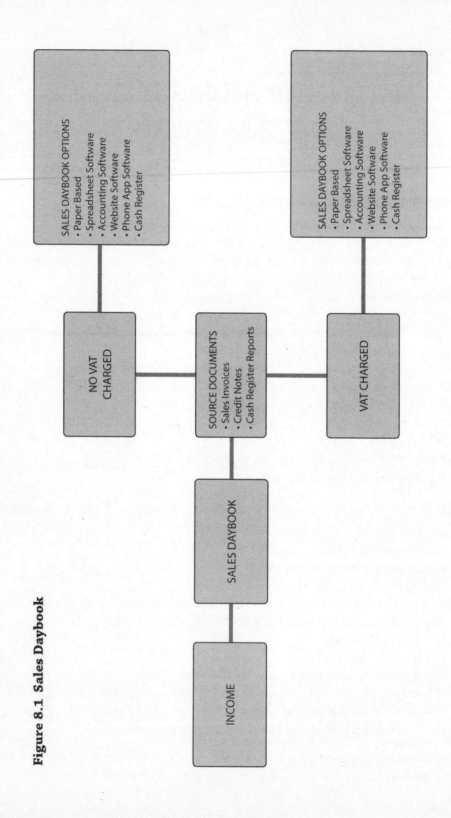

Figure 8.2
Sales Daybook – No VAT

SALES DAY BOOK			
DATE	CUSTOMER DETAILS	INVOICE NUMBER	£ GROSS AMOUNT
10-Jan-14	Mr Jones	1001	250
15-Jan-14	Mrs Smith	1002	950
20-Jan-14	John Fills	1003	450
25-Jan-14	Frank Marks	1004	250
Total			1,900

Figure 8.3
Sales Daybook — VAT

SALES DAYBOOK					
DATE	CUSTOMER DETAILS	INVOICE NUMBER	£ GROSS AMOUNT	VAT 20%	Net
03-Jan-14	ABC Ltd	1001	1,200	200	1,000
04-Jan-14	XYZ Ltd	1002	240	40	200
11-Jan-14	PPP Ltd	1003	120	20	100
15-Jan-14	LOL Ltd	1004	6,000	1,000	5,000
Total			7,560	1,260	6,300

The sales daybook for a VAT-registered retail business records basic details of all sales for a period including:
- The date of the sale(s)
- The monetary value of the sale(s) – gross amount
- The monetary value of VAT only and the rate of VAT charged
- The monetary value of the sale excluding VAT – net amount

> NOTE: If your business supplies goods and/or services at different VAT rates then it will be necessary to separate the VAT monetary amounts for the different VAT rates.

There are a number of sales daybook options available for a non-VAT-registered service and/or product-based business to evaluate in order to select the most appropriate option for the business.

Sales daybook options – non-VAT-registered businesses:
- Option 1 – Paper based
- Option 2 – Spreadsheet software based
- Option 3 – Accounting software based
- Option 4 – Website software based
- Option 5 – Phone app based
- Option 6 – Cash register based

SALES DAYBOOK – SOURCE DOCUMENTS

The data to be recorded in the sales daybook is obtained from a variety of source documents, such as:

Sales invoices – detail the monetary value and a description of the supply of a service rendered and/or products supplied to a customer. The relevant details contained on sales invoices can be transferred to a sales daybook.

Credit notes (issued) – detail the monetary value of refunds due to customers. The relevant details contained on credit notes can be transferred to a sales daybook. The value of sales will be reduced by the value of credit notes issued.

Cash register reports – for a business dealing with cash sales, such as a retail business, the cash register will produce reports on sales that can be transferred to a sales daybook. Alternatively, some cash registers are capable of automatically generating a sales daybook based on sales registered through the till.

SALES DAYBOOK – NO VAT CHARGED: PAPER BASED

A sales daybook that is paper based involves the use of any paper record, for example an A4 writing pad or a hardback analysis book with pre-printed columns. It is recommended to use a hardback analysis book as this is produced for the purpose of recording financial data. The set-up of a paper-based sales daybook is a straightforward process. Purchase a hardback analysis book as suggested and write in the column headings to collect the appropriate data. See Figure 8.4 for the basic headings required.

Figure 8.4
Sales Daybook Headings

Date	Customer Name	Invoice Number	£ Amount

Example

Jane offers a website design service to clients and charges her time out on an hourly rate. She is using a paper-based invoice system as described in the sales invoicing chapter. Each time she attends the office of a client she handwrites an invoice on a pre-printed invoice pad and presents it to her client. In the month of January she has issued four invoices to her clients, see invoices noted in Figure 8.5 overleaf.

MICRO TASK

Can you produce the sales daybook for Jane's business based on the sales invoices produced for January?

- Set up a sales daybook for Jane's business, with the appropriate headings.
- Transfer the information contained on the sales invoices to the sales daybook.
- Check your answer against the solution provided below.

In order to produce the sales daybook for Jane's business, she needs to transfer the information contained on the sales invoices to the sales daybook. At the end of the month Jane would need to total all the sales figures in the sales daybook, to establish total sales for the month. If at the end of January Jane had no other sales invoices issued, she would total up the four invoices and close off the sales daybook for January as illustrated in Figure 8.6.

Jane can now establish that her total sales for the month of January were £1,100.

SALES DAYBOOK – NO VAT CHARGED: SPREADSHEET SOFTWARE BASED

A sales daybook that is spreadsheet based involves setting up a template to capture all the relevant sales transaction information. A spreadsheet sales daybook has the advantage of being able to calculate totals automatically, thus

Figure 8.5
Sales Invoices – Handwritten

JANE'S IT SERVICES			
INVOICE			
Customer Details			
Chairco Ltd	Invoice	1001	
Side Street	DATE	03-Jan-13	
Small Town	Account	CHAS ID	
DETAILS			Gross
Fees for services rendered			300
Total			300

Studio 25, IT Park, Smalltown - Ph 8745 6321 e mail info@jit.com

JANE'S IT SERVICES			
INVOICE			
Customer Details			
Comfy Chairs	Invoice	1002	
Laneway	DATE	04-Jan-13	
Small Town	Account	COML AN	
DETAILS			Gross
Fees for services rendered			450
Total			450

Studio 25, IT Park, Smalltown - Ph 8745 6321 e mail info@jit.com

JANE'S IT SERVICES			
INVOICE			
Customer Details			
Comfy Chairs	Invoice	1003	
Laneway	DATE	11-Jan-13	
Small Town	Account	COML AN	
Details	Unit Net		Gross
Fees for services rendered			200
Total			200

Studio 25, IT Park, Smalltown - Ph 8745 6321 e mail info@jit.com

JANE'S IT SERVICES			
INVOICE			
Customer Details			
Chairco Ltd	Invoice	1004	
Side Street	DATE	15-Jan-13	
Small Town	Account	CHAS ID	
Details	Unit Net		Gross
Fees for services rendered			150
Total			150

Studio 25, IT Park, Smalltown - Ph 8745 6321 e mail info@jit.com

Figure 8.6
Sales Daybook – Handwritten – Totalled

SALES DAY BOOK			
DATE	CUSTOMER DETAILS	INVOICE NUMBER	£ AMOUNT
03-Jan-13	Chairco Ltd	1001	300
04-Jan-13	Comfy Chairs	1002	450
11-Jan-13	Comfy Chairs	1003	200
15-Jan-13	Chairco Ltd	1004	150
Total			1,100

speeding up the process. The set-up of a spreadsheet software-based sales daybook is a straightforward process. Purchase the software and install it on your computer. Open up a new spreadsheet file and key in the column headings to collect the appropriate data. The basic headings required are shown in Figure 8.7.

Figure 8.7
Sales Daybook – Spreadsheet Template

SALES DAY BOOK			
DATE	CUSTOMER DETAILS	INVOICE NUMBER	£ AMOUNT
Total			

Figure 8.8
Sales Invoices – Handwritten

JANE'S IT SERVICES		
INVOICE		
Customer Details		
Chairco Ltd	Invoice	1001
Side Street	DATE	03-Jan-13
Small Town	Account	CHAS ID
DETAILS		Gross
Fees for services rendered		300
Total		300

Studio 25, IT Park, Smalltown - Ph 8745 6321 e mail info@jit.com

JANE'S IT SERVICES		
INVOICE		
Customer Details		
Comfy Chairs	Invoice	1002
Laneway	DATE	04-Jan-13
Small Town	Account	COMLAN
DETAILS		Gross
Fees for services rendered		450
Total		450

Studio 25, IT Park, Smalltown - Ph 8745 6321 e mail info@jit.com

JANE'S IT SERVICES			
INVOICE			
Customer Details			
Comfy Chairs		Invoice	1003
Laneway		DATE	11-Jan-13
Small Town		Account	COMLAN
Details	Unit Net		Gross
Fees for services rendered			200
Total			200

Studio 25, IT Park, Smalltown - Ph 8745 6321 e mail info@jit.com

JANE'S IT SERVICES			
INVOICE			
Customer Details			
Chairco Ltd		Invoice	1004
Side Street		DATE	15-Jan-13
Small Town		Account	CHAS ID
Details	Unit Net		Gross
Fees for services rendered			150
Total			150

Studio 25, IT Park, Smalltown - Ph 8745 6321 e mail info@jit.com

Example

Jane offers an IT website design service to clients and charges her time out on an hourly rate. She is using a paper-based invoice system as described in the sales invoicing chapter. Each time she attends the office of a client she handwrites an invoice on a pre-printed invoice pad and presents it to her client. In the month of January she has issued four invoices to clients, see invoices listed in Figure 8.8.

MICRO TASK

Can you produce the sales daybook for Jane's business based on the sales invoices produced for January?
- Set up a sales daybook on a spreadsheet for Jane's business with the appropriate headings.
- Transfer the information contained on the sales invoices to the sales daybook
- Check your answer against the solution provided below.

In order to produce the sales daybook for Jane's business, she needs to transfer the information contained on the sales invoices to the sales daybook spreadsheet. At the end of the month Jane would need to total all the sales figures in the sales daybook spreadsheet to establish total sales for the month. If at the end of January Jane had no other sales invoices issued, she would total up the four invoices by using the formulae option on the spreadsheet software. Once the total is calculated then she can close off the sales daybook for January, as illustrated in Figure 8.9.

Figure 8.9
Sales Daybook Spreadsheet – Totalled

SALES DAY BOOK			
DATE	CUSTOMER DETAILS	INVOICE NUMBER	AMOUNT
03-Jan-13	Chairco Ltd	1001	300
04-Jan-13	Comfy Chairs	1002	450
11-Jan-13	Comfy Chairs	1003	200
15-Jan-13	Chairco Ltd	1004	150
Total			1,100

Jane can now establish that her total sales for the month of January were £1,100.

SALES DAYBOOK – NO VAT CHARGED: ACCOUNTING SOFTWARE BASED

A sales daybook that is accounting software based is normally a highly efficient method of recording sales transactions. The sales daybook on accounting software is usually generated automatically when sales invoices are produced. Therefore, if you have decided to use accounting software to generate sales invoices you will save time. There are numerous accounting software packages available on the market that you would need to evaluate based on how user friendly they are, the cost and also your accounting requirement. In addition, you would need to evaluate how long it would take you to learn how to operate any given accounting software package.

SALES DAYBOOK – NO VAT CHARGED: WEBSITE SOFTWARE BASED

If you are selling via a website, it is possible to use the website software to generate a sales daybook based on sales invoices issued. There are numerous options available depending on the functionality of your website.

SALES DAYBOOK – NO VAT CHARGED: PHONE APP SOFTWARE BASED

There are a variety of phone apps available that will enable you to generate invoices for services rendered or products sold that will also create a sales daybook of sales transactions. Some apps are free, others charge a fee. You will need to review the phone apps available and select the most appropriate one for your business.

SALES DAYBOOK – NO VAT CHARGED: CASH REGISTER BASED

If your business is cash based, such as a retail business, then using a cash register to record sales is the best option. The process to set up a system to record sales involves a number of steps:

- Step 1 – Select the most appropriate cash register for your business based on funds available and your requirements
- Step 2 – Select the most appropriate sales daybook option
- Step 3 – Set up an internal control process to ensure cash from sales is safeguarded and fully accounted for

Step 1 – Select the most appropriate cash register for your business based on funds available and your requirements

There are many options available when selecting a cash register. The choice will depend on funds available and functionality required. A basic till will cost you less initially but may involve more work overall when producing information for sales analysis. A sophisticated till will cost more initially but should reduce work overall when producing information for sales analysis.

When you have selected the most appropriate cash register for your business, you/your staff need to learn how to use it properly. The most important report will be the Z report that you need to run at the end of each trading day. The Z report totals the sales for the day. At the end of each trading day it is important to run the Z report to establish two things:

- **The value of actual sales generated during the day**
- **The amount of cash in the cash register equals the amount of cash sales recorded**

Step 2 – Select the most appropriate sales daybook option

Different types of cash registers offer different levels of functionality. The more basic cash registers will result in additional manual processing of sales data. For example, if a basic cash register is being used, it may not be capable of separating cash sales from credit/debit card sales.

The options available for a sales daybook that is cash register based are as follows:

- **Cash register sales daybook: paper based**
- **Cash register sales daybook spreadsheet: software based**
- **Cash register sales daybook cash register: software based**

Cash register sales daybook: paper based

Purchase an analysis notebook to be used as a sales daybook. Set up the appropriate headings in the sales daybook as shown in Figure 8.10.

Figure 8.10

Sales Daybook Template Paper Based – Retail Business

SALES DAY BOOK			
DATE	£ AMOUNT	£ AMOUNT	£ AMOUNT
	Total Sales as per Z Report	Total Credit/Debit Card Sales	Total Cash Sales
Total			

At the end of each trading day print off the Z report to identify the total value of the sales for the day. If your business accepts payment by cash and credit/debit cards then the sales figure needs to be further analysed into cash sales and credit/debit card sales.

For a business using a basic till that accepts payments in cash and credit/debit cards the cash sales figure can be identified as follows:

1. Print off the Z report from the cash register at the end of the trading day
2. Print off the sales report from the credit/debit card terminal
3. Subtract the sales figure on the credit/debit card terminal report from the sales figure on the Z report. This figure is the amount of cash sales for the day

Enter the sales data into the sales daybook. Enter the total value of all sales for the day in one column. Enter the total value of credit/debit cards sales for the day into a separate column. Enter the total value of cash sales for the day into a separate column. The value of the cash sales for the day and the value of the credit/debit cards for the same day must equate the total sales for the day as per the Z report figure. Do this every day for the week. At the end of the week add up all the daily sales, to calculate the total sales for the week. Keep repeating the process of recording the sales. See Figure 8.11 as an example of a paper-based cash register sales daybook.

Figure 8.11
Sales Daybook Paper Based – Retail Business

SALES DAY BOOK			
DATE	£ AMOUNT	£ AMOUNT	£ AMOUNT
	Total Sales as per Z Report	Total Credit/Debit Card Sales	Total Cash Sales
03-Mar-14	1325	525	800
04-Mar-14	1385	485	900
05-Mar-14	1335	615	720
06-Mar-14	1760	660	1100
07-Mar-14	2405	980	1425
08-Mar-14	3450	1225	2225
Total	11,660	4,490	7,170

Cash register sales daybook spreadsheet: software based

Set up a spreadsheet to be used as a sales daybook. Insert the appropriate headings in the sales daybook as shown in Figure 8.12.

Figure 8.12
Sales Daybook Spreadsheet-Based Template –
Retail Business

SALES DAY BOOK			
DATE	£ AMOUNT	£ AMOUNT	£ AMOUNT
	Total Sales as per Z Report	Total Credit/Debit Card Sales	Total Cash Sales
Total			

At the end of each trading day print off the Z report to identify the total value of the sales for the day. If your business accepts payment by cash and credit/debit cards then the sales figure needs to be further analysed into cash sales and credit/debit card sales.

For a business using a basic cash register that accepts payments in cash and credit/debit cards the cash sales figure can be identified as follows:

1. **Print off the Z report from the till at the end of the trading day**
2. **Print off the sales report from the credit/debit card terminal**
3. **Subtract the sales figure on the credit/debit card terminal report from the sales figure on the Z report. This figure is the amount of cash sales for the day**

Enter the sales data into the sales daybook spreadsheet. Enter the total value of sales for the day in one column. Enter the total value of credit/debit cards sales for the day into a separate column. Enter the total value of cash sales for the day into a separate column. The value of the cash sales for the day and the value of the credit/debit cards for the same day must equate the total sales for the day as per the Z report figure. Do this every day for the week. At the end of the week add up all the daily sales to calculate the total sales for the week. Keep repeating the process of recording the sales. See Figure 8.13 for an example of a spreadsheet-based cash register sales daybook.

Figure 8.13

Sales Daybook Spreadsheet Based – Retail Business

SALES DAY BOOK			
DATE	£ AMOUNT	£ AMOUNT	£ AMOUNT
	Total Sales as per Z Report	Total Credit/Debit Card Sales	Total Cash Sales
03-Mar-14	1,325	525	800
04-Mar-14	1,385	485	900
05-Mar-14	1,335	615	720
06-Mar-14	1,760	660	1,100
07-Mar-14	2,405	980	1,425
08-Mar-14	3,450	1,225	2,225
Total	11,660	4,490	7,170

Cash register sales daybook: cash register software based

On sophisticated cash registers there can be the option to print off a sales daybook based on sales receipts issued for a given period. If your till has this function it will speed up processing sales figures for a given period. This means the report printed off from the cash register is the sales daybook for the period, negating the need for manual input onto a separate sales daybook. The more sophisticated cash registers can analyse sales into cash sales and credit/debit card sales and even sales by product type.

Step 3 – Set up an internal control process to ensure cash from sales is safeguarded and fully accounted for.

A simple internal control to put in place to safeguard cash is the use of cash sheets. Cash sheets identify sales for a period, normally a week. In addition, cash sheets identify any monies taken from cash sales and how such monies were spent.

For full details of how to set up and operate cash sheets, see chapter 5.

SALES DAYBOOK – VAT CHARGED: PAPER BASED

A sales daybook that is paper based involves the use of any paper record, for example an A4 writing pad or a hardback analysis book with pre-printed columns. It is recommended to use a hardback analysis book as this is produced for the purpose of recording financial data. The set-up of a paper-based sales daybook is a straightforward process. Purchase a hardback analysis book as suggested and write in the column headings to collect the appropriate data. The basic headings required are shown in Figure 8.14.

Figure 8.14

Sales Daybook Paper Based – VAT

Date	Customer Name	Invoice Number	£ Amount Gross (including VAT)	£ Amount VAT only	£ Amount Net (excluding VAT)

Example: business – VAT rate 5%

Simon offers the supply and fitting of stair lifts for elderly people. His business is VAT registered and his supplies satisfy the conditions allowing VAT to be charged at the 5% reduced rate. He is using a paper-based invoice system as described in the sales invoicing chapter. Each time he completes work for a client he handwrites an invoice on pre-printed invoice pads and presents it to his client. In the month of January he has issued four invoices to clients as shown in Figure 8.15.

> **MICRO TASK**
> Can you produce the sales daybook for Simon's business based on the sales invoices produced for January?
> - Set up a sales daybook for Simon's business with the appropriate headings
> - Transfer the information contained on the sales invoices to the sales daybook
> - Check your answer against the solution provided below.

In order to produce the sales daybook for Simon's business he needs to transfer the information contained on the sales invoices to the sales daybook. At the end of the month Simon would need to total all the sales figures in the sales daybook to establish total sales for the month. If at the end of January Simon had no other sales invoices issued, he would total up the four invoices and close off the sales daybook for January as illustrated in Figure 8.16.

Based on the entries in the sales daybook for the month of January, Simon can identify his total gross sales were £2,100 including VAT. The total VAT charged to customers was £100 and the net sales excluding VAT for the month was £2,000.

Figure 8.15
Sales Invoices – Simon's Stair Lifts

Invoice 1001

Simon's Stair Lifts
Suite 22, Business Corp. Pk, Big City
Ph 8765 4321

INVOICE

Customer Details			
Mrs Bloggs		Invoice	1001
Side Street		DATE	03-Jan-14
Small Town		Account	Bloggs

DETAILS			Gross
Supply & Fit			
1 x Stair Lift - Basic Model			300
Sub Total			300
VAT		5%	15
Total			315

VAT NO. GB 123 4567 89

Invoice 1002

Simon's Stair Lifts
Suite 22, Business Corp. Pk, Big City
Ph 8765 4321

INVOICE

Customer Details			
Mr Soap		Invoice	1002
Laneway		DATE	04-Jan-14
Small Town		Account	Soap

DETAILS			Gross
Supply & Fit			
1 x Stair Lift - Deluxe			600
Sub total			600
VAT		5%	30
Total			630

VAT NO. GB 123 4567 89

Invoice 1003

Simon's Stair Lifts
Suite 22, Business Corp. Pk, Big City
Ph 8765 4321

INVOICE

Customer Details			
Mary Parker		Invoice	1003
Laneway		DATE	11-Jan-14
Small Town		Account	Parks

	Details	Unit Net	Gross
Supply & Fit			
1 x Stair Lift - Express Installation			800
Sub Total			800
VAT		5%	40
Total			840

VAT NO. GB 123 4567 89

Invoice 1004

Simon's Stair Lifts
Suite 22, Business Corp. Pk, Big City
Ph 8765 4321

INVOICE

Customer Details			
Julie Smith		Invoice	1004
Side Street		DATE	15-Jan-14
Small Town		Account	Sitts

	Details	Unit Net	Gross
Supply & Fit			
1 x Stair Lift - Basic Model			300
Sub Total			300
VAT		5%	15
Total			315

VAT NO. GB 123 4567 89

Figure 8.16

Sales Daybook Paper Based – Simon's Stair Lifts – Totalled

SALES DAYBOOK

DATE	CUSTOMER DETAILS	INVOICE NUMBER	£ Gross Amount	VAT 5%	Net Amt
03-Jan-14	Mrs Bloggs	1001	315	15	300
04-Jan-14	Mr Soap	1002	630	30	600
11-Jan-14	Mary Parker	1003	840	40	800
15-Jan-14	Julie Smith	1004	315	15	300
Total			2,100	100	2,000

SALES DAYBOOK – VAT CHARGED: SPREADSHEET SOFTWARE BASED

A sales daybook that is spreadsheet based involves setting up a template to capture all the relevant sales transaction information for a period. A spreadsheet sales daybook has the advantage of being able to calculate totals automatically, thus speeding up the process.

The set-up of a spreadsheet software-based sales daybook is a straightforward process. Purchase the software and install it on your computer. Open up a new spreadsheet file and key in the column headings to collect the appropriate data. The basic headings required are shown in Figure 8.17.

Figure 8.17

Sales Daybook Spreadsheet Software Based – VAT

Sales daybook

DATE	CUSTOMER DETAILS	INVOICE NUMBER	Gross £ AMOUNT	VAT	Net Amount

Figure 8.18
Sales Invoices – Chris's Chairs

Chris's Chairs			
Unit 44, Business Corp. Pk, Big City			
Ph 8765 1234			
INVOICE			
Customer Details			
ABC Ltd		Invoice	1001
Side Street		DATE	03-Jan-14
Small Town		Account	ABC Ltd
DETAILS			Gross
2 x Canteen Chairs			150
Sub Total			150
VAT		20%	30
Total			180
VAT NO. GB 123 4567 89			

Chris's Chairs			
Unit 44, Business Corp. Pk, Big City			
Ph 8765 1234			
INVOICE			
Customer Details			
XYZ Ltd		Invoice	1002
Laneway		DATE	04-Jan-14
Small Town		Account	XYZ Ltd
DETAILS			Gross
1 x Office Chair - Leather			400
Sub total			400
VAT		20%	80
Total			480
VAT NO. GB 123 4567 89			

Chris's Chairs				
Unit 44, Business Corp. Pk, Big City				
Ph 8765 1234				
INVOICE				
Customer Details				
PPP Ltd			Invoice	1003
Laneway			DATE	11-Jan-14
Small Town			Account	PPP Ltd
	Details	Unit Net		Gross
1 x Office Chair - Cloth				120
Sub Total				120
VAT			20%	24
Total				144
VAT NO. GB 123 4567 89				

Chris's Chairs				
Unit 44, Business Corp. Pk, Big City				
Ph 8765 1234				
INVOICE				
Customer Details				
LOL Ltd			Invoice	1004
Side Street			DATE	15-Jan-14
Small Town			Account	LOL Ltd
	Details	Unit Net		Gross
1 x Executive Chair				300
Sub Total				300
VAT			20%	60
Total				360
VAT NO. GB 123 4567 89				

Example: product-based business – VAT rate 20%

Chris sells chairs from his small warehouse in an industrial estate. His business is VAT registered. He is using a paper-based invoice system as described in the sales invoicing chapter. Each time he sells a chair to a customer he writes an invoice on a pre-printed invoice pad and presents it to his customer. In the month of January he has issued four invoices to clients (see Figure 8.18).

> **MICRO TASK**
>
> **Can you produce the sales daybook for Chris's business based on the sales invoices produced for January?**
> - **Set up a sales daybook spreadsheet for Chris's business with the appropriate headings**
> - **Transfer the information contained on the sales invoices to the sales daybook**
> - **Check your answer against the solution provided below.**

In order to produce the sales daybook Chris needs to transfer the information contained on the sales invoices to the sales daybook spreadsheet. At the end of the month Chris would need to total all the sales figures in the sales daybook, to establish total sales for the month. If at the end of January Chris had no other sales invoices issued, he would total up the four invoices and close off the sales daybook spreadsheet as illustrated in Figure 8.19.

Figure 8.19
Sales Daybook Spreadsheet Software Based – Chris's Chairs – Totalled

SALES DAYBOOK					
DATE	CUSTOMER DETAILS	INVOICE NUMBER	£ GROSS AMOUNT	VAT 20%	Net
03-Jan-14	ABC Ltd	1001	180	30	150
04-Jan-14	XYZ Ltd	1002	480	80	400
11-Jan-14	PPP Ltd	1003	144	24	120
15-Jan-14	LOL Ltd	1004	360	60	300
Total			1,164	194	970

Based on the entries in the sales daybook spreadsheet for the month of January, Chris can identify his total gross sales were £1,164 including VAT. The total VAT charged to customers was £194 and the net sales excluding VAT for the month was £970.

SALES DAYBOOK – VAT CHARGED: ACCOUNTING SOFTWARE BASED

A sales daybook that is accounting software based is normally a highly efficient method to record sales transactions. The sales daybook is usually generated automatically when sales invoices are produced using the accounting software. Therefore, if you have decided to use accounting software to generate sales invoices you will save time. Another major advantage to using accounting software is that it is capable of dealing with VAT transactions and VAT at different rates. In addition, most accounting software packages have a module that can calculate VAT. There are numerous accounting software packages available on the market that you would need to evaluate based on the following:

- **How user friendly they are**
- **The cost**
- **Your accounting requirements**

In addition, you would need to consider how long it will take you to learn how to use any given accounting software package.

SALES DAYBOOK – VAT CHARGED: WEBSITE SOFTWARE BASED

If you are selling via a website, it is possible to use software to generate sales daybooks based on bookings and sales invoices issued. Another advantage of using such software is that most can also deal with VAT processing. There are numerous options available, depending on the functionality of your website, that can facilitate VAT processing.

SALES DAYBOOK – VAT CHARGED: PHONE APP BASED

There are a variety of phone apps available that will enable you to generate invoices for services rendered or products sold that will also create a sales daybook of sales transactions. Some apps are free, others charge a fee. There are numerous options available, depending on the functionality of the phone app, that can facilitate VAT processing.

SALES DAYBOOK – VAT CHARGED: CASH REGISTER BASED

If your business is cash based, such as a retail business, then using a cash register to record sales is the best option. The process to set up a system to record sales involves a number of steps:

- Step 1 – Select the most appropriate cash register for your business based on funds available and your requirements
- Step 2 – Select the most appropriate sales daybook option
- Step 3 – Set up an internal control process to ensure cash from sales is safeguarded and fully accounted for

Step 1 – Select the most appropriate cash register for your business based on funds available and your requirements.

There are many options available when selecting a cash register. The choice will depend on funds available and functionality required. A basic till cash register will cost you less initially but may involve more work overall, when producing information for sales and VAT analysis. A sophisticated cash register will cost more initially but should reduce work overall, when producing information for sales and VAT analysis.

When you have selected the most appropriate cash register for your business you/your staff need to learn how to use it properly. The most important report will be the Z report that you need run at the end of each trading day. The Z report totals the sales for the day. At the end of each trading day it is important to run the Z report to establish two things:

- The value of actual sales generated during the day
- The amount of cash in the cash register equals the amount of cash sales recorded

Step 2 – Select the most appropriate sales daybook option

Different types of cash registers offer different levels of functionality. The more basic cash registers will result in additional manual processing of sales data. For example, if a basic cash register is being used it may not be capable of separating cash sales from credit/debit card sales.

The options available for a sales daybook that is based on a cash register are as follows:

- Cash register sales daybook: paper based
- Cash register sales daybook: spreadsheet software based
- Cash register sales daybook: cash register software based

Cash register sales daybook: paper based

Purchase an analysis notebook to be used as a sales daybook. Set up the appropriate headings in the sales daybook as shown in Figure 8.20.

Figure 8.20

Sales Daybook Paper-Based Template VAT

SALES DAYBOOK

DATE	£ AMOUNT	£ AMOUNT	£ AMOUNT	£ AMOUNT	£ AMOUNT
	Total Sales as per Z Report	Total Credit/Debit Card Sales	Total Cash Sales	VAT	Total Sales Excluding VAT
Total					

At the end of each trading day print off the Z report to identify the total value of the sales for the day. If your business accepts payment by cash and credit/debit cards then the sales figure needs to be further analysed into cash sales and credit/debit card sales.

For a business using a basic cash register that accepts payments in cash and credit/debit cards, the cash sales figure can be identified as follows:

1. Print off the Z report from the cash register at the end of the trading day
2. Print off the sales report from the credit/debit card terminal
3. Subtract the sales figure on the credit/debit card terminal report from the sales figure on the Z report. This figure is the amount of cash sales for the day

Enter the sales data into the sales daybook. Enter the total value of sales for the day in one column. Enter the total value of credit/debit cards sales for the day into a separate column. Enter the total value of cash sales for the day into a separate column. The value of the cash sales for the day and the value of the credit/debit cards for the same day must equate the total sales for the day as per the Z report figure. Calculate the value of VAT relating to the total sales figure for the day. Insert the VAT figure into the appropriate column. Calculate the value of total sales excluding VAT and insert the figure into the appropriate column.

Do this every day for the week. At the end of the week add up all the daily sales to calculate the total sales for the week. Keep repeating the process of recording the sales. See Figure 8.21 for an example of a cash register sales daybook paper based.

Cash register sales daybook: spreadsheet software based

Set up a spreadsheet to be used as a sales daybook. Set up the appropriate headings in the sales daybook as shown in Figure 8.22.

At the end of each trading day print off the Z report to identify the total

Figure 8.21

Sales Daybook Paper-Based – VAT

SALES DAYBOOK

DATE	£ AMOUNT	£ AMOUNT	£ AMOUNT	£ AMOUNT	£ AMOUNT
	Total Sales as per Z Report	Total Credit/Debit Card Sales	Total Cash Sales	VAT 20%	Total Sales Excluding VAT
03-Mar-14	1,200	500	700	200	1,000
04-Mar-14	2,400	1,000	1,400	400	2,000
05-Mar-14	600	300	300	100	500
06-Mar-14	1,800	600	1,200	300	1,500
07-Mar-14	1,350	450	900	225	1,125
08-Mar-14	2,400	200	2,200	400	2,000
Total	9,750	3,050	6,700	1,625	8,125

value of the sales for the day. If your business accepts payment by cash and credit/debit cards then the sales figure needs to be further analysed into cash sales and credit/debit card sales.

For a business using a basic cash register that accepts payments in cash and credit/debit cards the cash sales figure can be identified as follows:

1. **Print off the Z report from the cash register at the end of the trading day**
2. **Print off the sales report from the credit/debit card terminal**
3. **Subtract the sales figure on the credit/debit card terminal report from the sales figure on the Z report. This figure is the amount of cash sales for the day**

Enter the sales data into the sales daybook spreadsheet. Enter the total value of sales for the day in one column. Enter the total value of credit/debit cards sales

Figure 8.22

Sales Daybook Spreadsheet-Based Template – VAT

SALES DAYBOOK

DATE	£ AMOUNT	£ AMOUNT	£ AMOUNT	£ AMOUNT	£ AMOUNT
	Total Sales as per Z Report	Total Credit/Debit Card Sales	Total Cash Sales	VAT	Total Sales Excluding VAT
Total					

for the day into a separate column. Enter the total value of cash sales for the day into a separate column. The value of the cash sales for the day and the value of the credit/debit cards for the same day must equate the total sales for the day as per the Z report figure. Calculate the value of VAT relating to the total sales figure for the day. Insert the VAT figure into the appropriate column. Calculate the value of total sales excluding VAT and insert the figure into the appropriate column.

Do this every day for the week. At the end of the week add up all the daily sales to calculate the total sales for the week. Keep repeating the process of recording the sales. See Figure 8.23 for an example of a cash register sales daybook spreadsheet based.

Figure 8.23
Sales Daybook Spreadsheet Based – VAT

SALES DAYBOOK					
DATE	£ AMOUNT	£ AMOUNT	£ AMOUNT	£ AMOUNT	£ AMOUNT
	Total Sales as per Z Report	Total Credit/Debit Card Sales	Total Cash Sales	VAT 20%	Total Sales Excluding VAT
03-Mar-14	1,200	500	700	200	1,000
04-Mar-14	2,400	1,000	1,400	400	2,000
05-Mar-14	600	300	300	100	500
06-Mar-14	1,800	600	1,200	300	1,500
07-Mar-14	1,350	450	900	225	1,125
08-Mar-14	2,400	200	2,200	400	2,000
Total	9,750	3,050	6,700	1,625	8,125

Cash register sales daybook: cash register software based

On the more sophisticated cash registers there can be the option to print off a sales daybook based on sales receipts issued for a given period. If your cash register has this function it will speed up the processing of sales figures for a given period. This means the report printed off from the cash register is the sales daybook for the period, negating the need for manual input onto a separate sales daybook. The more sophisticated cash registers can analyse sales into cash sales and credit/debit card sales. Such registers can also have a reporting function to calculate VAT on sales and even sales by product type.

Step 3 – Set up an internal control process to ensure cash from sales is safeguarded and fully accounted for.

A simple internal control to put in place to safeguard cash is the use of cash sheets. Cash sheets identify sales for a period, normally a week. In addition, cash sheets identify any monies taken from cash sales and how such monies were spent. For full details of how to set up and operate cash sheets, see chapter 5.

CHAPTER 9

How to record income transactions using a bank receipts book

BANK RECEIPTS BOOK – OVERVIEW

A bank receipts book is a record that lists transactions relating to monies received into a bank account for a given period, e.g., a day, a week, a month or a year. It is referred to as a bank receipts book because traditionally it was a paper notebook with rows and columns, used to record bank receipts. Effectively the contents of a bank receipts book is merely a list of monies received into a bank account for a given period. See Figure 9.1 for an overview of a bank receipts book.

An example of a bank receipts book for a VAT-registered business or a non-VAT-registered business would contain information such as that shown in Figure 9.2.

Figure 9.1
Bank Receipts Book – Overview

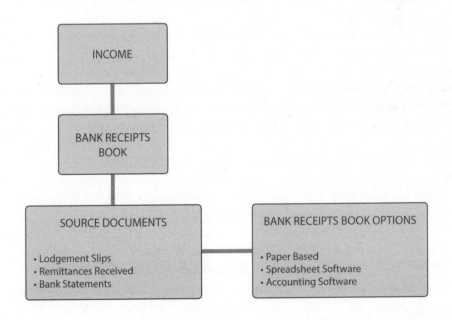

INCOME

BANK RECEIPTS BOOK

SOURCE DOCUMENTS

• Lodgement Slips
• Remittances Received
• Bank Statements

BANK RECEIPTS BOOK OPTIONS

• Paper Based
• Spreadsheet Software
• Accounting Software

Figure 9.2

Bank Receipts Book Example

BANK RECEIPTS BOOK					
DATE	NAME CUSTOMER/THIRD PARTY	RECEIPT TYPE / REF	AMOUNT £	SALES RECEIPTS £	OTHER RECEIPTS £

The basic information recorded in the bank receipts book would be:

- The date of the receipt of monies
- The source of the monies, for example the name of the customer making the payment or the name of the source of monies received from a third party, e.g., a bank loan
- The receipt reference or type, e.g., a cheque, a bank transfer, a cash lodgement
- The total amount of the receipt received
- The receipt amount relating to a sales receipt from a customer
- The receipt amount relating to a receipt from a source other than a customer

A bank receipts book is a record of all monies received by a business from any source into its bank account. The majority of monies received by a business will be from customers paying for services or products. Any other monies received by a business from third parties who are not customers will be recorded under the heading 'Other'. Examples of monies being received by a business that is not from customers would be bank loans, monies injected into the business by the owners or tax refunds.

The details noted in a bank receipts book would include the date of the receipt of monies, the name of the customer or third party who was the source of the money received, the receipt type, for example cash, cheque, electronic funds transfer (EFT) and the amount of money received.

BANK RECEIPTS BOOK – SOURCE DOCUMENTS

The data to be recorded in the bank receipts book is obtained from a variety of source documents, such as:

Lodgement slips – each time a physical lodgement of cash or cheques is made, a lodgement slip is created to record the transaction. The details contained on the lodgement slip would be: the date of the transaction, the total value of the lodgement and the name of the third party from whom the monies were received. Lodgement slips may be from a pre-printed lodgement book supplied by the bank to their customer. Lodgements slips may be generated from an automated teller machine (ATM) at a bank when a lodgement is made. Lodgements slips may be single dockets available at the bank when lodgements are being made. The details noted on lodgement slips need to be recorded in the bank receipts book. It is necessary to verify as part of a regular systematic check that lodgements made and recorded on the lodgement slips actually appear on a bank statement.

Remittance documents – a remittance is a document from a third party advising details of a payment. A customer remittance details the value of a payment being issued to a business, the invoices that the customer is paying and the method of payment, for example electronic funds transfer or cheque. The details of the customer remittance advice slip will need to be recorded in the bank receipts book. It is necessary to verify as part of a regular systematic check that the transfers noted on remittances actually appear on a bank statement and that the funds are actually credited to the bank account.

A remittance from a third party who is not a customer of the business will detail the value of monies being issued to the business, for example a loan from a bank. The details of the third party remittance advice slip will need to be recorded in the bank receipts book. It is necessary to verify as part of a regular systematic check that transfers noted on remittances actually appear on a bank statement and that the funds are actually credited to the bank account.

It is very important that sales receipts and non-sales receipts, i.e., other receipts, are separated. If they are not, it can happen that a non-sales receipt will be treated as a sales receipt, resulting in accounting errors, such as:

- **Customer accounts incorrectly showing a reduced amount of money owed**
- **Sales income for the business being stated at a higher amount than it should**

Bank statements – a bank statement will list all the monies received into the bank account for a given period. The receipts would normally have a reference noted, so the source of the receipt can be identified. Any receipts noted on the bank statement not previously entered into the bank receipts book would need to be recorded into the bank receipts book.

BANK RECEIPTS BOOK – PAPER BASED

A bank receipts book that is paper based involves the use of any paper record, for example an A4 writing pad or a hardback analysis book with pre-printed columns. It is recommended to use a hardback analysis book as this is produced for the purpose of recording financial data. To set up a paper-based bank receipts book is a straightforward process. Purchase a hardback analysis book as suggested and write in the column headings to collect the appropriate data. The basic headings required are shown in Figure 9.3.

Figure 9.3
Bank Receipts Book Paper-Based Template

BANK RECEIPTS BOOK					
DATE	NAME CUSTOMER/THIRD PARTY	RECEIPT TYPE / REF	AMOUNT £	SALES RECEIPTS £	OTHER RECEIPTS £

Example

John is an electrician who offers an electrical maintenance service to a number of factories in his town. He issues his invoices on a monthly basis. In January he issues a number of invoices and in February he receives a number of payments from his customers.

John receives a cash payment from his customer Jones Engineering of £250. John goes to the bank on 1 February and lodges the money into his business account. When he lodges the money, the bank clerk gives him a lodgement slip, receipt number 456, noting the details of the lodgement. Later that day John records the details of the lodgement slip number 456 in his bank receipts book. He also retains the lodgement slip on file for future reference. John will also verify that the payment was actually credited to his bank account when he receives his bank statement or views it online.

On 5 February John receives a remittance notice from AB Ltd, advising an electronic funds transfer of £800 has been issued to pay for a January invoice. John records the details of this remittance advice in his bank receipts book. He will also verify that the payment was actually credited to his bank account when he receives his bank statement or views it online.

John receives a cheque in the post on 7 February for £600 from Factory Outlet Ltd, with a remittance advice noting the January invoice the payment relates to. John lodges the cheque at the bank and receives a lodgement slip, number 789. Later that day John records the details of the lodgement slip number 789 in his bank receipts book. He also retains the lodgement slip on file for future reference. John will also verify that the payment was actually credited to his bank account when he receives his bank statement or views it online.

John receives a letter from his bank on 15 February advising that a loan he applied for has been approved. The letter is effectively a remittance advice, as it details the value of the funds credited to his bank account is £2,000. John records this receipt in the bank receipts book. John also retains the letter on file for future reference. He will also verify that the monies were actually credited to his bank account when he receives his statement or views it online.

John inputs the receipts for February in his bank receipts book as shown in Figure 9.4.

Figure 9.4
Bank Receipts Book – John, Electrical Engineer

BANK RECEIPTS BOOK

DATE	NAME CUSTOMER/THIRD PARTY	RECEIPT TYPE / REF	AMOUNT £	SALES RECEIPTS £	OTHER RECEIPTS £
01-Feb-14	Jones Engineering	ref 456 cash	250.00	250.00	
05-Feb-14	AB Ltd	EFT	800.00	800.00	
07-Feb-14	Factory Outlet Ltd	ref 789 cheque	600.00	600.00	
15-Feb-14	Bank	Bank loan	2,000.00		2,000.00
Total			3,650.00	1,650.00	2,000.00

Based on the bank receipts book John can identify that his customers paid him £1,650 and he received a loan from the bank of £2,000 in the month of February. It is very important that the sales receipts and the non-sales receipts, i.e., the loan, are separately identified.

John would need to check that the amount he received from his customers equates to the amount due on outstanding invoices.

In addition, as part of his internal controls, John should write on the sales invoices the date that they have been paid and the method of payment, for example cash, cheque, electronic funds transfer.

BANK RECEIPTS BOOK – SPREADSHEET SOFTWARE BASED

A bank receipts book that is spreadsheet based involves setting up a template to capture all the relevant information. A spreadsheet bank receipts book has the advantage of being able to calculate totals automatically, resulting in faster processing. The set-up of a spreadsheet software-based bank receipts book is a straightforward process. Purchase the software and install it on your computer. Open up a new spreadsheet file and key in the column headings to collect the appropriate data. The basic headings required are shown in Figure 9.5.

Figure 9.5

Bank Receipts Book Spreadsheet Software-Based Template

BANK RECEIPTS BOOK					
DATE	NAME CUSTOMER/THIRD PARTY	RECEIPT TYPE / REF	AMOUNT £	SALES RECEIPTS £	OTHER RECEIPTS £

Example

Peter runs a printing business offering products to local businesses in his town. He issues his invoices on a monthly basis. In January, he issues a number of invoices and in February he receives a number of payments from his customers.

Peter receives a text message from his uncle Jim on 5 February advising that the loan of £5,000 they had discussed has been lodged by his uncle into Peter's bank account. The text message is effectively a remittance advice as it details the value of the funds credited to his bank account. Peter records this receipt in the bank receipts book. Peter will also verify that the payment was actually credited to his bank account when he receives his bank statement or views it online.

On 6 February Peter receives a remittance notice from XY Ltd advising an electronic funds transfer of £475 has been issued to pay for a January invoice. Peter records the details of this remittance advice in his bank receipts book. Peter will also verify that the payment was actually credited to his bank account when he receives his bank statement or views it online.

Peter receives a cash payment from his customer Mr Smith of £250. Peter goes to the bank on 10 February and lodges the money into his business account. When he lodges the money, the bank clerk gives him a lodgement slip receipt, number 333, noting the details of the lodgement. Later that day Peter records the details of the lodgement slip number 333 in his bank receipts book. He retains the lodgement slip on file for future reference. Peter will also verify that the payment was actually credited to his bank account when he receives his bank statement or views it online.

Peter receives a cheque in the post on 20 February for £600, from Super Fit Ltd, with a remittance advice noting the January invoice the payment relates to. Peter lodges the cheque at the bank and receives a lodgement slip, number 666. Later that day Peter records the details of the lodgement slip number 666 in his bank receipts book. He retains the lodgement slip on file for future reference. Peter will also verify that the payment was actually credited to his bank account when he receives his bank statement or views it online.

MICRO TASK
- **Can you set up a bank receipts book to record the bank receipt transactions for Peter?**
- **Compare your bank receipts book for Peter against the solution below.**

Peter inputs the receipts for February into his spreadsheet software-based bank receipts book as shown in Figure 9.6.

Figure 9.6
Bank Receipts Book Spreadsheet Software Based – Peter

BANK RECEIPTS BOOK					
DATE	NAME CUSTOMER/THIRD PARTY	RECEIPT TYPE / REF	AMOUNT £	SALES RECEIPT £	OTHER RECEIPTS £
05-Feb-14	Uncle Jim	text message	5,000.00		5,000.00
06-Feb-14	XY Ltd	EFT	475.00	475.00	
10-Feb-14	Smith	ref 333 cash	250.00	250.00	
20-Feb-14	Super Fit Ltd	ref 666 cheque	600.00	600.00	
Total			6,325.00	1,325.00	5,000.00

Based on the bank receipts book spreadsheet Peter can identify that in the month of February he received £1,325 from his customers and also a loan of £5,000 from his uncle.

BANK RECEIPTS BOOK – ACCOUNTING SOFTWARE BASED

Using accounting software to record receipts is normally highly efficient. In addition to automatically generating various reports, accounting software can utilize the data for other purposes once it has been input. For example, a receipt from a customer input onto accounting software can increase the bank balance by the amount received and simultaneously reduce the amount owed by the relevant customer. There are numerous accounting software packages available on the market that you would need to evaluate based on how user friendly they are, the cost and also your accounting requirements.

CHAPTER 10

How to record income transactions – summary

INCOME TRANSACTIONS SUMMARY

A bookkeeping system needs to systematically record all income transactions. The income of a business can be recorded using the following records:
- **Sales daybook**
- **Bank receipts book**

The choice between using a manual system and a computerized system will depend upon several factors including: sales volume, costs, IT skills level and image.

A sales daybook identifies total sales for a period of time. The sales figures for a business are essential to have available to be able to monitor the progress of the business.

A bank receipts book records all monies received by a business. Money receipts can be obtained from customers or from other third parties such as a bank or investors.

Small businesses tend to operate with little financial information about their business. Having accurate sales figures is the absolute minimum that is required to have any hope of controlling a business. Different business sectors can approach the recording of sales in a variety of ways. The option to select is the one that is most suitable for the business you are currently running. The best option is usually the most automated.

MICRO QUIZ

Q1: A sales daybook for a VAT-registered business and a non-VAT-registered business records the exact same information.

    True or False?

Q2: Source documents such as sales invoices are used to capture sales transactions.

    True or False?

Q3: A sales daybook is a list of all sales invoices for a given period.

    True or False?

Q4: The end-of-day Z report from a cash register identifies the total sales for the day.

    True or False?

Q5: A cash sheet is not an effective internal control to monitor cash payments from cash sales.

    True or False?

Q6: Lodgement slips are a source document used to identify transactions to be recorded in the bank receipts book.

    True or False?

Q7: A bank receipts book for a VAT-registered business does not need to record the VAT element of a bank receipt.

    True or False?

Q8: It is not possible to use a paper-based record system with a software-based record system.

    True or False?

Q9: The more automated a system is for recording sales the better.

    True or False?

Q10: EFT stands for electronic financial transaction.

    True or False?

Micro quiz – solutions

Q1: False

Q2: True

Q3: True

Q4: True

Q5: False

Q6: True

Q7: True

Q8: False

Q9: True

Q10: False

Expenditure – how to record expenditure transactions

CHAPTER 11

How to record expenditure transactions

Figure 11.1
Expenditure Overview

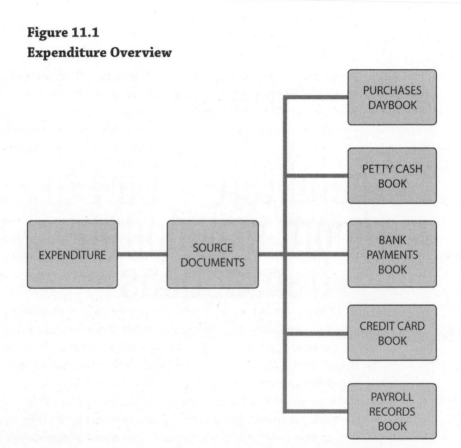

EXPENDITURE OVERVIEW – SOURCE DOCUMENTS

Source documents are the starting point to identify expenditure transactions. Source documents are documents that record the activities of a business. The activities recorded can be financial or non-financial. Source documents can be produced internally by a business, such as a delivery docket to record quantities of goods supplied or a sales invoice to record the monetary value of services rendered and/or goods supplied to a customer. Source documents can also be received by a business from third parties, such as purchase invoices detailing the value of goods or services obtained from a supplier or bank statements detailing banking transactions for a period. The details of expenditure transactions are identified from source documents and recorded in various expenditure records. See figure 11.1 for an overview of expenditure.

The expenditure records illustrated in this section include:

- **Purchases daybook**
- **Petty cash book**
- **Bank payments book**
- **Credit card book**
- **Payroll records book**

The number of expenditure records that need to be maintained by a business depends on the amount of different types of expenditure that the business incurs. The majority of businesses need to maintain at least three expenditure records, i.e., purchases daybook, petty cash book and a bank payments book. If a business does not use a credit card, then it does not need a credit card book. If a business does not have any staff, then it does not need a payroll records book.

Expenditure transactions are recorded in a variety of ways depending on a number of factors:

- **If the expenditure incurred is due to a purchase of goods or services then expenditure would be recorded in the purchases daybook. The purchases daybook is a list detailing such information as the date of the purchase invoice from the supplier, the supplier name, the supplier invoice number, the monetary value of the transaction and VAT details if applicable**
- **If the expenditure incurred is paid by cash for a low-value transaction, then it is recorded in the petty cash book. The petty cash book is a list of low-value purchase transactions. It records basic details of transactions including the date, the name of the payee, the monetary amount and any other relevant information deemed necessary**
- **If the expenditure incurred is paid from the bank account, then it is recorded in the bank payments book. The bank payments book lists information such as the date of the transaction, the name of the payee and the monetary value. It will also detail supplementary information, for example a reference to the type of payment (cheque/direct debit/ standing order), and any other relevant details**
- **If the expenditure incurred is paid by credit card, then it is recorded in the credit card book. The credit card book is a list of credit card transactions recording details including the date, the name of the payee, any other relevant details, for example supplier invoice numbers, and the monetary value of the transaction**
- **If the expenditure relates to payroll it is necessary to maintain a payroll records book that show the calculations for net wages and taxes. The actual payments relating to payroll that need to be recorded depends**

on how the payment is made. If the payment for payroll is issued from the bank, then it is recorded in the bank payments book. If the payment for payroll is issued from cash sales, then it is recorded on cash sheets and subsequently the petty cash book

The records generated to record expenditure transactions can be affected by the circumstances of a business. A business may supply a service and/or product, a business may be VAT registered, a business may be a sole trader, a partnership or a limited company. The recording of expenditure transactions needs to be adjusted to record the relevant information for the circumstances of the business.

This topic, expenditure, is divided into five sections relating to expenditure records. For the maximum return on your time you should only read the material that is relevant to the circumstances of your business. If your business is not VAT registered then you can ignore material relating to VAT-registered businesses and vice versa.

Purchases daybook

A purchases daybook is a record that lists expenditure transactions for a given period, e.g., a day, a week, a month or a year. Expenditure transactions are purchases made by a business of goods and/or services from other businesses.

Petty cash book

A petty cash book is a record that lists minor cash expenditure transactions for a given period, e.g., a day, a week, a month or a year. Minor cash expenditure transactions are purchases made by a business for goods and/or services from other businesses of low monetary value, paid for by cash.

Bank payments book

A bank payments book is a record that lists payment transactions issued from a bank account for a given period, e.g., a day, a week, a month or a year. Bank payment transactions are payments issued through a bank account by cheque, transfers or any other means.

Credit card book

A credit card book is a record that lists payment transactions issued from a credit card account for a given period, e.g., a day, a week, a month or a year. Credit card payment transactions are payments issued through a credit card account. Receipt transactions affecting the credit card account are also recorded in the credit card book.

Payroll records book

A payroll records book details relevant information relating to payroll, for example staff gross pay, staff net pay and taxes deducted for the period. It is not necessary to maintain a book, either paper based or software based, to record the aforementioned details. Payroll information can be produced from payroll software and reports can be retained as a record of payroll transactions. The payroll reports are effectively the payroll records book.

Paper-based systems versus software-based systems

For every expenditure your business incurs, you have the choice to record the transaction in a paper-based system or a software-based system. It is your decision to choose which system is most appropriate for your business and you need to evaluate the relative pros and cons of each.

There are advantages and disadvantages associated with both paper-based systems and software-based systems. The choice between each type of system is not mutually exclusive. It is possible to use a paper-based system in conjunction with a software-based system.

You may favour a paper-based system if you have an IT phobia or you may favour a software-based system if you have a high-volume business and require a system that enables faster processing. You may start off with a paper-based system and then migrate to a software-based system as your business expands.

In order to facilitate your decision-making process consider the following factors when evaluating which type of system is most appropriate for your business:

Purchases volume

A low purchase volume business can be adequately controlled using a paper-based system. A high purchase volume business is more suited to software-based systems.

Costs

Paper-based systems are relatively cheap to set up and maintain, although it would be important to consider the time spent processing, as this is also a cost to your business. Software-based systems can be inexpensive due to the volume of software providers in the marketplace.

IT skills level

You need to consider if you have adequate IT knowledge to allow you to set up and run a software-based system. If not, you can learn the basics to get you started. You need to consider the time required for you to increase your IT knowledge levels, as this is also a cost to your business.

Image

You need to consider the image you portray to your suppliers. If you are using a paper-based system, will this make your business look antiquated? Handwritten paperwork does not look as professional as computer-generated documents.

CHAPTER 12

How to record expenditure transactions in a purchases daybook

Figure 12.1
Expenditure – Purchases Daybook

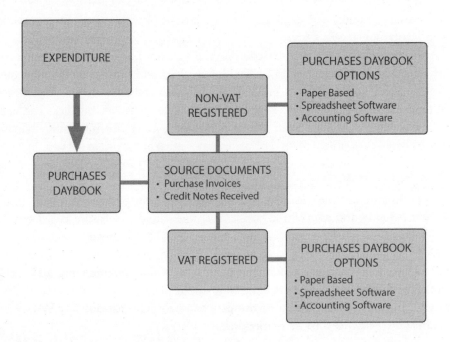

PURCHASES DAYBOOK – OVERVIEW

A purchases daybook is a record that lists expenditure transactions for a given period, e.g., a day, a week, a month or a year. Expenditure transactions are purchases made by a business of goods and/or services. It is referred to as a purchases book because traditionally it was a paper notebook with rows and columns used to record purchases. It is referred to as a purchases daybook because the book was traditionally updated on a daily basis. Effectively the contents of a purchases daybook is merely a list of purchase invoices received from suppliers for a given period. If credit notes are received from suppliers, then the value of purchases noted in the purchases daybook is reduced by the value of the credit notes. See Figure 12.1 for an overview of expenditure relating to the purchases of the day.

An example of a purchases daybook for a non-VAT-registered business would contain information such as shown in Figure 12.2.

Figure 12.2
Purchases Daybook – Non-Vat-Registered Business

PURCHASES DAYBOOK

Date	Supplier	Invoice No.	Description	Gross Amount	Goods for Resale	Office Rent	Stationery	Telecoms	Insurance
05-May-14	Acme Supplies Ltd	AS 1445	Chairs	2,400	2,400				
07-May-14	Stationery Plus	SP 5689	Various	150			150		
13-May-14	Telecoms Tech	889 TT	Landline	114				114	
22-May-14	Big Lets Ltd	444555	Office rent	1,200		1,200			
23-May-14	Acme Supplies Ltd	AS 1498	Chairs	3,600	3,600				
26-May-14	Triple A Insurance	Q1 - 88	Insurance	650					650
				8,114	6,000	1,200	150	114	650

The purchases daybook for a non-VAT-registered business records basic details of purchases for a period, such as the following:
- **The date of the purchase**
- **The name of the supplier**
- **The supplier invoice number that relates to the purchase**
- **A brief description of goods or services purchased**
- **The gross monetary value of the purchase, which includes any VAT charged**
- **The gross monetary value of the purchase, which includes any VAT charged, allocated to an appropriate category**

An example of a purchases daybook for a VAT-registered business would contain information as detailed in Figure 12.3.

The purchases daybook for a VAT-registered business records basic details of purchases for a period, such as the following:
- **The date of the purchase**
- **The name of the supplier**
- **The supplier invoice number that relates to the purchase**
- **A brief description of goods or services purchased**
- **The gross monetary value of the purchase including VAT**
- **The monetary value of the VAT only, i.e., VAT amount**

Figure 12.3

Purchases Daybook – Vat-Registered Business

PURCHASES DAYBOOK											
Date	Supplier	Invoice No.	Description	Gross Amount	VAT	Net Amount	Goods for Resale	Office Rent	Stationery	Telecoms	Insurance
05-May-14	Acme Supplies Ltd	AS 1445	Chairs	2,400	400	2,000	2,000				
07-May-14	Stationery Plus	SP 5689	Various	150	25	125			125		
13-May-14	Telecoms Tech	889 TT	Landline	114	19	95				95	
22-May-14	Big Lets Ltd	444555	Office rent	1,200	200	1,000		1,000			
23-May-14	Acme Supplies Ltd	AS 1498	Chairs	3,600	600	3,000	3,000				
26-May-14	Triple A Insurance	Q1 - 88	Insurance	650	0	650					650
				8,114	1,244	6,870	5,000	1,000	125	95	650

- The net monetary value, i.e., the purchase price excluding VAT
- The net monetary value purchase price allocated to an appropriate category, i.e., the purchase price excluding VAT

Purchases daybook options

There are a number of purchases daybook options available and it is necessary to evaluate which option is best suited so you can select the most appropriate option for the business.

- Option 1 – Paper based
- Option 2 – Spreadsheet software based
- Option 3 – Accounting software based

In order to facilitate your decision making when evaluating a manual system or a software system you should review paper-based systems versus software-based systems, noted in chapter 11.

A purchases daybook identifies the total value of all purchases for a period of time. The purchases figures for a business are essential to have available to be able to control the finances of the business. Small businesses tend to operate with little financial information about their businesses. Having accurate purchases figures helps a business to keep track of its spending. Different business sectors can approach the recording of purchases in the purchases daybook in a variety of ways. The option to select is the one that is most suitable for the business you are currently running. The best option is usually the most automated.

One minor complication arises when a business is registered for VAT (value added tax). If a business is registered for VAT it is necessary to account for the VAT and detail it in the purchases daybook. VAT rates differ depending on the products or services supplied and the VAT status of suppliers.

Purchases daybook – source documents

The data to be recorded in the purchases daybook is obtained from a variety of source documents, such as:

Purchase invoices – a purchase invoice is a document that details the monetary value and a description of goods and/or services supplied to a business. The relevant details contained on purchase invoices can be transferred to a purchases daybook. Credit notes (received) – a credit note received from a supplier is a document that details the monetary value of a refund from a supplier. The relevant details contained on credit notes can be transferred to a purchases daybook. The value of purchases will be reduced by the value of credit notes received.

Purchases daybook – non-VAT-registered business: paper based

What do you need to record purchases manually for a non-VAT-registered business using a paper-based purchases daybook?
1. A lever arch folder to file purchase invoices
2. An accounts analysis book to record purchases

Set-up

- The spine of the lever arch folder should be clearly marked as 'Purchase Invoices Unpaid' and the financial year should be noted on the spine, e.g., 'Year 2014', so it is clearly visible
- The lever arch folder should be divided alphabetically with an alphabetical divider
- The accounts analysis book being used as a purchases daybook should have the appropriate headings noted in columns, including the following: date, supplier name, supplier invoice number, description of

Figure 12.4

Purchases Daybook Paper Based – Non-VAT Registered

PURCHASES DAYBOOK									
Date	Supplier	Invoice No.	Description	Gross Amount	Goods For Resale	Rent	Stationery	Telecoms	Insurance

goods or services, gross monetary amount. Other columns should be used to categorize the nature of purchases as appropriate, such as goods for resale (if your business is product based), office rent, stationery, telecoms, insurance, etc. The number of other categories you use depends on the level of detail you require. Figure 12.4 is an example of a purchases daybook with relevant header columns noted

NOTE: If you are running a service-based business you can omit the column noted as 'Goods for Resale'.

The process

Each time a purchase invoice is received from a supplier for goods or services supplied it should be filed at the front of the 'Purchase Invoices Unpaid' lever arch folder, i.e., not filed alphabetically. The purchase invoices are merely held at the front of the file until a batch of purchase invoices can be processed.

When a batch of purchase invoices has accumulated at the front of the folder, they can then be processed. This should be part of a regular routine, carried out on a daily, weekly or monthly basis. Take the batch of purchase invoices out of the lever arch folder and record the details of these invoices in the purchases daybook. For each purchase invoice you will need to record the relevant information in the columns in the purchases daybook. Record details, including the date, the name of the supplier, a brief description of the supply of goods or services, the gross monetary amount and the category that best fits the nature of the purchase, for example rent, stationery, telecoms, insurance, etc.

Each time you have entered in the details of a purchase invoice write the letter 'E' in a circle in red ink at the top right-hand corner of the purchase invoice. This simple process will enable you to know immediately if you have entered any given purchase invoice into the purchases daybook. When all the purchase invoices in the batch have been entered into the purchases daybook, all of these purchase invoices should have the letter 'E' in a circle in red ink at the top right-hand corner. These invoices should then be filed alphabetically in the 'Purchase Invoices Unpaid' lever arch folder.

Example – non-VAT-registered business: Andrew, architect

Andrew is an architect who operates as a sole trader who is not registered for VAT and runs his business from a city centre office. During any given month he will receive invoices for goods and services he has obtained from his suppliers.

Andrew has agreed credit terms with suppliers of 30 days, meaning goods and services purchased in January are paid for in February.

As he receives invoices during the month he places them at the front of the 'Purchase Invoices Unpaid' lever arch folder. At the end of the month Andrew can then process the purchase invoices as a batch. Andrew enters the details of

Figure 12.5
Purchase Invoices – Andrew, Architect

Office Supplies Ltd
INVOICE

Customer Details
Andrew Architect
Main Street
Large Town

	Invoice	4596
	DATE	05-Jan-14
	Account	AA01

Qty	Details	Net	VAT	Gross
			20%	
10	Boxes of A4	375	75	450

Total				450

VAT No. 1122 12345

Speak Now PLC
INVOICE

Customer Details
Andrew Architect
Main Street
Large Town

	Invoice	99856
	DATE	08-Jan-14
	Account	ANDARC

Details	Net	VAT	Gross
		20%	
Provision of telecoms	145	29.00	174

Total			174

VAT No. 3344 12345

J B LANDLORD
INVOICE

Customer Details
Andrew Architect
Main Street
Large Town

	Invoice	A01
	DATE	08-Jan-14
	Account	Andrew

Details	Net	VAT	Gross
		20%	
Rent for January	500	100	600

Total			600

VAT No. 5566 12345

Triple A Insurance
INVOICE

Customer Details
Andrew Architect
Main Street
Large Town

	Invoice	145
	DATE	14-Jan-14
	Account	Classic

Details	Net	Gross
Insurance	1,000	1,000

Total		1,000

each purchase invoice into the purchases daybook, noting the date, the supplier name, the invoice number, a description of the goods or services, the gross monetary amount and then enters the monetary amount in the appropriate analysis column.

During the month of January Andrew receives the purchase invoices as detailed in Figure 12.5.

At the end of the month Andrew processes all the purchase invoices received and records the details in the purchases daybook. After he has written the details of an invoice in the purchases daybook he writes the letter 'E' in red ink with a circle around it, in the top right-hand corner of the purchase invoice. The letter 'E' written in red and circled is a visual reminder to Andrew that he has entered the details of the invoice in the purchases daybook. This will stop him entering the invoice twice or searching the purchases daybook to verify if the invoice has been written in. Andrew then files the invoices in the 'Purchase Invoices Unpaid' folder, in alphabetical order.

MICRO TASK

Can you record the purchase transactions in the purchases daybook for Andrew's business?
- Set up the purchases daybook based on the templates previously explained
- Input the transactions into the purchases daybook
- Compare your purchases daybook for Andrew to the solution below.

After the purchase invoice details have been entered into the purchases daybook it would show what is illustrated in Figure 12.6.

Figure 12.6
Purchases Daybook Paper Based – Andrew, Architect

	PURCHASES DAYBOOK								

Date	Supplier	Invoice No.	Description	Gross Amount	Rent	Stationery	Telecoms	Insurance
05-Jan-14	Office Supplies Ltd	4596	Boxes of A4	450.00		450.00		
08-Jan-14	Speak Now PLC	99856	Provision of telecoms	174.00			174.00	
08-Jan-14	J B LANDLORD	A01	Rent for January	600.00	600.00			
14-Jan-14	Triple A Insurance	145	Insurance	1,000.00				1,000.00
Total				2,224.00	600.00	450.00	174.00	1,000.00

Andrew's business is not VAT registered, therefore he records the gross amount of each invoice that includes VAT, where charged by the supplier, in both the total column, i.e., gross amount column, and also in the analysis columns.

Based on the details in the purchases daybook Andrew can identify that he purchased goods and services of £2,224, comprising rent £600, stationery £450, telecoms £174 and insurance £1,000.

Purchases daybook – non-VAT-registered business: spreadsheet software

What do you need to record purchases using spreadsheet software for a non-VAT-registered service or product-based business?

1. A lever arch folder
2. A computer
3. Spreadsheet software

Set-up

- The spine of the lever arch folder should be clearly marked as 'Purchase Invoices Unpaid' and also the financial year should be noted on the spine, e.g., 'Year 2014', so it is clearly visible
- The lever arch folder should be divided alphabetically with an alphabetical divider
- Create a spreadsheet file and name it 'Purchases Daybook' and include the trading year, for example 'Purchases Daybook 2014'
- The spreadsheet file being used as a purchases daybook should have the appropriate headings noted in columns. Headings should include the following: date, supplier name, supplier invoice number, description of

Figure 12.7
Purchases Daybook Spreadsheet Software Based – Template

PURCHASES DAYBOOK								
Date	Supplier	Invoice No.	Description	Gross Amount	Rent	Stationery	Telecoms	Insurance

goods or services, gross monetary amount. Other columns should be used to categorize the nature of purchases as appropriate, for example goods for resale (if your business is product based), rent, stationery, telecoms, insurance, etc. The number of other categories you use depends on the level of detail you require. Detailed in Figure 12.7 is an example of a purchases daybook spreadsheet with relevant header columns noted

---

NOTE: If you are running a service-based business you can omit the column noted as 'Goods for Resale'.

The process

Each time a purchase invoice is received from a supplier for goods or services supplied, it should be filed at the front of the 'Purchase Invoices Unpaid' lever arch folder, i.e., not filed alphabetically, merely held at the front of the file until a batch of purchase invoices can be processed.

When a batch of purchase invoices has accumulated at the front of the file, they can then be processed. This should be part of a regular routine, carried out on a daily, weekly or monthly basis. Take the batch of purchase invoices out of the lever arch folder and record the details of these invoices in the purchases daybook spreadsheet. For each purchase invoice you will need to record the relevant information in the columns in the purchases daybook spreadsheet. Record details, for example the date, the name of the supplier, invoice number, a brief description of the supply of goods or services, the gross monetary amount and the category that best fits the nature of the purchase, for example rent, stationery, telecoms, insurance, etc.

Each time you have entered in the details of a purchase invoice, write the letter 'E' in a circle in red ink at the top right-hand corner of the purchase invoice. This simple process will enable you to know immediately if you have entered any given purchase invoice into the purchases daybook spreadsheet. When all the purchase invoices in the batch have been entered into the purchases daybook spreadsheet, all of these purchase invoices should have the letter 'E' in a circle in red ink at the top right-hand corner. These invoices should then be filed alphabetically in the 'Purchase Invoices Unpaid' lever arch file.

Example – non-VAT-registered business: Classic Chairs

Classic Chairs is a business that buys and sells chairs and is not registered for VAT. Each time the business purchases chairs for its stock, it will receive a purchase invoice from its supplier. The purchase invoice will detail the quantity of product purchased and the cost of the products. The shop will also receive invoices from suppliers for goods and services supplied that are not intended for resale by the shop, for example stationery.

Figure 12.8
Purchase Invoices – Classic Chairs

Super Chairs Ltd
INVOICE

Customer Details			
Classic Chairs	Invoice	SC111	
Main Street	DATE	13-Jan-14	
Large Town	Account	CC	

Qty	Details	Net	VAT	Gross
			20%	
1	Leather Chair	400	80	480
Total				480

VAT No. 1234 55555

Wooden Chairs Ltd
INVOICE

Customer Details			
Classic Chairs	Invoice	WC222	
Main Street	DATE	15-Jan-14	
Large Town	Account	MS01	

Details	Net	VAT	Gross
		20%	
Wooden Stools	155	31	186
Total			186

VAT No. 1234 66666

Big Chairs Ltd
INVOICE

Customer Details			
Classic Chairs	Invoice	BC333	
Main Street	DATE	16-Jan-14	
Large Town	Account	CC01	

Details	Net	VAT	Gross
		20%	
Executive Chair	755	151	906
Total			906

VAT No. 1234 77777

Office Supplies
INVOICE

Customer Details			
Classic Chairs	Invoice	OF444	
Main Street	DATE	18-Jan-14	
Large Town	Account	Classic	

Details	Net	VAT	Gross
		20%	
20 Boxes of A4	110	22	132
Total			132

VAT No. 1234 8888

Classic Chairs has agreed credit terms with suppliers of 30 days, meaning goods and services purchased in January are paid for in February.

If the shopkeeper wants to record all the purchases for the week, he could place all the purchase invoices received during the week into the front of the 'Purchase Invoices Unpaid' lever arch folder and at the end of the week process them as a batch.

The shopkeeper would enter the details of each purchase invoice into the purchases daybook spreadsheet, noting the date, the supplier name, the invoice number, a description of the goods or services, the gross monetary amount and then enter the gross monetary amount in the appropriate analysis column.

During a week, the shopkeeper received the invoices as detailed in Figure 12.8.

At the end of the week the shopkeeper processes all of the purchase invoices received and records the details in the purchases daybook spreadsheet. After he has written the details of an invoice in the purchases daybook spreadsheet, he writes the letter 'E' in red ink with a circle around it in the top right-hand corner of the purchase invoice. The letter 'E' written in red and circled is a visual reminder that he has written the details of the invoice in the purchases daybook spreadsheet. This will stop him entering the invoice twice or searching the purchases daybook spreadsheet to verify if the purchase invoice has been written in. The shopkeeper then files the purchase invoices in the 'Purchase Invoices Unpaid' file in alphabetical order.

MICRO TASK

Can you record the purchase transactions in the purchases daybook for Classic Chairs?

- Set up the purchases daybook based on the templates previously explained
- Input the transactions into the purchases daybook
- Compare your purchases daybook for Classic Chairs to the solution below.

After the purchase invoice details have been entered into the purchases daybook spreadsheet it would show as indicated in Figure 12.9.

Classic Chairs is not VAT registered, therefore it records the gross amount of each invoice that includes VAT, where charged by the supplier, in both the total column, i.e., the gross amount column, and also in the analysis columns.

Based on the details in the purchases daybook the shopkeeper can identify that he purchased goods and services for the week of £1,704. The purchases can be further analysed into separate categories, i.e., goods for resale of £1,572 and stationery of £132.

Figure 12.9

Purchases Daybook Spreadsheet Based – Classic Chairs

PURCHASES DAYBOOK

Date	Supplier	Invoice No.	Description	Gross Amount	Goods for Resale	Rent	Stationery	Telecoms	Insurance
13-Jan-14	Super Chairs Ltd	SC111	Leather Chair	480.00	480.00				
15-Jan-14	Wooden Chairs Ltd	WC222	Wooden Stools	186.00	186.00				
16-Jan-14	Big Chairs Ltd	BC333	Executive Chair	906.00	906.00				
18-Jan-14	Office Supplies	OF444	20 Boxes of A4	132.00			132.00		
Total				1,704.00	1,572.00	0.00	132.00	0.00	0.00

Purchases daybook – non-VAT-registered business: accounting software

What do you need to record purchases using accounting software for a non-VAT-registered product or service-based business?

1. A lever arch file
2. A computer
3. Accounting software

Set-up

- The spine of the lever arch folder should be clearly marked as 'Purchase Invoices Unpaid' and also the financial year should be noted on the spine, e.g., 'Year 2014', so it is clearly visible
- The lever arch file should be divided alphabetically with an alphabetical divider
- The accounting software should be loaded onto the computer. All accounting packages operate on the same general principles. The purchases daybook on accounting software requires certain information to be input concerning the contents of purchase invoices. Details such as the following would need to be input: date of invoice, supplier invoice number, supplier name, description of goods or services purchased, monetary value

The process

Each time a purchase invoice is received from a supplier for goods and services supplied it should be filed at the front of the 'Purchase Invoices Unpaid' lever arch file, i.e., not filed alphabetically, merely held at the front of the file until a batch of purchase invoices can be processed.

When a batch of purchase invoices has accumulated at the front of the folder, they can then be processed. This should be part of a regular routine, carried out on a daily, weekly or monthly basis. Take the batch of purchase invoices out of the lever arch folder and record the details of these invoices in the purchases daybook module on the accounting software. For each invoice you will need to record the relevant information as prompted by the accounting software. Basic details such as the following would need to be recorded: the date of the purchase invoice, the name of the supplier, the invoice number, the monetary amount and the category that best fits the nature of the purchase. The way accounting software categorizes expenditure is by using nominal codes. These nominal codes are part of the set-up process and it would be necessary to follow the instructions from the software provider when setting these up.

Each time you have entered in the details of the purchase invoice write the letter 'E' in a circle in red ink at the top right-hand corner of the purchase invoice. This simple process will enable you to know immediately if you have entered any given purchase invoice into the purchases daybook on the accounting software. When all purchase invoices in the batch have been entered into the purchases daybook module of the accounting software, all of these purchase invoices should have the letter 'E' in a circle in red ink at the top right-hand corner. These invoices should then be filed alphabetically in the 'Purchase Invoices Unpaid' lever arch file.

After the details of the purchase invoices have been input onto the accounting software it will be possible to run reports to review the purchases daybook. The purchases daybook report will list all the purchase invoices that have been input detailing items, for example the date of each invoice, the supplier names, the gross monetary value. You should also be able to run other reports that will display information in a variety of different ways; for example, you could run a purchases daybook for a single supplier over a particular date range.

Due to the vast array of accounting software programs available it is only practical to review the general features of accounting software in this section as detailed above.

Purchases daybook – VAT-registered business: paper based

What do you need to record purchases manually for a VAT-registered business using a paper-based purchases daybook?

1. A lever arch folder to file purchase invoices
2. An accounts analysis book to record purchases

Set-up

- The spine of the lever arch folder should be clearly marked as 'Purchase Invoices Unpaid' and the financial year should be noted on the spine, e.g., 'Year 2014', so it is clearly visible

- The lever arch folder should be divided alphabetically with an alphabetical divider
- The accounts analysis book being used as a purchases daybook should have the appropriate headings noted in columns, such as the following: date, supplier name, supplier invoice number, description of goods or services, gross monetary amount, VAT amount, net amount, i.e., VAT-exclusive value. Other columns, noted at net value amounts, should be used to categorize the nature of purchases as appropriate, e.g., goods for resale (if your business is product based), rent, stationery, telecoms, insurance, etc. The number of other categories you use depends on the level of detail you require. Detailed in Figure 12.10 is an example of a purchases daybook with relevant header columns noted

Figure 12.10

Purchases Daybook Paper-Based Template – VAT

PURCHASES DAYBOOK										
Date	Supplier	Invoice No.	Description	Gross Amount	VAT Amount	Net Amount	Rent	Stationery	Telecoms	Insurance

The process

Each time a purchase invoice is received for goods and/or services from a supplier, it should be filed at the front of the 'Purchase Invoices Unpaid' lever arch folder, i.e., not filed alphabetically, merely held at the front of the file until a batch of purchase invoices can be processed.

When a batch of purchase invoices has accumulated at the front of the file, they can then be processed. This should be part of a regular routine, carried out on a daily, weekly or monthly basis. Take the batch of purchase invoices out of the lever arch folder and record the details of these invoices in the purchases daybook. For each invoice you will need to record the relevant information in the columns in the purchases daybook. Record details such as the date, the name of the supplier, the invoice number, the gross monetary amount, VAT amount, net amount excluding VAT and the category that best fits the nature of the purchase, for example goods for resale (if your business is product based), rent, stationery, telecoms, insurance, etc.

Each time you have entered in the details of the purchase invoice write the letter 'E' in a circle in red ink at the top right-hand corner of the purchase invoice. This simple process will enable you to know immediately if you have entered any given purchase invoice into the purchases daybook. When all the purchase invoices in the batch have been entered into the purchases daybook all of these purchase invoices should have the letter 'E' in a circle in red ink at the top right-hand corner. These invoices should then be filed alphabetically in the 'Purchase Invoices Unpaid' lever arch file.

Example – VAT registered: Andrew, Architect

Andrew is an architect who operates as a sole trader who is registered for VAT and runs his business from a city centre office. During any given month he will receive invoices for goods and services he has obtained from his suppliers.

Andrew has agreed credit terms with suppliers of 30 days, meaning goods and services purchased in January are paid for in February. As he receives invoices during the month, he places all the purchase invoices received during each day at the front of the 'Purchase Invoices Unpaid' lever arch folder. At the end of the month Andrew can then process the purchase invoices as a batch. Andrew enters the details of each purchase invoice into the purchases daybook, noting the date, the supplier name, the invoice number, a description of the goods or services, the gross monetary amount, the VAT amount, the net amount and then enters the monetary amount excluding VAT in the appropriate analysis column.

During the month of January Andrew receives the invoices shown in Figure 12.11.

At the end of the month Andrew processes all the invoices received and records the details in the purchases daybook. After he has written the details of an invoice in the purchases daybook he writes the letter 'E' in red ink with a circle around it in the top right-hand corner of the purchase invoice. The letter 'E' written in red and circled is a visual reminder to Andrew that he has written the details of the invoice in the purchases daybook. This will stop him entering the invoice twice or searching the purchases daybook to verify if the purchase invoice has been written in. Andrew then files the invoices in the 'Purchase Invoices Unpaid' folder in alphabetical order.

MICRO TASK

Can you record the purchase transactions in the purchases daybook for Andrew's business?

- Set up the purchases daybook based on the templates previously explained
- Input the transactions into the purchases daybook
- Compare your purchases daybook for Andrew to the solution below.

Figure 12.11

Purchase Invoices – Andrew, Architect – VAT Registered

Office Supplies Ltd
INVOICE

Customer Details

Andrew Architect	Invoice	4596
Main Street	DATE	05-Jan-14
Large Town	Account	AA01

Qty	Details	Net	VAT	Gross
			20%	
10	Boxes of A4	375	75	450

| Total | | | | 450 |

VAT No. 1122 12345

Speak Now PLC
INVOICE

Customer Details

Andrew Architect	Invoice	99856
Main Street	DATE	08-Jan-14
Large Town	Account	ANDARC

Details	Net	VAT	Gross
		20%	
Provision of telecoms	145	29.00	174

| Total | | | 174 |

VAT No. 3344 12345

J B LANDLORD
INVOICE

Customer Details

Andrew Architect	Invoice	A01
Main Street	DATE	08-Jan-14
Large Town	Account	Andrew

Details	Net	VAT	Gross
		20%	
Rent for January	500	100	600

| Total | | | 600 |

VAT No. 5566 12345

Triple A Insurance
INVOICE

Customer Details

Andrew Architect	Invoice	145
Main Street	DATE	14-Jan-14
Large Town	Account	Classic

Details	Net	Gross
Insurance	1,000	1,000

| Total | | 1,000 |

After the invoice details have been entered into the purchases daybook it would show what appears in Figure 12.12.

Figure 12.12
Purchases Daybook Paper Based – Andrew, Architect –
VAT Registered

PURCHASES DAYBOOK

Date	Supplier	Invoice No.	Description	Gross Amount	VAT Amount	Net Amount	Rent	Stationery	Telecoms	Insurance
05-Jan-14	Office Supplies Ltd	4596	Boxes of A4	450.00	75.00	375.00		375.00		
08-Jan-14	Speak Now PLC	99856	Provision of telecoms	174.00	29.00	145.00			145.00	
08-Jan-14	J B LANDLORD	A01	Rent for January	600.00	100.00	500.00	500.00			
14-Jan-14	Triple A Insurance	145	Insurance	1,000.00	0.00	1,000.00				1,000.00
Total				2,224.00	204.00	2,020.00	500.00	375.00	145.00	1,000.00

Andrew's business is VAT registered, therefore he records the gross amount, the VAT amount, and the amount excluding VAT, i.e., net amount. In addition, when Andrew analyses his expenditure in the other columns he notes the monetary amount excluding VAT.

Based on the details in the purchases daybook Andrew can identify that he purchased goods and services of £2,224 including VAT. He was charged VAT of £204 by his suppliers for the month. He purchased goods and services of £2,020 excluding VAT. Purchases of goods and services included: rent £500, excluding VAT; stationery £375, excluding VAT; telecoms services of £145 excluding VAT and insurance £1,000, no VAT applicable.

> NOTE: Where a purchase invoice is received and it does not state VAT or show a VAT registration number, then it can be assumed that VAT has not been charged, therefore no VAT is due to be reclaimed. This is shown in the above example regarding the invoice received from Triple A insurance for £1,000.

Purchases daybook – VAT-registered business: spreadsheet software

What do you need to record purchases using spreadsheet software for a VAT-registered business?

1. A lever arch folder

2. A computer

3. Spreadsheet software installed on computer

Set-up

- The spine of the lever arch folder should be clearly marked as 'Purchase Invoices Unpaid' and also the financial year should be noted on the spine, e.g. 'Year 2014', so it is clearly visible
- The lever arch file should be divided alphabetically with an alphabetical divider
- Create a spreadsheet file and name it 'Purchases Daybook' and include the trading year, for example 'Purchases Daybook 2014'
- The spreadsheet file being used as a purchases daybook should have the appropriate headings noted in columns, including the following: date, supplier name, supplier invoice number, description of goods or services, gross monetary amount, VAT amount, net amount, i.e., monetary value excluding VAT. Other columns noted at net value amounts should be used to categorize the nature of purchases as appropriate, e.g., goods for resale (if your business is product based), rent, stationery, telecoms, insurance, etc. The number of other categories you use depends on the level of detail you require. Detailed in Figure 12.13 is an example of a purchases daybook spreadsheet with relevant header columns noted

Figure 12.13
Purchases Daybook Spreadsheet Software-Based Template

PURCHASES DAYBOOK											
Date	Supplier	Invoice No.	Description	Gross Amount	VAT Amount	Net Amount	Goods For Resale	Rent	Stationery	Telecoms	Insurance

> NOTE: If you are running a service-based business you can omit the column noted as 'Goods for Resale'.

The process

Each time a purchase invoice is received from a supplier for goods or services supplied it should be filed at the front of the 'Purchase Invoices Unpaid' lever arch folder, i.e., not filed alphabetically, merely held at the front of the file until a batch of purchase invoices can be processed.

When a batch of purchase invoices has accumulated at the front of the folder, they can then be processed. This should be part of a regular routine, carried out on a daily, weekly or monthly basis. Take the batch of purchase invoices out of the lever arch file and record the details of these invoices in the purchases daybook spreadsheet. For each purchase invoice you will need to record the relevant information in the columns in the purchase daybook spreadsheet. Record details such as the date, the name of the supplier, invoice number, a brief description of the supply of goods or services, the gross monetary amount, VAT amount, net amount, i.e., monetary amount excluding VAT, and the category that best fits the nature of the purchase, for example rent, stationery, telecoms, insurance, etc.

Each time you have entered in the details of a purchase invoice write the letter 'E' in a circle in red ink at the top right-hand corner of the purchase invoice. This simple process will enable you to know immediately if you have entered any given purchase invoice into the purchases daybook spreadsheet. When all the purchase invoices in the batch have been entered into the purchases daybook spreadsheet all of these purchase invoices should have the letter 'E' in a circle in red ink at the top right-hand corner. These invoices should then be filed alphabetically in the 'Purchase Invoices Unpaid' lever arch file.

Example – VAT-registered business: Classic Chairs

Classic Chairs is a business that buys and sells chairs and is registered for VAT. Each time the business purchases chairs for its stock, it will receive a purchase invoice from its supplier. The purchase invoice will detail the quantity of product purchased and the cost of the products. The shop will also receive invoices from suppliers for goods and services supplied that are not intended for resale by the shop, for example stationery.

Classic Chairs has agreed credit terms with suppliers of 30 days, meaning goods and services purchased in January are paid for in February.

If the shopkeeper wants to record all the purchases for the week, he could place all the purchase invoices received during the week into the front of the 'Purchase Invoices Unpaid' lever arch file and at the end of the week process them as a batch.

The shopkeeper would enter the details of each purchase invoice into the purchases daybook spreadsheet, noting the date, the supplier name, the invoice number, a description of the goods or services, the gross monetary amount, the VAT amount, the net amount, i.e., the monetary value excluding VAT, and then enter the net amounts in the appropriate analysis column.

During a week, the shopkeeper received the invoices indicated in Figure 12.14.

At the end of the week the shopkeeper processes all of the purchase invoices received and records the details in the purchases daybook spreadsheet. After he has written the details of an invoice in the purchases daybook spreadsheet, he writes the letter 'E' in red ink with a circle around it in the top right-hand corner of the purchase invoice. The letter 'E' written in red and circled is a visual

Figure 12.14
Purchase Invoices – Classic Chairs – VAT Registered

Super Chairs Ltd	Wooden Chairs Ltd
INVOICE	INVOICE

Super Chairs Ltd

Customer Details			
Classic Chairs	Invoice	SC111
Main Street	DATE	13-Jan-14
Large Town	Account	CC

Qty	Details	Net	VAT 20%	Gross
1	Leather Chair	400	80	480
Total				480

VAT No. 1234 55555

Wooden Chairs Ltd

Customer Details			
Classic Chairs	Invoice	WC222
Main Street	DATE	15-Jan-14
Large Town	Account	MS01

Details	Net	VAT 20%	Gross
Wooden Stools	155	31	186
Total			186

VAT No. 1234 66666

Big Chairs Ltd

Customer Details			
Classic Chairs	Invoice	BC333
Main Street	DATE	16-Jan-14
Large Town	Account	CC01

Details	Net	VAT 20%	Gross
Executive Chair	755	151	906
Total			906

VAT No. 1234 77777

Office Supplies

Customer Details			
Classic Chairs	Invoice	OF444
Main Street	DATE	18-Jan-14
Large Town	Account	Classic

Details	Net	20%	Gross
20 Boxes of A4	110	22	132
Total			132

VAT No. 1234 8888

reminder that he has written the details of the invoice in the purchases daybook spreadsheet. This will stop him entering the invoice twice or searching the purchases daybook spreadsheet to verify if the purchase invoice has been written in. The shopkeeper then files the purchase invoices in the 'Purchase Invoices Unpaid' file in alphabetical order.

MICRO TASK

Can you record the purchase transactions in the purchases daybook for Classic Chairs?

- Set up the purchases daybook based on the templates previously explained
- Input the transactions into the purchases daybook
- Compare your purchases daybook for Classic Chairs to the solution below.

After the purchase invoice details have been entered into the purchases daybook spreadsheet it would show as in Figure 12.15

Figure 12.15
Purchases Daybook Spreadsheet Based – Classic Chairs – VAT Registered

PURCHASES DAYBOOK									
Date	Supplier	Invoice No.	Description	Gross Amount	VAT Amount	Net Amount	Goods For Resale	Rent	Stationery
13-Jan-14	Super Chairs Ltd	SC111	Leather Chair	480.00	80.00	400.00	400.00		
15-Jan-14	Wooden Chairs Ltd	WC222	Wooden Stools	186.00	31.00	155.00	155.00		
16-Jan-14	Big Chairs Ltd	BC333	Executive Chair	906.00	151.00	755.00	755.00		
18-Jan-14	Office Supplies	OF444	20 Boxes of A4	132.00	22.00	110.00			110.00
				1,704.00	284.00	1,420.00	1,310.00	0.00	110.00

Classic Chairs is VAT registered, therefore it records the gross amount of each invoice that includes VAT, the VAT amount and the net amount, excluding VAT.

Based on the details in the purchases daybook the shopkeeper can identify that he purchased goods for the week of £1,704 including VAT. The business was charged £284 of VAT. The value of the purchases excluding VAT was £1,420. The purchases can be further analysed into separate categories, i.e., goods for resale of £1,310 excluding VAT and stationery of £110 excluding VAT.

Purchases daybook – VAT-registered business: accounting software

What do you need to record purchases using accounting software for a VAT-registered product or service-based business?

1. A lever arch file
2. A computer
3. Accounting software installed on computer

Set-up

- The spine of the lever arch folder should be clearly marked as 'Purchase Invoices Unpaid' and also the financial year should be noted on the spine, e.g. 'Year 2014', so it is clearly visible
- The lever arch file should be divided alphabetically with an alphabetical divider
- The accounting software product should be loaded onto your computer. All accounting packages operate on the same general principles. The purchases daybook on accounting software requires certain information to be input concerning the contents of purchase invoices; for example, date of invoice, supplier invoice number, supplier name, description of goods or services purchased, monetary value, VAT amount, net amount

The process

Each time a purchase invoice is received from a supplier for goods and services supplied, it should be filed at the front of the 'Purchase Invoices Unpaid' lever arch file, i.e., not filed alphabetically, but merely held at the front of the file until a batch of purchase invoices can be processed.

When a batch of purchase invoices has accumulated at the front of the folder, they can then be processed. This should be part of a regular routine, carried out on a daily, weekly or monthly basis. Take the batch of purchase invoices out of the lever arch folder and record the details of these invoices in the purchases daybook module on the accounting software. For each invoice you will need to record the relevant information as prompted by the accounting software; for example, the date of the purchase invoice, the name of the supplier, the monetary amount, VAT amount, net amount and the category that best fits the nature of the purchase.

The way accounting software categorizes expenditure is by using nominal codes. These nominal codes are part of the set-up process and it would be necessary to follow the instructions from the software provider when setting these up.

Each time you have entered in the details of the purchase invoice write the letter 'E' in a circle in red ink at the top right-hand corner of the purchase invoice. This simple process will enable you to know immediately if you have entered any given purchase invoice into the purchases daybook on the accounting software. When all purchase invoices in the batch have been entered into the purchases daybook module of the accounting software, all of these purchase invoices should have the letter 'E' in a circle in red ink at the top right-hand corner. These invoices should then be filed alphabetically in the 'Purchase Invoices Unpaid' lever arch folder.

After the details of the purchase invoices have been input onto the accounting software it will be possible to run reports to review the purchases daybook. The purchases daybook report will list all the purchase invoices that have been input, detailing items including: the date of each invoice, the supplier names, the gross monetary value, VAT amount, net amount. You should also be able to run other reports that will display information in a variety of different ways; for example, you could run a purchases daybook for a single supplier over a particular date range.

Due to the vast array of accounting software programs available it is only practical to review the general features of accounting software in this section as detailed above.

CHAPTER 13

How to record expenditure transactions in a petty cashbook

Figure 13.1
Expenditure – Petty Cash

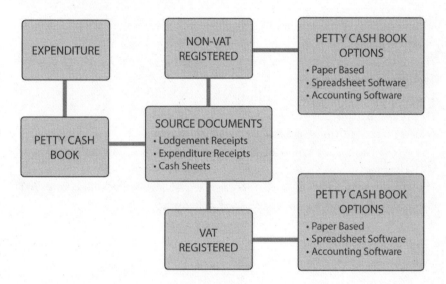

PETTY CASH BOOK – OVERVIEW

A petty cash book is a record that lists minor cash expenditure transactions for a given period, e.g., a day, a week, a month or a year. Minor cash expenditure transactions are purchases made by a business for goods and services from other businesses, of low monetary value, paid by cash. It is referred to as a petty cash book because traditionally it was a paper notebook with rows and columns used to record minor cash purchases. Effectively the contents of a petty cash book is a list of minor cash expenditure receipts received from suppliers for a given period and also a list of cash lodgements into petty cash. See Figure 13.1 for an overview of petty cash expenditure.

An example of a petty cash book for a non-VAT-registered business would contain information as illustrated in Figure 13.2.

Figure 13.2
Petty Cash Book Example – Non-VAT-Registered Business

PETTY CASH BOOK									
DATE	PAYEE / SOURCE	DESCRIPTION	MONEY IN	MONEY OUT	FUEL	SUBSISTENCE	STAMPS	OTHER	BALANCE
01-Mar-14	BUSINESS BANK A/C	Lodgement	200.00						200.00
05-Mar-14	SERVICE STATION	FUEL		72.00	72.00				128.00
07-Mar-14	POST OFFICE	STAMPS		6.00			6.00		122.00
15-Mar-14	BIG EATS LTD	LUNCH		10.00		10.00			112.00
25-Mar-14	WINDOW SHOP	WINDOW LOCK		14.40				14.40	97.60
			200.00	102.40	72.00	10.00	6.00	14.40	97.60

The petty cash book for a non-VAT-registered business records basic details of minor cash expenditure for a period, such as the following:

- The date and details of any monies lodged into petty cash to pay for cash expenditures
- The date of the cash expenditure
- The name of the payee
- A brief description of goods or services purchased
- The gross monetary value of the cash expenditure, which includes any VAT charged
- The gross monetary value of the cash expenditure including any VAT charged, allocated to an appropriate category

An example of a petty cash book for a VAT-registered business would contain information as illustrated in Figure 13.3.

Figure 13.3
Petty Cash Book Example – VAT-Registered Business

PETTY CASH BOOK											
DATE	PAYEE / SOURCE	DESCRIPTION	MONEY IN	MONEY OUT	VAT AMOUNT	NET AMOUNT	FUEL	SUBSISTENCE	STAMPS	OTHER	BALANCE
01-Mar-14	BUSINESS BANK A/C	Lodgement	200.00								200.00
05-Mar-14	SERVICE STATION	FUEL		96.00	16.00	80.00	80.00				104.00
07-Mar-14	POST OFFICE	STAMPS		6.00	0.00	6.00			6.00		98.00
15-Mar-14	BIG EATS LTD	LUNCH		10.00	1.67	8.33		8.33			88.00
25-Mar-14	WINDOW SHOP	WINDOW LOCK		14.40	2.40	12.00				12.00	73.60
			200.00	126.40	20.07	106.33	80.00	8.33	6.00	12.00	73.60

The petty cash book for a VAT-registered business records basic details of purchases for a period, such as the following:

- **The date and details of any monies lodged into petty cash to pay for cash expenditures**
- **The date of the cash expenditure**
- **The name of the payee**
- **A brief description of goods or services purchased**
- **The gross monetary value of the cash expenditure, which includes any VAT charged**
- **The monetary value of the VAT only, i.e., the VAT amount**
- **The net monetary value, i.e., the purchase price excluding VAT.**
- **The net monetary value of the purchase allocated to an appropriate category; i.e. the purchase price excluding VAT**

There are a number of petty cash book options available and it is necessary to evaluate which option is best suited to your business.

- **Option 1 – Paper based**
- **Option 2 – Spreadsheet software based**
- **Option 3 – Accounting software based**

In order to facilitate your decision making when evaluating a manual system or a software system you should review paper-based systems versus software based systems, noted in chapter 11.

> **NOTE: A complication arises when a business is registered for VAT (value added tax). If a business is registered for VAT it is necessary to account for the VAT and detail it in the petty cash book. VAT rates differ depending on the products or services supplied and the VAT status of suppliers.**

How to operate a petty cash book

When a payment is made using petty cash, an invoice or receipt should be obtained. The invoice or receipt obtained should be filed in a 'Petty Cash' lever arch folder. The petty cash folder should be divided into monthly sections. Due to the minor nature of the expenditure, it might be appropriate to have a plastic pocket folder for each month of the year. Petty cash invoices/receipts can be placed in the plastic pocket folder and filed in the 'Petty Cash' lever arch folder.

Recording petty cash transactions

Each time a payment is made using petty cash, the details need to be recorded in the petty cash book. Regardless of which petty cash system is being operated – paper based, spreadsheet software based or accounting software based – the type of details to be recorded are basically the same. The only difference relates to how the information is input.

The following list illustrates the type of detail that should be recorded concerning petty cash transactions:

- **Date** – the actual date of the transaction
- **Money in** – if money is being put into the petty cash then the amount of money needs to be recorded. It can be helpful to record the source of the money in, for example the business bank account, a director, the business owner, a staff member, cash from cash sales as noted on cash sheets (see chapter 5)
- **Payee** – the name of the person, company, organization, to whom the payment is being issued
- **Description** – a brief description of the transaction should be noted
- **Money out**, i.e., the gross amount of expenditure per transaction, i.e., the total value of the payment being issued for each transaction
- **Other details** noted in the petty cash book to categorize expenditure are created as required, fuel, subsistence, stamps. In a paper-based or spreadsheet software-based petty cash book, columns are created to accommodate the extra expense categories. In an accounting software-based petty cash book, additional nominal codes are created. Nominal codes are used by accounting software to categorize expenditure
- **For a non-VAT-registered business** transactions are recorded at gross value, i.e., inclusive of VAT
- **For a VAT-registered business** VAT is recorded separately
- **Balance** – the balance of cash available to spend can be calculated by adding any opening balance to monies in and deducting the figure noted as monies out. An accounting software-based petty cash book will calculate the balance automatically

Petty cash book – source documents

The data to be recorded in the petty cash book is obtained from a variety of source documents, such as:

Lodgement receipts – when money is lodged into petty cash, a lodgement receipt is created to note details of the value of money placed into petty cash, the source of the cash and the date of the transaction.

Expenditure receipts – an expenditure receipt is a receipt obtained from a supplier when a payment is made from petty cash to validate the expenditure.

Cash sheets – a cash sheet is a document that can be used to trace the composition of cash lodgements into petty cash that originate from cash sales. It can also be used to identify the details of how such money was spent. See chapter 5 for full details of cash sheets. It is a document mainly used in retail businesses that deal with cash sales.

Petty cash book – non-VAT-registered business: paper based

What do you need to set up a paper-based petty cash book for a non-VAT-registered business?

1. A lever arch folder to file petty cash expenditure receipts and lodgement receipts
2. A petty cash tin to store petty cash
3. An accounts analysis book to record petty cash payments and cash receipts

Set-up

- The spine of the lever arch folder should be clearly marked as 'Petty Cash' and also the financial year should be noted on the spine, e.g., 'Year 2014', so it is clearly visible
- This folder should be subdivided into twelve months for the financial year, e.g., January to December
- The accounts analysis book being used as a petty cash book should have the appropriate headings noted
- The headings noted in the columns of the petty cash book will depend on the circumstances of the business and the type of petty cash expenditure incurred
- Standard column headings would be as follows: date of transaction, details of payee or source of receipt, description of transaction, money in, money out (i.e., gross monetary value of monies spent). Other columns should be used to categorize the nature of the payments, such as fuel, subsistence, stamps, etc. The number of categories you use depends on the level of detail you require. A useful column heading is 'Other': into this column items can be entered that you are unsure of how to categorize. Such items can be dealt with at a later date when

Figure 13.4
Petty Cash Book Template Paper Based – Non-VAT-Registered Business

PETTY CASH BOOK									
DATE	PAYEE / SOURCE	DESCRIPTION	MONEY IN	MONEY OUT	FUEL	SUBSISTENCE	STAMPS	OTHER	BALANCE

more information may be available relating to them. Alternatively, such expenditure could be categorized as general expenditure
- The final column should be noted as 'Balance'. This column is used to calculate the amount of cash that is left at the end of a period

Figure 13.4 is an example of a petty cash book with relevant header columns noted for a non-VAT-registered business.

Petty cash book – non-VAT-registered business: spreadsheet software

What do you need to set up a spreadsheet software-based petty cash book for a non-VAT-registered business?
1. A lever arch folder to file petty cash expenditure receipts and lodgement receipts
2. A petty cash tin to store petty cash
3. A computer
4. Spreadsheet software installed on computer

Set-up

- The spine of the lever arch folder should be clearly marked as 'Petty Cash' and also the financial year should be noted on the spine, e.g., 'Year 2014', so it is clearly visible
- This folder should be subdivided into twelve months for the financial year, e.g., January to December
- A new spreadsheet file should be set up to be used as a petty cash book. The file should be named 'Petty Cash Book' and the trading year should be noted, for example '2014'
- The spreadsheet should have the appropriate headings noted in columns. The headings noted in the columns of the spreadsheet software-based petty cash book will depend on the circumstances of the business, and the type of petty cash expenditure incurred
- Standard column headings would be as follows: date of transaction, payee/source, description of transaction, money in, money out, i.e., gross monetary amount. Other columns should be used to categorize the nature of the payments, such as fuel, subsistence, stamps, etc. The number of categories you use depends on the level of detail you require. A useful column heading is 'Other': into this column items can be entered that you are unsure of how to categorize. Such items can be dealt with at a later date when more information may be available relating to them. Alternatively, such expenditure could be categorized as general expenditure
- The final column should be noted as 'Balance'. This column is used to calculate the amount of cash that is left at the end of a period

Figure 13.5 is an example of a spreadsheet software-based petty cash book with relevant header columns noted.

Figure 13.5
Petty Cash Book Template Spreadsheet Software Based

PETTY CASH BOOK									
DATE	PAYEE / SOURCE	DESCRIPTION	MONEY IN	MONEY OUT	FUEL	SUBSISTENCE	STAMPS	OTHER	BALANCE

Petty cash book – non-VAT-registered business: illustrative example

This illustrative example is applicable to both a paper-based petty cash book and a spreadsheet software-based petty cash book.

Andrew is an architect who operates as a sole trader; he is not registered for VAT and runs his business from a city centre office. During any given month he will spend petty cash to pay for incidental products and services.

During the month of March Andrew transacts the following petty cash items:

1. On 1 March he withdraws £200 from the business bank account and places it into the petty cash tin. He places a note in the petty cash folder for the relevant month noting that £200 has been lodged into petty cash from the business bank account
2. On 5 March he takes out £100 from the petty cash tin, goes to the local service station and spends £72 on fuel for a business trip. He places the receipt in the 'Petty Cash' lever arch folder and the change back into the petty cash tin
3. On 7 March he takes £6 out of the petty cash tin and uses the money to purchase stamps at the post office. He places the receipt for the stamps into the petty cash lever arch folder
4. On 15 March he takes out £10 from the petty cash tin to pay for food during a site visit. On his return to the office he places the receipt into the 'Petty Cash' lever arch folder
5. On 25 March Andrew pays £14.40 from petty cash for a window lock for the office window. He places the receipt for £14.40 into the 'Petty Cash' lever arch folder

Andrew needs to record each of the above transactions in the petty cash book. In order to record the transactions, he retrieves the documents and receipts from the petty cash folder for the month of March. Each time he enters an item into the petty cash book, he writes the letter 'E' with a circle around it in red ink on the petty cash document/receipt to note that it has been recorded in the petty cash book.

If Andrew handwrites the petty cash transactions into the paper-based petty cash book the result will be as shown in Figure 13.6.

If Andrew inputs the petty cash transactions into a spreadsheet software-based petty cash book the result will be as shown in Figure 13.7.

Figure 13.6
Petty Cash Book Paper Based – Andrew, Architect

PETTY CASH BOOK

DATE	PAYEE / SOURCE	DESCRIPTION	MONEY IN	MONEY OUT	FUEL	SUBSISTENCE	STAMPS	OTHER	BALANCE
01-Mar-14	BUSINESS BANK A/C	Lodgement	200.00						200.00
05-Mar-14	SERVICE STATION	FUEL		72.00	72.00				128.00
07-Mar-14	POST OFFICE	STAMPS		6.00			6.00		122.00
15-Mar-14	BIG EATS LTD	LUNCH		10.00		10.00			112.00
25-Mar-14	WINDOW SHOP	WINDOW LOCK		14.40				14.40	97.60
			200.00	102.40	72.00	10.00	6.00	14.40	97.60

NOTE: The date recorded in the petty cash book is the ACTUAL date of the transaction, NOT the date the transaction is entered into the petty cash book.

Review of transactions recorded in the petty cash book:
- All transactions are dated on the date that the actual transaction took place
- All receipts note the source of money receipts into petty cash, for example business bank account, business owner
- All payment transactions detail who the payee is, i.e., the recipient of the payment
- All payments note a brief description of goods or services paid for
- All transactions have the gross monetary amount recorded
- All payment transactions are allocated to an analysis column. In this example the payments are analysed into fuel, subsistence, stamps, other

Figure 13.7
Petty Cash Book Spreadsheet Software Based –
Andrew, Architect

PETTY CASH BOOK									
DATE	PAYEE / SOURCE	DESCRIPTION	MONEY IN	MONEY OUT	FUEL	SUBSISTENCE	STAMPS	OTHER	BALANCE
01-Mar-14	BUSINESS BANK A/C	Lodgement	200.00						200.00
05-Mar-14	SERVICE STATION	FUEL		72.00	72.00				128.00
07-Mar-14	POST OFFICE	STAMPS		6.00			6.00		122.00
15-Mar-14	BIG EATS LTD	LUNCH		10.00		10.00			112.00
25-Mar-14	WINDOW SHOP	WINDOW LOCK		14.40				14.40	97.60
			200.00	102.40	72.00	10.00	6.00	14.40	97.60

The balance column identifies the amount of petty cash actually available to spend. It is calculated by adding the opening balance of cash to any monies in and deducting expenditure, monies out, for the period.

In the case of Andrew there was no opening balance and the total of monies received was £200 less the total of monies spent of £102.40, leaving cash available of £97.60.

Based on the payment transactions recorded in the petty cash book, Andrew can identify that his business paid £102.40 from petty cash for the month of March. In addition, Andrew can identify from the analysis columns that the following petty cash payments were issued in the month of March:

- **£72 was spent on fuel**
- **£10 was spent on subsistence**
- **£6 was spent on stamps**
- **£14.40 was spent on other items, i.e., the money spent on the window lock**

Petty cash book – non-VAT-registered business: accounting software

What do you need to record petty cash payments and lodgements using accounting software for a non-VAT-registered business?

1. **A lever arch folder to file petty cash expenditure receipts and lodgement receipts**
2. **A petty cash tin to store petty cash**
3. **A computer**
4. **Accounting software installed on computer**

- The spine of the lever arch folder should be clearly marked as 'Petty Cash' and also the financial year should be noted on the spine, e.g., 'Year 2014', so it is clearly visible
- The folder should be subdivided into twelve months for the financial year, e.g., January to December
- The accounting software product should be loaded onto your computer. Each different accounting package operates on the same general principles
- The petty cash book on accounting software can be set up in a variety of ways. It may be set up and operated as a bank account. Alternatively, it may involve entering the transactions directly onto the nominal ledger, using journal debits and credits. Whatever set-up you use will depend on the software
- The petty cash payments being issued need to be input onto the accounting software, noting certain details of each payment transaction. Details would include: the date of the transaction, the payee, the monetary amount of the payment. The payments would also be allocated to different expense categories using nominal codes. Nominal codes are used by accounting software to group transactions

Petty cash book – VAT-registered business: paper based

What do you need to set up a paper-based petty cash book for a VAT-registered business?

1. A lever arch folder to file petty cash expenditure receipts and lodgement receipts
2. A petty cash tin to store petty cash
3. An accounts analysis book to record petty cash payments and cash receipts

Set-up

- The spine of the lever arch folder should be clearly marked as 'Petty Cash' and also the financial year should be noted on the spine, e.g., 'Year 2014', so it is clearly visible
- This folder should be subdivided into twelve months for the financial year, e.g., January to December
- The accounts analysis book being used as a petty cash book should have the appropriate headings noted
- The headings noted in the columns of the petty cash book will depend on the circumstances of the business, relating to items such as VAT or the type of petty cash expenditure incurred
- Standard column headings would be as follows: date of transaction,

details of payee or source of receipt, description of transaction, money in, money out (i.e., gross monetary value of monies spent), VAT amount, net amount (i.e., monetary value of the expenditure transaction excluding VAT). Other columns should be used to categorize the nature of the payments, such as fuel, subsistence, stamps, etc. The number of categories you use depends on the level of detail you require. A useful column heading is 'Other': into this column items can be entered that you are unsure of how to categorize. Such items can be dealt with at a later date when more information may be available relating to them. Alternatively, such expenditure could be categorized as general expenditure

- The final column should be noted as 'Balance'. This column is used to calculate the amount of cash that is left at the end of a period

Figure 13.8 is an example of a petty cash book with relevant header columns noted for a VAT–registered business.

Petty cash book – VAT-registered business: spreadsheet

Figure 13.8
Petty Cash Book Paper-Based Template – VAT

PETTY CASH BOOK											
DATE	PAYEE / SOURCE	DESCRIPTION	MONEY IN	MONEY OUT	VAT AMOUNT	NET AMOUNT	FUEL	SUBSISTENCE	STAMPS	OTHER	BALANCE

software

What do you need to set up a spreadsheet software-based petty cash book for a VAT-registered business?

1. A lever arch folder to file petty cash expenditure receipts and lodgement receipts
2. A petty cash tin to store petty cash
3. A computer
4. Spreadsheet software installed on computer

Set-up

- The spine of the lever arch folder should be clearly marked as 'Petty Cash' and also the financial year should be noted on the spine, e.g., 'Year 2014', so it is clearly visible
- This folder should be subdivided into twelve months for the financial year, e.g., January to December
- A new spreadsheet file should be set up to be used as a petty cash book. The file should be named 'Petty Cash Book' and the trading year should be noted, for example '2014'
- The headings noted in the columns of the spreadsheet software petty cash book will depend on the circumstances of the business, relating to items such as the type of petty cash expenditure incurred
- Standard column headings would be as follows: date of transaction, payee/source, description of transaction, money in, money out (i.e., gross monetary amount), VAT amount, net amount (i.e., monetary value of expenditure excluding VAT). Other columns should be used to categorize the nature of the payments, such as fuel, subsistence, stamps, etc. The number of categories you use depends on the level of detail you require. A useful column heading is 'Other': into this column items can be entered that you are unsure of how to categorize. Such items can be dealt with at a later date when more information may be available relating to them. Alternatively, such expenditure could be categorized as general expenditure
- The final column should be noted as 'Balance'. This column is used to calculate the amount of cash that is left at the end of a period

Figure 13.9 is an example of a spreadsheet software-based petty cash book with relevant header columns noted.

Figure 13.9
Petty Cash Book Spreadsheet Software Based – VAT

PETTY CASH BOOK											
DATE	PAYEE / SOURCE	DESCRIPTION	MONEY IN	MONEY OUT	VAT AMOUNT	NET AMOUNT	FUEL	SUBSISTENCE	STAMPS	OTHER	BALANCE

Petty cash book – VAT-registered business: illustrative example

This illustrative example is applicable to both a paper-based petty cash book and a spreadsheet software-based petty cash book.

Andrew is an architect who operates as a sole trader. He is registered for VAT and runs his business from a city centre office. During any given month he will spend petty cash to pay for incidental products and services.

During the month of March Andrew transacted the following petty cash items:

1. On 1 March he withdraws £200 from the business bank account and places it into the petty cash tin. He places a note in the petty cash folder for the relevant month noting that £200 has been lodged into petty cash from the business bank account

2. On 5 March he takes out £100 from the petty cash tin, goes to the local service station and spends £72 on fuel for his car for a business trip. He places the receipt in the 'Petty Cash' lever arch folder and the change back into the petty cash tin

3. On 7 March he takes £6 out of the petty cash tin and uses the money to purchase stamps at the post office. He places the receipt for the stamps into the 'Petty Cash' lever arch folder

4. On 15 March he takes out £10 from the petty cash tin to pay for lunch during a site visit. On his return to the office he places the receipt into the 'Petty Cash' lever arch folder

5. On 25 March Andrew pays £14.40 from petty cash for a window lock for the office window. He places the receipt for £14.40 into the 'Petty Cash' lever arch folder

Andrew needs to record each of the above transactions in the petty cash book. In order to record the transactions, he retrieves the documents and receipts from the petty cash folder for the month of March. Each time he enters an item into the petty cash book, he writes the letter 'E' with a circle around it in red ink on the petty cash document/receipt to note that it has been recorded in the petty cash book.

> **MICRO TASK**
> Can you produce the petty cash book for Andrew to record the transactions noted above?
> • Compare your petty cash book for Andrew to the solution noted below.

If Andrew handwrites the petty cash transactions into the paper-based petty cash book the result will be as shown in Figure 13.10.

Figure 13.10

Petty Cash Book Paper Based – Andrew, Architect – VAT Registered

PETTY CASH BOOK

DATE	PAYEE/SOURCE	DESCRIPTION	MONEY IN	MONEY OUT	VAT AMOUNT	NET AMOUNT	FUEL	SUBSISTENCE	STAMPS	OTHER	BALANCE
01-Mar-14	BUSINESS BANK	Lodgement	200.00								200.00
05-Mar-14	SERVICE STATION	FUEL		72.00	12.00	60.00	60.00				128.00
07-Mar-14	POST OFFICE	STAMPS		6.00	0.00	6.00			6.00		122.00
15-Mar-14	BIG EATS LTD	LUNCH		10.00	1.67	8.33		8.33			112.00
25-Mar-14	WINDOW SHOP	WINDOW LOCK		14.40	2.40	12.00				12.00	97.60
			200.00	102.40	16.07	86.33	60.00	8.33	6.00	12.00	97.60

If Andrew inputs the petty cash transactions into a spreadsheet software-based petty cash book the result will be as shown in Figure 13.11.

> NOTE: The date recorded in the petty cash book is the ACTUAL date of the transaction, NOT the date the transaction is entered into the petty cash book.

Review of transactions recorded in the petty cash book:
- All transactions are dated on the date that the actual transaction took place
- All receipts note the source of money receipts into petty cash, for example business bank account, business owner
- All payment transactions detail who the payee is, i.e., the recipient of the payment

Figure 13.11

Petty Cash Book Spreadsheet Software Based – Andrew, Architect – VAT Registered

PETTY CASH BOOK

DATE	PAYEE / SOURCE	DESCRIPTION	MONEY IN	MONEY OUT	VAT AMOUNT	NET AMOUNT	FUEL	SUBSISTENCE	STAMPS	OTHER	BALANCE
01-Mar-14	BUSINESS BANK A/C	LODGEMENT	200.00								200.00
05-Mar-14	SERVICE STATION	FUEL		72.00	12.00	60.00	60.00				128.00
07-Mar-14	POST OFFICE	STAMPS		6.00	0.00	6.00			6.00		122.00
15-Mar-14	BIG EATS LTD	LUNCH		10.00	1.67	8.33		8.33			112.00
25-Mar-14	WINDOW SHOP	WINDOW LOCK		14.40	2.40	12.00				12.00	97.60
			200.00	102.40	16.07	86.33	60.00	8.33	6.00	12.00	97.60

- All payments note a brief description of goods or services paid for
- All transactions have the gross monetary amount recorded
- All payments record the VAT charged
- All payments record the net of VAT amount, i.e., the value of the payment excluding VAT
- All payment transactions are allocated to an analysis column. In this example the payments are analysed into fuel, subsistence, stamps, other. All the payment transactions noted in the analysis columns are noted at the VAT-exclusive amount

The balance column identifies the amount of petty cash actually available to spend. It is calculated by adding the opening balance of cash to any monies in and deducting expenditure for the period.

In the case of Andrew there was no opening balance and the total of monies received was £200 less the total of monies spent of £102.40, leaving cash available of £97.60.

Based on the payment transactions recorded in the petty cash book Andrew can identify that his business paid £102.40 from petty cash for the month of March. In addition, Andrew can identify from the analysis columns that the following petty cash payments were issued in the month of March:
- £60 was spent on fuel excluding VAT
- £8.33 was spent on subsistence excluding VAT
- £6 was spent on stamps, VAT not applicable
- £12 was spent on other items excluding VAT, i.e., the money spent on the window lock

Petty cash book – VAT-registered business: accounting software

What do you need to record petty cash payments and lodgements using accounting software for a VAT-registered business?
1. A lever arch folder to file petty cash expenditure receipts and lodgement receipts
2. A petty cash tin to store petty cash
3. A computer
4. Accounting software installed on computer

Set-up

- The spine of the lever arch folder should be clearly marked as 'Petty Cash' and also the financial year should be noted on the spine, e.g., 'Year 2014', so it is clearly visible
- This folder should be subdivided into twelve months for the financial year, e.g., January to December

- The accounting software product should be loaded onto your computer. All accounting packages operate on the same general principles
- The petty cash book on accounting software can be set up in a variety of ways. It may be set up and operated as a bank account. Alternatively, it may involve entering the transactions directly onto the nominal ledger, using journal debits and credits. Whatever set-up you use will depend on the software
- The petty cash payments being issued need to be input onto the accounting software, noting certain details of each payment transaction. Details would include: the date of the transaction, the payee, the monetary amount of the payment. The payments would also be allocated to different expense categories using nominal codes. Nominal codes are used by accounting software to group transactions. A VAT-registered business would also need to input VAT details of each transaction

CHAPTER 14

How to record expenditure transactions in a bank payments book

Figure 14.1

Expenditure – Bank Payments Book

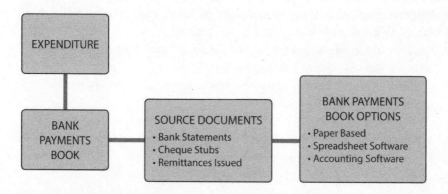

BANK PAYMENTS BOOK – OVERVIEW

A bank payments book is a record that lists payment transactions issued from a bank account for a given period, e.g., a day, a week, a month or a year. Bank payment transactions are payments issued through a bank account by cheque, transfers or any other means. It is referred to as a bank payments book because

Figure 14.2

Bank payments book

BANK PAYMENTS BOOK										
DATE	PAYEE	PAYMENT TYPE	PAYMENT REFERENCE	GROSS AMOUNT	PURCHASES DAYBOOK PAYMENTS	Wages	Drawings	Bank Charges	Credit Card	Other
05-Feb-14	Big Suppliers Ltd	Chq No. 889	Invoice 9999	850.00	850.00					
10-Feb-14	J Jonrd	EFT	Payroll	980.00		980.00				
16-Feb-14	Mr Smith	ATM	Cash withdrawal	150.00			150.00			
20-Feb-14	Big Bank Plc	DD	Bank charges	32.00				32.00		
25-Feb-14	Credit Card Co.	EFT	January A/C	885.00					885.00	
27-Feb-14	Funds for Dogs	Chq No. 890	Donation	50.00						50.00
				2,947.00	850.00	980.00	150.00	32.00	885.00	50.00

151

traditionally it was a paper notebook with rows and columns used to record payments issued. See Figure 14.1 for an overview of bank payment expenditure. Effectively the contents of a bank payments book is a list of payments issued through a bank account by any means. Figure 14.2 is an example of a bank payments book.

If expenditure incurred is paid from the bank account, then it is recorded in the bank payments book. The bank payments book is a list detailing information relating to bank payments; for example, the date of the transaction, the name of the payee and the monetary value. Also recorded would be supplementary details, for example a reference to the type of payment (cheque/direct debit/standing order) and any other relevant details, such as invoice numbers.

Depending on the type of business you are running you can record payments from the bank account in a variety of ways. A number of options are listed below:

- **You can record bank payments manually, i.e., maintaining a handwritten list of all bank payments for a given period**
- **You can use basic software, for example a spreadsheet, to record lists of all bank payments for a given period**
- **You can use accounting software that creates a bank payments book, recording all bank payments input**

In order to facilitate your decision making when evaluating a manual system or a software system you should review paper-based systems versus software-based systems, noted in chapter 11.

A bank payments book is a list of all monies spent from the bank account. Payments can be made in a variety of ways, for example cheque, electronic funds transfer (EFT), bankers' draft, standing orders, direct debits, visa delta, ATM (automated teller machine), cash withdrawals. The bank payments book can be used to analyse the different types of payments issued. Payments can be categorized under a variety of different headings, such as supplier payments/purchases daybook, wages, drawings, bank charges, credit card account, bank loan repayments, hire purchase repayments. The ability to maintain detailed and accurate records of how money is spent through the bank account will allow greater financial control to be exercised over the business.

The bank payments book is linked to the purchases daybook (see chapter 12) when payments are issued from the bank account to pay for purchase invoices recorded in the purchases daybook. The interaction between the bank payments book and the purchases daybook depends on the type of system being used:

- **Paper-based and spreadsheet software-based bank payments books interact as follows: bank payments issued to pay for goods or services supplied, where the purchase invoices are recorded in the purchases daybook, are allocated to the purchases daybook payments column in the bank payments book**

- An accounting software bank payment book interacts as follows: bank payments issued to pay for goods or services supplied, where the purchase invoices are recorded in the purchases daybook, are allocated to the creditors' ledger/purchases daybook when inputting the payment on the accounting software

If goods and services are supplied on credit, i.e., payment is not issued immediately on receipt of goods or services, then the procedure to process the paperwork, record the purchases and subsequent bank payment is as follows:
- The purchase invoice is recorded in the purchases daybook when goods/services are received
- The purchase invoice is filed in the purchases invoice unpaid file until due for payment
- The purchase invoice is retrieved from the 'Purchase Invoices Unpaid' file when due for payment
- Payment is issued from the bank account to pay the monies due noted on the purchase invoice
- The payment is recorded in the bank payments book, in the purchases daybook payment column, for a paper-based or spreadsheet software-based bank payments book. For an accounting software-based bank payments book, the payment is entered as required by the software
- The purchase invoice is marked with the payment details: the date of payment, method of payment
- The purchase invoice is filed in the purchase invoice paid file

If goods and services are supplied without credit, i.e., payment is due immediately on receipt of goods or services, then the procedure to process the paperwork, record the purchase and the bank payment is as follows:
- The purchase invoice is recorded in the purchases daybook when goods/services are received
- The payment is issued from the bank account
- The payment is recorded in the bank payments book, in the purchases daybook payment column, for a paper-based or spreadsheet software-based bank payments book. For an accounting software-based bank payments book, the payment is entered as required by the software
- The purchase invoice is marked with the payment details: the date of payment, method of payment
- The purchase invoice is filed in the purchase invoice paid folder

NOTE: The VAT element of purchases is dealt with via the purchases daybook, see chapter 12.

The layout and detail contained in a bank payments book will differ from business to business due to the different circumstances that can exist. This section will explain how to set up a bank payments book utilizing a paper-based system, a spreadsheet-based system or an accounting software-based system.

Bank payments book – source documents

The data to be recorded in the bank payments book is obtained from a variety of source documents, such as:

Bank statements – these detail the banking transactions of a business for a given period. Each will detail the value of monies received into the bank account and the value of monies paid out of the bank account.

Cheque stubs – these detail the value of a cheque issued, the date the cheque was issued and details of the payee.

Remittances issued – documents issued by a business when paying a supplier, detailing the purchase invoices that the business is paying a supplier.

Each time the details of a bank payment are entered, it is necessary to record on the source document that the transaction has been recorded. The simplest method is to write the letter 'E' in red ink with a circle around it on the source document (see Figure 14.3).

Figure 14.3
'E'

If a payment is issued by cheque, then on the cheque stub write the letter 'E' in red ink with a circle around it. This will immediately indicate that a record has been made of the cheque payment in the bank payments book.

If a payment is made by electronic funds transfer (EFT), direct debit (DD), or standing order (SO) then write the letter 'E' in red ink with a circle around it on the bank statement next to the transaction. This will immediately indicate that a record has been made of the payment in the bank payments book.

Bank payments book – paper based

What do you need to set up a paper-based bank payments book?

1. A lever arch folder to file paid purchase invoices

2. An accounts analysis book to record payments from the bank account

Set-up

- The spine of the lever arch folder should be clearly marked as 'Purchase Invoices Paid' and also the financial year should be noted on the spine, e.g., 'Year 2014', so it is clearly visible
- The lever arch folder should be divided alphabetically with an alphabetical divider
- The accounts analysis book being used as a bank payments book should have the appropriate headings noted in the columns
- Standard column headings would be as follows: date of payment, payee, payment type, payment reference, gross monetary amount. Other columns should be used to categorize the nature of the payments, for example supplier payments/purchase daybook payments (see chapter 12), wages, drawings, bank charges, credit card account, bank loan repayments, hire purchase repayments, PAYE taxes paid, VAT paid, other taxes paid. The number of other categories you use depends on the level of detail you require. A useful column heading is 'Other': into this column items can be entered that you are unsure of how to categorize. These items can be dealt with at a later date when more information may be available relating to them

How to operate a paper-based bank payments book

Each time a payment is issued from the bank account the details need to be recorded in the bank payments book.

The following list illustrates the type of detail that should be recorded:

Date – the actual date of the payment

Payee – the name of the person, company, organization to whom the payment is being issued

Payment type – if a cheque payment, then the cheque number; if an electronic funds transfer; then 'EFT' is noted; if a payment is by direct debit then 'DD' is noted; if payment is by standing order; then 'SO' is noted. Payment type should describe the payment so it can be traced

Payment reference – if appropriate, a reference can be noted to further detail the payment, for example a supplier invoice number; or if a payment is issued to pay a credit card bill, then the credit card bill statement date or month should be noted

Gross amount – the total value of the payment being issued

Purchases daybook payments (supplier payments) – any payments issued to suppliers for invoices recorded in the purchases daybook should be noted in this column. (NOTE – refer to the purchase daybook section of this book for full details of how to set up and maintain a purchase daybook. See chapter 12)

Other columns – additional columns in the bank payments book are created as required, for example wages, drawings, i.e., monies taken by the owner of the business for his/her private use, credit card account, bank loan repayments, hire purchase payments, PAYE taxes paid, VAT paid, other taxes paid, other

Bank payments book – spreadsheet software

What do you need to set up a spreadsheet software-based bank payments book?

1. A lever arch folder to file 'Purchase Invoices Paid'
2. A computer
3. Spreadsheet software installed on computer

Set-up

- The spine of the lever arch folder should be clearly marked as 'Purchase Invoices Paid' and also the financial year should be noted on the spine, e.g. 'Year 2014', so it is clearly visible
- The lever arch file should be divided alphabetically with an alphabetical divider
- A new spreadsheet file should be set up to be used as a bank payments book and should have the appropriate headings noted in columns. The file should be named 'Bank Payments Book'. Also the trading year should be noted, e.g., 'Bank Payments Book 2014'
- Standard column headings would be as follows: date of payment, payee, payment type, payment reference, gross monetary amount. Other columns should be used to categorize the nature of the payments, such as purchases daybook payments/supplier payments (see chapter 12 re purchases daybook), wages, drawings, bank charges, credit card account, bank loan repayments, hire purchase repayments, PAYE taxes paid, VAT paid, other taxes paid, other. The number of other categories you use depends on the level of detail you require. A useful column heading is

Figure 14.4
Spreadsheet Software-Based Bank Payments Book

BANK PAYMENTS BOOK										
DATE	PAYEE	PAYMENT TYPE	PAYMENT REFERENCE	GROSS AMOUNT	PURCHASES DAYBOOK PAYMENTS	Wages	Drawings	Bank Charges	Credit Card	Other

'Other': into this column items can be entered that you are unsure of how to categorize; these items can be dealt with at a later date when more information may be available relating to them

Figure 14.4 is an example of a spreadsheet software-based bank payment book with relevant header columns noted.

NOTE: If you are using online banking it is possible to download the transactions from the banking website directly into a spreadsheet. This can save considerable time as it avoids the inputting of raw data. However you will still need to set up the bank payments book as described above in order to analyse the payments in the appropriate columns. This will involve downloading the data from the online software and sorting the data.

How to operate a spreadsheet software-based bank payments book

Each time a payment is issued from the bank account the details need to be recorded in the spreadsheet bank payments book.

The following list illustrates the type of detail that should be recorded:

Date – the actual date of the payment

Payee – the name of the person, company, organization, to whom the payment is being issued

Payment type – if a cheque payment, then the cheque number; if an electronic funds transfer; then 'EFT' is noted; if a payment is by direct debit; then 'DD' is noted, if payment is by standing order; then 'SO' is noted. Payment type should describe the payment so it can be traced

Payment reference – if appropriate a reference can be noted to further detail the payment, for example a reference to a supplier invoice number; or if a payment is issued to pay a credit card bill, then the credit card bill statement date or month should be noted

Gross amount – the total value of the payment being issued

Purchases daybook payments (supplier payments) – any payments issued to suppliers for invoices recorded in the purchases daybook should be noted in this column (see chapter 12)

Other columns – additional columns in the bank payments book are created as required, for example wages, drawings, i.e., monies taken by the owner of the business for his/her private use, credit card account, bank loan repayments, hire purchase payments, PAYE paid, VAT paid, other taxes paid

Bank payments book – illustrative example

This illustrative example is applicable to both a paper-based bank payments book and a spreadsheet software-based bank payments book.

Andrew is an architect who operates as a sole trader and runs his business from a city centre office. During any given month he will issue payments to various third parties for goods and services or payments against liabilities such as loans.

Andrew records his payments at the end of the month. On 31 March he needs to record the following payments in the bank payments book:

1. **Cheque number 475 for £450, issued on 5 March to Office Supplies for stationery products he obtained in January noted on invoice number 4596**
2. **Electronic funds transfer of wages for £1,200 issued on 10 March to Joe Bloggs, his member of staff**
3. **Andrew used the ATM cash card to withdraw £100 for his own personal use on 16 March**
4. **The bank took a payment of £55 by direct debit on 20 March for bank charges as noted on the bank statement**
5. **On 25 March, Andrew issued an EFT (electronic funds transfer) payment of £1,285 to pay for the credit card bill, relating to the previous month of February**
6. **Andrew issued a short-term loan to Joe Bloggs, his staff member, on 30 March for £500 by cheque number 476**

Andrew needs to record each of the above transactions in his bank payments book. In addition, he also needs to mark the source documents to indicate that the payment transaction has been recorded in the bank payments book.

Transaction 1 – On the cheque stub of cheque number 475 Andrew will mark it with the letter 'E' in red ink with a circle around it, to record that the cheque payment of £450 has been noted in the bank payments book.

Transaction 2 – On the paper bank statement, Andrew will mark the electronic funds transfer (EFT) transaction of £1,200 with the letter 'E' in red ink with a circle around it, to record that the EFT has been recorded in the bank payments book.

Transaction 3 – On the paper bank statement Andrew will mark the ATM withdrawal of £100 with the letter 'E' in red ink with a circle around it, to note that the payment has been recorded in the bank payments book.

Transaction 4 – On the paper bank statement Andrew will mark the direct debit payment of £55 with the letter 'E' in red ink with a circle around it, to record that the direct debit payment has been recorded in the bank payments book.

Transaction 5 – On the paper bank statement Andrew will mark the electronic funds transfer (EFT) payment of £1,285 with the letter 'E' in red ink with a circle around it, to note that the EFT payment has been recorded in the bank payments book.

Transaction 6 – On the cheque stub of cheque number 476 Andrew will write the letter 'E' in red ink with a circle around it, to record that the cheque payment of £500 has been noted in the bank payments book.

> **MICRO TASK**
> **Can you produce the bank payments book to reflect the transaction noted above?**
> • **Compare the bank payments book you have produced against the solution noted below.**

The bank payments book will record transactions 1 to 6 above as follows:

> **NOTE: The date recorded in the bank payment book is the ACTUAL date of the transaction, NOT the date the transaction is entered into the bank payments book.**

If Andrew handwrites the bank payment transactions into the paper-based bank payments book the result will be as shown in Figure 14.5.

If Andrew inputs the bank payment transactions into a spreadsheet software-based bank payments book the result will be as shown in Figure 14.6.

Figure 14.5
Bank Payments Book Paper Based – Andrew, Architect

BANK PAYMENTS BOOK

DATE	PAYEE	PAYMENT TYPE	PAYMENT REFERENCE	GROSS AMOUNT	PURCHASES DAYBOOK PAYMENTS	Wages	Drawings	Bank Charges	Credit Card	Other
05-Mar-14	Office Supplies	Chq No. 475	Invoice 4596	450.00	450.00					
10-Mar-14	Joe Bloggs	EFT	Feb Payroll	1,200.00		1,200.00				
16-Mar-14	Andrew	ATM	Cash withdrawal	100.00			100.00			
20-Mar-14	Bank Plc	DD	Bank charges	55.00				55.00		
25-Mar-14	Credit Card Co.	EFT	Feb a/c	1,285.00					1,285.00	
30-Mar-14	Joe Bloggs	Chq No. 476	Loan to Joe	500.00						500.00
				3,590.00	450.00	1,200.00	100.00	55.00	1,285.00	500.00

Figure 14.6
Bank Payments Book Spreadsheet Software Based – Andrew, Architect

| BANK PAYMENTS BOOK | | | | | | | | | | |

DATE	PAYEE	PAYMENT TYPE	PAYMENT REFERENCE	GROSS AMOUNT	PURCHASES DAYBOOK PAYMENTS	Wages	Drawings	Bank Charges	Credit Card	Other
05-Mar-14	Office Supplies	Chq No. 475	Invoice 4596	450.00	450.00					
10-Mar-14	Joe Bloggs	EFT	Feb Payroll	1,200.00		1,200.00				
16-Mar-14	Andrew	ATM	Cash withdrawal	100.00			100.00			
20-Mar-14	Bank Plc	DD	Bank charges	55.00				55.00		
25-Mar-14	Credit Card Co.	EFT	Feb a/c	1,285.00					1,285.00	
30-Mar-14	Joe Bloggs	Chq No. 476	Loan to Joe	500.00						500.00
				3,590.00	450.00	1,200.00	100.00	55.00	1,285.00	500.00

Review of transactions recorded in the bank payments book:
- **All transactions are dated on the date that the actual transaction took place**
- **All transactions detail the payee, i.e., the recipient of the payment**
- **All transactions detail the payment type, such as cheque with number, electronic funds transfer, direct debit, Visa Debit, standing order, ATM**
- **All transactions record a payment reference, such as the invoice number, docket number or some other reference, to identify what source document the payment relates to**
- **All transactions have the gross monetary amount recorded**
- **All transactions are allocated to an analysis column. In this example the payments are analysed into purchases daybook (see chapter 12), wages, drawings, bank charges, credit card, other**

Based on the payment transactions recorded in the bank payments book Andrew can identify that his business paid out of the bank account a total of £3,590 for the month of March. In addition, Andrew can identify from the analysis columns that the following payments were issued in the month of March:
- **Purchases daybook payment of £450, i.e., payment to a trade supplier who previously supplied goods on credit in January and waited until March for payment**
- **Payment of £1,200 paid in wages to Joe Bloggs**
- **Payment of £100 taken by Andrew as drawings**
- **Payment of £55 taken by the bank as bank charges**
- **Payment of £1,285 to pay the previous month's credit card bill**
- **Payment of £500 issued as a loan to staff member Joe Bloggs**

NOTE: Transaction 1 – Purchases daybook payment
For full details of the purchase daybook refer to chapter 12.

The payment to Office Supplies of £450 is allocated to the purchases daybook column as the purchase invoice had been entered into the purchase daybook. The purchase invoice relating to these goods was dated January, when the goods were delivered, and the payment is only being issued in March.

The purchase invoice from Office Supplies of £450 would be held in the 'Purchase Invoices Unpaid' folder. When payment is being issued, the invoice would be retrieved from the 'Purchase Invoices Unpaid' folder, the amount due identified and the payment issued by cheque. Then the date of payment and the cheque number would be written in red ink on the physical purchase invoice as a record that the invoice has been paid. The purchase invoice would then be filed alphabetically in the 'Purchase Invoices Paid' folder.

Bank payments book – accounting software

What do you need to set up an accounting software-based bank payments book for a business?

1. A lever arch file
2. A computer
3. Accounting software installed on computer

Set-up

- The spine of the lever arch folder should be clearly marked as 'Purchase Invoices Paid' and also the financial year should be noted on the spine, for example 'Year 2014', so it is clearly visible
- The lever arch file should be divided alphabetically with an alphabetical divider
- The accounting software product should be loaded onto your computer. All accounting packages operate on the same general principles
- The bank payments book on accounting software is often referred to as 'Bank'. The payments being issued via the bank need to be input onto the accounting software, noting certain details of each payment transaction, for example the date of the transaction, the payee, the monetary amount of the payment

How to operate an accounting software-based bank payments book

Each time a payment is issued from the bank account the details need to be recorded on the accounting software in the bank module. The following list illustrates the type of detail that should be recorded:

Date – the actual date of the payment

Payee – the name of the person, company, organization to whom the payment is being issued

Payment type – if a cheque payment, then the cheque number; if an electronic funds transfer; then 'EFT' is noted; if a payment is by direct debit; then 'DD' is noted; if payment is by standing order; then 'SO' is noted. The payment type should describe the payment so it can be traced

Payment reference – if appropriate, a reference can be noted to further detail the payment, for example a reference to a supplier invoice number

Gross amount – the total value of the payment being issued

Purchases daybook payments/supplier payments – if you are issuing a payment for a purchase invoice that you have input on the accounting software already, then the payment can be directly allocated against the invoice

Payment analysis – accounting software uses codes to group similar types of transactions together. These codes are known as nominal codes and need to be set up when the software is loaded up for the first time or alternatively as and when required, as payments are being input

After the details of the payments have been input onto the accounting software it will be possible to run reports to review the bank payments book. The bank payments book report will list all the payments issued over the particular date range selected that have been input, detailing the date of each payment, the payee names and the gross monetary value. You should be able to run other reports that will display information in a variety of different ways; for example, you could run a bank payment book report for a single supplier, over a particular date range.

Due to the vast array of accounting software programs available it is only practical to review the general features of accounting software in this section as detailed above.

CHAPTER 15

How to record expenditure transactions in a credit card book

Figure 15.1
Expenditure – credit card book

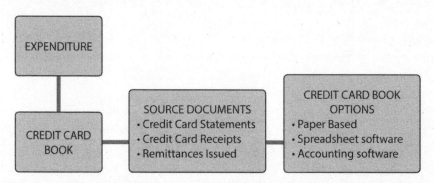

CREDIT CARD BOOK – OVERVIEW

A credit card book is a record that lists payment transactions issued from a credit card account and lodgements received reducing the liability for a given period, e.g. a day, a week, a month or a year. Credit card payment transactions are payments issued through a credit card account. See Figure 15.1 for an overview of credit card expenditure. It is referred to as a credit card book because traditionally it was a paper notebook with rows and columns used to record payments issued. Effectively the contents of a credit card book is a list of payments issued through a credit card account and monies lodged to the credit card account to reduce the balance due. A credit card book would contain information as shown in Figure 15.2.

If expenditure incurred is paid from the credit card account, then it is recorded in the credit card book. The credit card book is a list of credit card transactions recording information, including the name of the payee or receipt details and the monetary value. In addition, supplementary details can be recorded, for example a reference to an invoice number. Credit card payments can also be analysed into categories, such as purchases daybook payments/supplier payments, drawings, fees, interest, other.

Depending on the type of business you are running you can record payments from the credit card account in a variety of ways. A number of options are listed below:

Figure 15.2 Credit Card Book Example

CREDIT CARD BOOK

DATE	PAYEE/RECEIPT DETAILS	PAYMENT/RECEIPT REFERENCE	GROSS AMOUNT	PURCHASES DAYBOOK PAYMENTS	Drawings	Credit Card Fees	Credit Card Interest	Payments	Balance
	Opening Balance		344.86						344.86
05-Mar-14	Office Supplies	Invoice 1998	414.00	414.00					758.86
16-Mar-14	Esso Service Station	Van	38.40	38.40					797.26
20-Mar-14	Insure It Ltd	ref 8787	300.00	300.00					1,097.26
22-Mar-14	Payment	credit card	-344.86					-344.86	752.40
25-Mar-14	Apple Store	music	9.99		9.99				762.39
22-Mar-14	Late payment fee	credit card	12.00			12.00			774.39
22-Mar-14	Interest charge	credit card	2.56				2.56		776.95
28-Mar-14	Esso Service Station	Car	66.78	66.78					843.73
			843.73	819.18	9.99	12.00	2.56	-344.86	

- You can record credit card expenditure manually, i.e., maintaining a handwritten list of all credit card expenditure and receipts for a given period
- You can use basic software, for example a spreadsheet; to record lists of all credit card expenditure and transactions for a given period
- You can use accounting software that creates a credit card book, recording all credit card expenditure and transactions for a given period

In order to facilitate your decision making when evaluating a manual system or a software system you should review paper-based systems versus software-based systems, noted in chapter 11.

The credit card book can be used to analyse the different types of payments issued. Payments can be categorized under a variety of different headings: for example, purchases daybook payments, i.e., payments to suppliers; drawings, i.e., monies taken from the business by the owner of the business for personal use; credit card fees; credit card interest; other. The ability to maintain detailed and accurate records of how money is spent through the credit card book will allow greater financial control to be exercised over the business.

The credit card book is linked to the purchases daybook (see chapter 12) when payments are issued from the credit card account to pay for purchase invoices recorded in the purchases daybook. The interaction between the credit card book and the purchases daybook depends on the type of system being used:

- Paper-based and spreadsheet software-based credit card books interact as follows: credit card payments issued to pay for goods or services supplied, where the purchase invoices are recorded in the purchases daybook, are allocated to the purchases daybook payments column in the credit card book
- An accounting software credit card book interacts as follows: credit card payments issued to pay for goods or services supplied, where the purchase invoices are recorded in the purchases daybook, are allocated to the creditors' ledger/purchases daybook when inputting the payment on the accounting software

If goods and services are supplied on credit, i.e., payment is not issued immediately on receipt of goods or services, then the procedure to process the paperwork, record the purchases and subsequent credit card payment is as follows:

- The purchase invoice is recorded in the purchases daybook when goods/services are received
- The purchase invoice is filed in the 'Purchase Invoices Unpaid' folder until due for payment
- The purchase invoice is retrieved from the 'Purchase Invoices Unpaid'

folder when due for payment
- The payment is issued by credit card
- The payment is recorded in the credit card book, in the purchases daybook payment column, for a paper-based or spreadsheet software-based bank payments book. For an accounting software-based credit card book, the payment is entered as required by the software
- The purchase invoice is marked with the payment details, the date of payment and method of payment, i.e., credit card
- The purchase invoice is filed in the 'Purchase Invoices Paid' folder

If goods and services are supplied without credit, i.e., payment is due immediately on receipt of goods or services, then the procedure to process the paperwork, record the purchase and the credit card payment is as follows:
- The purchase invoice is recorded in the purchases daybook when goods/services are received
- The payment is issued from the credit card account
- The payment is recorded in the credit card book, in the purchases daybook payment column, for a paper-based or spreadsheet software-based credit card book. For an accounting software-based credit card book, the payment is entered as required by the software
- The purchase invoice is marked with the payment details: the date of payment, method of payment
- The purchase invoice is filed in the 'Purchase Invoices Paid' folder

> NOTE: The VAT element of purchases is dealt with via the purchases daybook, see chapter 12.

The layout and detail contained in a credit card book will differ from business to business due to the different circumstances that can exist. This section will explain how to set up a credit card book utilizing a paper-based system, a spreadsheet-based system or an accounting software-based system.

Credit card book – source documents

The data to be recorded in the credit card book is obtained from a variety of source documents, such as:

Credit card statement – this is a document that details credit card payment transactions and receipts for a given period. It will detail the value of all payments issued and also show monies received to pay against the balance due on the credit card.

Credit card receipt – a receipt obtained when payment is issued by credit card.

Remittance issued – this is a document issued by a business when paying a supplier or creditor. The document details the purchase invoices that the business is paying a supplier or details the debt to which the payment relates.

Credit card book – paper based

What do you need to set up a paper-based credit card book?

1. A lever arch folder to file credit card statements
2. An accounts analysis book to record payments from and lodgements to the credit card

Set-up

- The spine of the lever arch folder should be clearly marked as 'Credit Card Statements' and also the financial year should be noted on the spine, for example 'Year 2014', so it is clearly visible. This file should be subdivided into twelve months for the financial year, e.g., January to December
- The accounts analysis book being used as a credit card book should have the appropriate headings noted
- The headings noted in the columns of the credit card book will depend on the circumstances of the business
- Standard column headings would be as follows: date of transaction, payee/receipt details, payment/receipt reference, gross monetary amount. Other columns should be used to categorize the nature of the payments, such as purchases daybook payments (see chapter 12 re purchases daybook), drawings, i.e., credit card payments relating to private expenditure that is not related to the business, credit card fees, credit card interest, payments, balance. A useful column heading is 'Other': into this column items can be entered that you are unsure of how to categorize. These items can then be dealt with at a later date when more information may be available relating to them

Figure 15.3 is an example of a credit card book with relevant header columns noted.

Figure 15.3
Paper-Based Credit Card Book Template

CREDIT CARD BOOK									
DATE	PAYEE/RECEIPT DETAILS	PAYMENT / RECEIPT REFERENCE	GROSS AMOUNT	PURCHASES DAYBOOK PAYMENTS	Drawings	Credit Card Fees	Credit Card Interest	Payments	Balance

How to operate a paper-based credit card book

Each time a payment is issued by credit card the details need to be recorded in the credit card book.

The following list illustrates the type of detail that should be recorded:

Date – the actual date of the credit card payment

Payee – the name of the person, company, organization, to whom the payment is being issued

Receipt details – if a receipt is recorded on the credit card statement then the source of the receipt needs to be noted, for example a payment issued by the credit card holder to clear the prior month's credit card balance

Payment reference – if appropriate, a reference can be noted to further detail the payment, for example a reference to a supplier invoice number

Gross amount – the total value of the payment being issued for all transactions noted on a credit card statement needs to be recorded

Purchases daybook payments (supplier payments) – any payments issued to suppliers for invoices recorded in the purchases daybook should be noted in this column (NOTE – refer to the purchase daybook section of this book for full details of how to set up and maintain a purchases daybook. See chapter 12)

Other columns – additional columns in the credit card book are created as required, for example drawings, i.e., monies taken by the owner of the business for his/her private use, credit card fees, credit card interest, payments to the credit card company

Balance – this column is used to record the running balance due on the credit card

Credit card book: paperwork and filing

If the purchase invoice being paid by credit card relates to an invoice for goods and/or services that was recorded in the purchases daybook, then the purchase invoice will be found in the 'Purchase Invoices Unpaid' lever arch folder (see chapter 12 for full details).

If the purchase invoice being paid by credit card relates to an invoice for goods and/or services that are being supplied without credit, then the purchase invoice will be presented for immediate payment at the time of supply of the goods and/or service.

When a payment is made by credit card, the purchase invoice being paid should be clearly marked in red ink 'paid by credit card' and also the date of payment should be noted on the purchase invoice. The purchase invoice that has been paid by credit card should be filed alphabetically in the 'Purchase Invoices Paid' lever arch folder as set up in chapter 14.

When the credit card statement has been received for a given month, the transactions detailed on it need to be checked to ensure that all payments are legitimate payments issued by the credit card holder. For each payment transaction detailed on the statement, there should be corresponding paperwork, i.e., invoices/receipts. Each time a transaction on the credit card statement is matched with an invoice/receipt, the credit card transaction noted on the statement should be ticked using red ink to clearly identify it has been checked.

Each time a transaction on the credit card statement is recorded in the credit card book the credit card statement transaction should be marked with a letter 'E' and circled in red ink. This will highlight that the transaction has been processed.

Credit card book – spreadsheet software

What do you need to set up a spreadsheet software-based credit card book?
1. A lever arch folder to file credit card statements
2. A computer
3. Spreadsheet software installed on computer

Set-up

- The spine of a lever arch folder should be clearly marked as 'Credit Card Statements' and also the financial year should be noted on the spine, for example 'Year 2014', so it is clearly visible. This file should be subdivided into twelve months for the financial year, e.g., January to December
- A new spreadsheet file should be set up to be used as a credit card book and should have the appropriate headings noted in columns. The file should be named 'Credit Card Book' and the trading year should also be part of the file name, for example 'Credit Card Book 2014'

Figure 15.4
Spreadsheet Software-Based Credit Card Book

CREDIT CARD BOOK									
DATE	PAYEE/RECEIPT DETAILS	PAYMENT/RECEIPT REFERENCE	GROSS AMOUNT	PURCHASES DAYBOOK PAYMENTS	Drawings	Credit Card Fees	Credit Card Interest	Payments	Balance

- Standard column headings would be as follows: date of transaction, payee/receipt details, payment/receipt reference, gross monetary amount. Other columns should be used to categorize the nature of the payments, such as purchases daybook payments, i.e., supplier payments (see chapter 12), drawings, i.e., credit card payments relating to private expenditure that are not related to the business, credit card fees, credit card interest, payments, balance. A useful column heading is 'Other': into this column items can be entered that you are unsure of how to categorize. These items can then be dealt with at a later date when more information may be available relating to them

Figure 15.4 is an example of a spreadsheet software-based credit card book with relevant header columns noted.

> NOTE: If you are using online credit card banking, it is possible to download the transactions from the credit card website directly into a spreadsheet. This can save considerable time as it avoids the inputting of raw data. However you will still need to set up the credit card book as described above in order to analyse the payments in the appropriate columns.

How to operate a spreadsheet software-based credit card book

Each time a payment is issued by credit card the details need to be recorded in the credit card book. The following list illustrates the type of detail that should be recorded:

Date – the actual date of the credit card payment

Payee – the name of the person, company, organization to whom the payment is being issued

Receipt details – if a receipt is recorded on the credit card statement then the source of the receipt needs to be noted, for example a payment issued by the credit card holder to clear the prior month's balance

Payment reference – if appropriate, a reference can be noted to further detail the payment, for example a reference to a supplier invoice number

Gross amount – the total value of the payment being issued for all transactions noted on a credit card statement needs to be recorded

Purchases daybook payments (supplier payments) – any payments issued to suppliers for invoices recorded in the purchases daybook should be noted in this column. (NOTE – refer to the purchase daybook section of this book for full details of how to set up and maintain a purchases daybook. See chapter 12)

Other columns – additional columns in the credit card book are created as required, for example drawings, i.e., monies taken by the owner of the business for his/her private use, credit card fees, credit card interest, payments to the credit card company

Balance – this column is used to record the running balance due on the credit card

Credit card book: paperwork and filing

If the purchase invoice being paid by credit card relates to an invoice for goods and/or services that was recorded in the purchases daybook, then the purchase invoice will be found in the 'Purchase Invoices Unpaid' lever arch folder (see chapter 12 for full details).

If the purchase invoice being paid by credit card relates to an invoice for goods and/or services that are being supplied without credit, then the purchase invoice will be presented for immediate payment at the time of supply of the goods and/or service.

When a payment is made by credit card, the purchase invoice being paid should be clearly marked in red ink 'paid by credit card' and also the date of payment should be noted on the purchase invoice. The purchase invoice that has been paid by credit card should be filed alphabetically in the 'Purchase Invoices Paid' lever arch folder as set up in chapter 14.

When the credit card statement has been received for a given month, the transactions detailed on it need to be checked to ensure that all payments are legitimate payments issued by the credit card holder. For each payment transaction detailed on the statement, there should be corresponding paperwork, i.e., invoices/receipts. Each time a transaction on the credit card statement is matched with an invoice/receipt, the credit card transaction noted on the statement should be ticked using red ink to clearly identify it has been checked.

Each time a transaction on the credit card statement is recorded in the credit card book the credit card statement transaction should be marked with a letter 'E' and circled in red ink. This will highlight that the transaction has been processed.

Credit card book – accounting software

What do you need to record credit card payments and transactions using accounting software?

1. A lever arch folder
2. A computer
3. Accounting software installed on computer

Set-up

• The spine of the lever arch folder should be clearly marked as 'Credit Card Statements' and also the financial year should be noted on the spine, for example 'Year 2014', so it is clearly visible. This folder should be subdivided into twelve months for the financial year, e.g., January to December

- The accounting software product should be loaded onto your computer. All accounting packages operate on the same general principles
- The credit card book on accounting software can be set up in a variety of ways. It may be set up and operated as a bank account or you may input the transactions directly onto the nominal ledger using journal debits and credits to input transactions. Whatever set-up you use will depend on the software
- The credit card payments being issued need to be input onto the accounting software, noting certain details of each payment transaction, such as the date of the transaction, the payee, the monetary amount of the payment
- Accounting software categorizes transactions using nominal codes and these will need to be set up to capture the data for further analysis. It will be necessary to follow the instructions as per the accounting software supplier to set up the nominal codes. The nominal codes act in the same way as the columns on the paper-based or spreadsheet-based credit card books above. Examples of categories of transactions would be drawings, purchases daybook payments (supplier payments), credit card fees, credit card interest

How to operate a credit card book using accounting software

Each time a payment is issued by credit card the details need to be recorded in the accounting software credit card book.

The following list illustrates the type of detail that should be recorded:

Date – the actual date of the credit card payment

Payee – the name of the person, company, organization to whom the payment is being issued

Receipt details – if a receipt is recorded on the credit card statement, then the source of the receipt needs to be noted, for example a payment issued by the credit card holder to clear the prior month's balance

Payment reference – if appropriate, a reference can be noted to further detail the payment, such as a reference to a supplier invoice number

Gross amount – the total value of the payment being issued for all transactions noted on a credit card statement needs to be recorded

Credit card book: paperwork and filing

If the purchase invoice being paid by credit card relates to an invoice for goods and/or services that was recorded in the purchases daybook, then the purchase invoice will be found in the 'Purchase Invoices Unpaid' lever arch folder (see chapter 12 for full details).

If the purchase invoice being paid by credit card relates to an invoice for goods and/or services that are being supplied without credit, then the purchase invoice will be presented for immediate payment at the time of supply of the goods and/or service.

When a payment is made by credit card, the purchase invoice being paid should be clearly marked 'paid by credit card' in red ink and also the date of payment should be noted on the purchase invoice. The purchase invoice that has been paid by credit card should be filed alphabetically in the 'Purchase Invoices Paid' lever arch folder as set up in chapter 14.

When the credit card statement has been received for a given month, the transactions detailed on it need to be checked to ensure that all payments are legitimate payments issued by the credit card holder. For each payment transaction detailed on the statement, there should be corresponding paperwork, i.e., invoices/receipts. Each time a transaction on the credit card statement is matched with an invoice/receipt, the credit card transaction noted on the statement should be ticked using red ink to clearly identify it has been checked.

Each time a transaction on the credit card statement is recorded in the credit card book the credit card statement transaction should be marked with a letter 'E' and circled in red ink. This will highlight that the transaction has been processed.

After the details of credit card transactions have been input onto the accounting software, it will be possible to run reports to review the credit card book. The credit card book report will list all the payments issued and lodgements over the particular date range selected that have been input. Standard reports will detail such items as the date of each payment, the payee names, the gross monetary value. You should also be able to run other reports that will display information in a variety of different ways.

Due to the vast array of accounting software programs available it is only practical to review the general features of accounting software in this section as detailed above.

Credit card book – illustrative example

This illustrative example is applicable to a paper-based credit card book, a spreadsheet software-based credit card book and an accounting software-based credit card book.

Andrew is an architect who operates as a sole trader and runs his business from a city centre office. During any given month he will issue payments by credit card to various third parties for goods and services.

During the month of March Andrew issued the following credit card payments:

1. Credit card payment of £174 issued on 5 March to Telecoms for services rendered in January noted on invoice number 99856; i.e., he obtained

credit terms in relation to this supply of services

2. Credit card payment of £8.99 issued on 10 March to Apple online music store
3. Esso were paid £70.75 by credit card on 16 March for fuel
4. Paid £600 to J B Landlord for rent on 20 March
5. Andrew issued a payment on 25 March to the credit card company for £1,285 from the business bank account to pay the previous month's balance due on the credit card account
6. On 27 March Andrew purchased some downloads from the Apple online store for £9.99
7. Esso were paid £65.85 by credit card on 28 March for fuel

For each payment issued Andrew marks the source document, such as the purchase invoice/receipt, noting 'paid by credit card' in red ink and also noting the date of the payment.

Andrew receives his credit card statement in April that reflects the credit card payments he issued in March. In addition, the credit card statement for March will record the payment he issued from the bank account to pay the credit card bill for February. Also noted on the credit card statement will be transactions that have been generated by the credit card company, for example, fees and interest.

The credit card statement for March is as shown in Figure 15.5.

Figure 15.5

Credit Card Statement – Andrew, Architect

CREDIT CARD STATEMENT	Mar-14	
	Balance from previous statement	1,285.00
05-Mar-14	Telecoms plc	174.00
10-Mar-14	Apple Store	8.99
16-Mar-14	Esso Service Station	70.75
20-Mar-14	J B Landlord	600.00
25-Mar-14	Payment Received Thank You	-1,285.00
26-Mar-14	Late payment fee	15.00
26-Mar-14	Interest charge	3.22
27-Mar-14	Apple Store	9.99
28-Mar-14	Esso Service Station	65.85
	New balance this statement	947.80

On receipt of the credit card statement Andrew needs to review the following:

1. **Balance brought forward from previous statement, if such a balance exists**
2. **All credit card payment transactions noted on the credit card statement**
3. **Any payments made to reduce the balance due to the credit card company**
4. **Any charges imposed by the credit card company**

Andrew will need to check that the opening balance brought forward from the previous statement is correct, by checking the figure on the March statement against the balance on the February statement. If both figures match he will place a red tick next to the opening balance figure. If there is a discrepancy Andrew will need to establish the reason for it.

Andrew needs to check he has a purchase invoice/receipt for each payment noted on the statement. He should be able to find these invoices in the 'Purchase Invoices Paid' lever arch folder. These purchase invoices should have written 'paid by credit card' on them in red ink and also the date of the payment. For each transaction noted on the credit card statement for which Andrew has identified an invoice/receipt in the 'Purchase Invoices Paid' lever arch folder, he should place a red tick on the credit card statement to indicate that the transaction has been checked against a source document. If a payment on the credit card statement cannot be verified as an expense incurred by Andrew, he

Figure 15.6

Credit Card Statement – Andrew, Architect – Ticked

CREDIT CARD STATEMENT	Mar-14		
	Balance from previous statement	✓	1,285.00
05-Mar-14	Telecoms plc	✓	174.00
10-Mar-14	Apple Store	✓	8.99
16-Mar-14	Esso Service Station	✓	70.75
20-Mar-14	J B Landlord	✓	600.00
25-Mar-14	Payment Received Thank You	✓	-1,285.00
26-Mar-14	Late payment fee	✓	15.00
26-Mar-14	Interest charge	✓	3.22
27-Mar-14	Apple Store	✓	9.99
28-Mar-14	Esso Service Station	✓	65.85
	New balance this statement		947.80

would need to query it with the credit card company.

Andrew will need to check that any payments he has issued to reduce monies due to the credit card company are noted on the statement and place a red tick against the payment if it is correct.

When Andrew has ticked off all the transactions the credit card statement will reflect same, as noted in Figure 15.6.

Andrew needs to record the transactions on the credit card statement for March into the credit card book so the information can be analysed. Andrew has several options to consider concerning the credit card book:

- **Use a paper-based credit card book**
- **Use a spreadsheet software-based credit card book**
- **Use an accounting software-based credit card book**

As Andrew records the transactions noted on the credit card statement he needs to mark each credit card payment transaction on the credit card statement. He marks the transactions with the letter 'E' with a circle around it in red ink, to record the fact that the transaction has been recorded in the credit card book. After the entries have been made the credit card statement will look like Figure 15.7.

Figure 15.7
Credit Card Statement – Andrew, Architect – Ticked
and Entered

CREDIT CARD STATEMENT	Mar-14			
	Balance from previous statement	✓	Ⓔ	1,285.00
05-Mar-14	Telecoms plc	✓	Ⓔ	174.00
10-Mar-14	Apple Store	✓	Ⓔ	8.99
16-Mar-14	Esso Service Station	✓	Ⓔ	70.75
20-Mar-14	J B Landlord	✓	Ⓔ	600.00
25-Mar-14	Payment Received Thank You	✓	Ⓔ	-1,285.00
26-Mar-14	Late payment fee	✓	Ⓔ	15.00
26-Mar-14	Interest charge	✓	Ⓔ	3.22
27-Mar-14	Apple Store	✓	Ⓔ	9.99
28-Mar-14	Esso Service Station	✓	Ⓔ	65.85
	New balance this statement			947.80

> NOTE: The date recorded in the credit card book is the ACTUAL date of the transaction, NOT the date the transaction is entered into the credit card book.

MICRO TASK
Can you record the credit card transactions in the credit card book for Andrew's business?
- Set up the credit card book based on the templates previously explained
- Input the transactions into the credit card book
- Compare your credit card book for Andrew to the solution below.

Depending on the credit card book that Andrew decides to operate, the outcomes shown in Figure 15.8 (paper based) or Figure 15.9 (spreadsheet software) are possible.

Figure 15.8
Credit Card Book – Andrew, Architect – Paper Based

CREDIT CARD BOOK

DATE	PAYEE/RECEIPT DETAILS	PAYMENT / RECEIPT REFERENCE	GROSS AMOUNT	PURCHASE DAYBOOK PAYMENTS	Drawings	Credit Card Fees	Credit Card Interest	Payments	Balance
	Opening Balance		1,285.00						1,285.00
05-Mar-14	Telecoms plc	Inv 99856	174.00	174.00					1,459.00
10-Mar-14	Apple Store	music	8.99		8.99				1,467.99
16-Mar-14	Esso	fuel	70.75	70.75					1,538.74
20-Mar-14	J B Landlord	Inv A01	600.00	600.00					2,138.74
25-Mar-14	Credit Card Co	Business Bank	-1,285.00					-1,285.00	853.74
26-Mar-14	Credit Card Co	Fee	15.00			15.00			868.74
26-Mar-14	Credit Card Co	Interest	3.22				3.22		871.96
27-Mar-14	Apple Store	music	9.99		9.99				881.95
28-Mar-14	Esso	fuel	65.85	65.85					947.80
			947.80	910.60	18.98	15.00	3.22	-1,285.00	

Figure 15.9

Credit Card Book – Andrew, Architect – Spreadsheet Software Based

CREDIT CARD BOOK									
DATE	PAYEE/RECEIPT DETAILS	PAYMENT / RECEIPT REFERENCE	GROSS AMOUNT	PURCHASE DAYBOOK PAYMENTS	Drawings	Credit Card Fees	Credit Card Interest	Payments	Balance
	Opening Balance		1,285.00						1,285.00
05-Mar-14	Telecoms plc	Inv 99856	174.00	174.00					1,459.00
10-Mar-14	Apple Store	music	8.99		8.99				1,467.99
16-Mar-14	Esso	fuel	70.75	70.75					1,538.74
20-Mar-14	J B Landlord	Inv A01	600.00	600.00					2,138.74
25-Mar-14	Credit Card Co.	Business Bank A/C	-1,285.00					-1,285.00	853.74
26-Mar-14	Credit Card Co.	Fee	15.00			15.00			868.74
26-Mar-14	Credit Card Co.	Interest	3.22				3.22		871.96
27-Mar-14	Apple Store	music	9.99		9.99				881.95
28-Mar-14	Esso	fuel	65.85	65.85					947.80
			947.80	910.60	18.98	15.00	3.22	-1,285.00	

Credit card book – Andrew, architect: accounting software based

If Andrew uses an accounting software-based credit card book then the report layout will be dependent on the software used. However he will be able to obtain the same detail as illustrated in Figure 15.8.

A review of transactions recorded in the credit card book will reveal the same information for all three options: paper based / spreadsheet software based / accounting software based.

- All transactions are dated on the date that the actual transaction took place
- All transactions detail who the payee is, i.e., the recipient of the payment, except for opening balance transactions
- All receipts detail the source of the receipt
- All transactions record a reference, e.g., an invoice number
- All transactions have the gross monetary amount recorded
- All transactions are allocated to an analysis column or a nominal code if using accounting software. In this example, for paper-based and spreadsheet software-based credit card books, the payments are analysed into the purchases daybook (see chapter 12), drawings, credit card fees, credit card interest, payments and balance

Based on the payment transactions recorded in the credit card book Andrew can identify that his business paid by credit card £947.80 for the month of March. In addition, Andrew can identify from the analysis columns for paper-based and spreadsheet software-based credit card books that the following credit card payments/receipts were issued in the month of March:

- **Purchases daybook payments of £910.60, i.e., payments to suppliers**
- **Payment of £18.98 relating to drawings, i.e., monies spent for private use**
- **Payment of £15.00 fee charged by the credit card company**
- **Payment of £3.22 interest charged by the credit card company**
- **Receipt of £1,285 received by the credit card company to pay for prior month's credit card bill**

All of the above information would also be available from an accounting software-based credit card book. The information would be generated by running reports contained in the accounting software.

NOTE: The payments for fuel, £70.75 and £65.85, will be recorded in the purchases daybook as a normal purchase invoice received by a supplier. If Andrew's business is registered for VAT, then the VAT element of these purchases will be accounted for in the purchases daybook.

CHAPTER 16

How to record expenditure in a payroll records book

It is beyond the scope of this book to cover tax law in relation to payroll; however, this section will briefly address several important issues concerning payroll as follows: payroll software, payroll information requirements, payroll pitfalls and the payroll records book.

PAYROLL SOFTWARE

If your business pays wages for staff members then you are required to operate a payroll under the PAYE (pay as you earn) tax system. Due to the complexity of tax legislation it is highly recommended that you use dedicated payroll software to calculate the appropriate tax deductions from staff pay.

PAYROLL INFORMATION REQUIREMENTS

The payroll software that you select should be capable of producing the following information/documents at the very minimum:
- **Staff net pay for a given period**
- **Total tax due to the tax authorities for the period**
- **Staff payslips**

PAYROLL PITFALLS

Dealing with payroll for the uninitiated can lead to problems, as noted below:
- **Failing to calculate taxes correctly**
- **Failing to file and pay taxes on time, resulting in interest charges**
- **Failing to maintain proper staff holiday records**
- **Failing to ensure appropriate pay rates are paid**

PAYROLL RECORDS BOOK

A payroll records book would detail relevant information relating to payroll including staff gross pay, staff net pay and taxes deducted for the period. Such information can be produced from payroll software. In order to have easy access to payroll information, it would be recommended that reports that detail the relevant information be printed off and held in a payroll file for future reference. This payroll file will, in essence, be a payroll records book.

CHAPTER 17

How to record expenditure transactions – summary

Expenditure by a business requires certain records to be maintained to ensure a complete record of all expenditure. The type of expenditure records that need to be maintained depends upon business circumstances and also the payment methods being used.

BUSINESS CIRCUMSTANCES

If your business is VAT registered you will be required to account for the VAT relating to goods and services purchased. Accounting for VAT can add an additional complexity to record keeping. VAT relating to purchases will be separately identified in the purchases daybook and the petty cash book. If your business is not VAT registered you can avoid the need to account for VAT, thus simplifying record keeping.

If your business employs staff, then you will be required to operate a payroll. Payroll will add an additional complexity to record keeping. If your business does not employ staff, it can avoid the need to maintain a payroll, thus simplifying record keeping.

If your business generates cash sales then you will need to maintain records to monitor and control cash. Cash sheets will enable you to keep detailed records of cash sales and the expenditure from such cash sales. If your business does not generate cash sales it can avoid the need to record these, thus simplifying record keeping. See chapter 5 for details concerning cash sheets.

PAYMENT METHODS

Business expenditure can be captured using the following records:

- **Purchases daybook**
- **Petty cash book**
- **Bank payments book**
- **Credit card book**
- **Payroll records book**

Purchases daybook

This is a record of goods and services purchased by a business. It analyses expenditure into categories, to enable different types of expenditure to be monitored.

Petty cash book

This is a record of all minor cash payments and cash lodgements used to pay for these. It analyses expenditure into categories, to enable different types of expenditure to be monitored.

Bank payments book

This is a record of all payments issued from the bank account. It analyses expenditure into categories, to enable different types of expenditure to be monitored.

Credit card book

This is a record of all payments issued by credit card. It analyses expenditure into categories, to enable different types of expenditure to be monitored.

Payroll records book

This is a record of payroll costs. It analyses the expenditure into net pay, gross pay and relevant taxes.

It is possible to avoid the need for certain expenditure records by not using certain payment methods.

- **If in the unlikely circumstances your business never makes any miscellaneous cash purchases, then it is not necessary to maintain a petty cash book**
- **If your business does not use a credit card to pay for goods and/or services, then it can avoid maintaining a credit card book**
- **If your business does not employ staff, then it is not necessary to maintain a payroll records book**

The choice between using a manual system and a computerized system for recording expenditure will depend upon the following: sales volume, costs, IT skills level, image. For a detailed examination of the advantages and disadvantages concerning manual systems versus computer systems for recording expenditure see chapter 11.

MICRO QUIZ

Q1: A purchases daybook lists all expenditure relating to payments issued by credit card.
> True or False?

Q2: A purchases daybook records the gross value of purchases, i.e., the value including VAT if the business is not registered for VAT and is charged VAT by a supplier.
> True or False?

Q3: A bank payments book records all payments issued via the bank account.
> True or False?

Q4: Payments issued via the bank account relating to the purchases daybook are recorded at gross value, i.e., the value including VAT, and the VAT is accounted for in the purchases daybook for VAT-registered businesses.
> True or False?

Q5: A credit card book records all purchases and expenditure that have been incurred by a credit card.
> True or False?

Q6: A credit card book should not separate out payments for personal use or record same as drawings.
> True or False?

Q7: A petty cash book records material cash expenditure for a given period.
> True or False?

Q8: A petty cash book should record the source of cash receipts.
> True or False?

Q9: A business that does not make miscellaneous cash payments does not need to maintain a petty cash book.
> True or False?

Q10: Payroll records are optional if a business employs staff.
> True or False?

MICRO QUIZ – SOLUTIONS

Q1: False
Q2: True
Q3: True
Q4: True
Q5: True
Q6: False
Q7: False
Q8: True
Q9: True
Q10: False

SECTION 5

Value Added Tax (VAT)

CHAPTER 18

Value Added Tax

VALUE ADDED TAX (VAT) – OVERVIEW

Value added tax (VAT) adds a percentage tax to the cost of the supply of certain goods or services. The percentage of VAT charged can depend upon the type of goods or services supplied. For the majority of VAT-registered businesses, VAT is relatively straightforward. In essence, VAT is charged on the supply of goods and/or services to customers and this sales VAT (output VAT) is owed to the tax authorities. The amount of sales VAT (output VAT) due can be reduced by deducting purchase VAT (input VAT) the business has been charged for goods and services it has purchased. See Figure 18.1 for an overview of VAT.

VAT and your business

VAT relates to charging tax on taxable supplies, i.e., any supply of goods or services made in the UK that is not exempt from VAT. The question that you need to answer in relation to your business is as follows: are the goods and/or services your business supplies to customers a taxable supply, i.e., liable for a VAT charge? If the answer is yes, then you need to address the following:

- When is there an obligation to register for VAT?
- Is there a benefit to voluntary registration for VAT, prior to being obligated to register for VAT?
- What is the procedure for VAT registration?
- What rate of VAT needs to be charged?
- What information should be detailed on VAT invoices or VAT receipts?
- What VAT records need to be maintained?
- How is VAT charged on the sale of a product/service?
- How is VAT calculated?
- How is VAT calculated using the standard VAT calculation method?
- How is VAT calculated using the cash-accounting scheme?
- How is VAT calculated using the flat-rate scheme for small businesses?
- How is VAT calculated using the margin scheme for second-hand goods?
- What are the features of retail VAT schemes?
- What is the annual accounting scheme?
- How is a VAT return form completed?
- How is a VAT return filed?
- When must a VAT return be filed and paid?
- What type of pitfalls exist concerning VAT?

Figure 18.1
VAT Overview

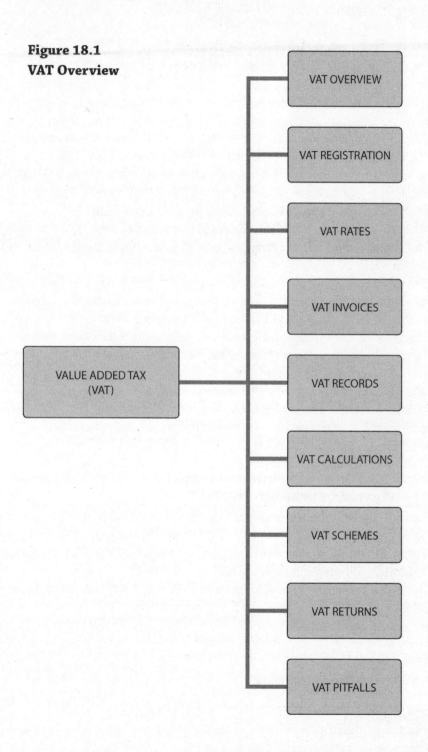

VAT registration

When is there an obligation to register for VAT?

If the goods and/or services your business supplies are liable to VAT, then you will be obligated to register for VAT if the value of your taxable supplies breaches the registration threshold. For a business trading in the domestic market the key issue relates to the value of taxable supplies. If the value of your taxable supplies in a twelve-month period or less exceeds £81,000 then VAT registration is compulsory.

The VAT registration threshold of £81,000 is effective from 1 April 2014. It is important to note that the VAT registration threshold is subject to change. Previously the registration threshold was £79,000, effective 1 April 2013; £77,000, effective 1 April 2012; and £73,000, effective 1 April 2011.

Alternatively, if at any time it is expected that taxable supplies in the next 30 days will breach the VAT registration threshold then there is an obligation to register for VAT.

The threshold relates to a rolling twelve-month period so it is necessary to be aware of cumulative sales, in case the threshold is breached. For example, if the taxable supplies for a period January to December were £70,000, then the business is below the threshold. However, by rolling the sales period forward by one month, February to January, and if taxable supplies were £85,000, then the sales would breach the VAT registration threshold.

Other conditions apply whereby there is an obligation to register for VAT concerning matters such as distance sales or acquisitions. For full details concerning VAT registration refer to www.hmrc.gov.uk and review 'Notice 700/1 – Should I be registered for VAT?'

Is there a benefit to voluntary registration for VAT, prior to being obligated to register for VAT?

If the goods and/or services your business supplies are liable to VAT then you will be obligated to register for VAT if your taxable supplies breach certain thresholds. However, if your business has not breached the VAT registration threshold then you may still register for VAT voluntarily.

The issues you need to consider prior to voluntary VAT registration relate to the following:

- **Fixed-asset purchases**
- **Image**
- **VAT-registered customers**
- **Non-VAT-registered customers**

Fixed-asset purchases

If the business will incur VAT on the purchases of fixed assets during the set-up phase, then the business can benefit from reclaiming VAT. This is particularly the case if the business is buying fixed assets such as computer equipment or machinery.

Image

If your business is not registered for VAT and selling taxable supplies, then customers and suppliers will be aware that your sales are below the VAT threshold. This may hinder your business as your business could be classed as insignificant in the marketplace, especially if you are dealing with large companies.

VAT-registered customers

If the business sells services and/or products to VAT-registered individuals or businesses then the VAT can be reclaimed by such customers. Customers who are VAT-registered are less concerned with being charged VAT, as they can claim it back.

Non-VAT-registered customers

If the customers of the business are not VAT registered, then these customers will not be able to reclaim the VAT charged and it may make your service or goods more expensive for them to buy. If your business is competing with VAT-registered businesses, then you may be in a position to undercut the competitors' prices if your business remains non-VAT registered.

What is the procedure for VAT registration?

If your business is obligated to register for VAT or you want to voluntarily register for VAT, then it is necessary to notify the tax authorities. Log on to www.hmrc.gov.uk and follow the instructions concerning VAT registration. The details you will need to supply will relate to such matters as contact details, business activities engaged in, bank account details, details concerning voluntary or compulsory registration.

VAT rates

What rate of VAT needs to be charged?

VAT is charged at different rates depending on the goods or services supplied. VAT rates are noted below:
- **VAT exempt: VAT not applicable**
- **Zero rate: 0%**
- **Reduced rate: 5%**
- **Standard rate: 20%**

> **NOTE: It is vitally important to be certain of the VAT rate that should be charged by a business on the goods or services it supplies. It is not always clear what VAT rate should be charged. If in doubt, seek clarification from the tax authorities or your professional advisor.**

Detailed below are non-exhaustive lists of examples of goods and services that are VAT exempt or charged at various VAT rates. The descriptions are of a general nature as certain rules and restrictions can apply.

Exempt
- Sporting events and physical education activities, such as athletics, badminton, boxing, cricket, cycling, equestrian, karate, motor sports, sailing, yoga – supplied by eligible bodies e.g. non-profit making organisations
- Betting, bingo and lotteries
- Certain cultural services
- Certain charitable fundraising events
- Burial or cremation services
- Certain health services
- Certain educational services
- Certain public postal services provided by the Royal Mail
- Certain financial services
- Certain insurance services

Zero rate 0%
- Food (however certain types of food are excluded, for example, food supplied in the course of catering, restaurant meals, cafes or hot takeaway food)
- The sale of donated goods by charity shops
- Certain equipment for disabled people
- Prescribed medicine
- Books, newspapers, magazines
- Exports
- Children's clothes and shoes
- Protective boots and helmets
- Passenger transport (certain restrictions apply)

Reduced rate 5%
- Children's car seats
- Supplies of fuel and power for domestic use
- Residential conversions and renovations (certain restrictions apply)
- Certain sanitary products
- Installation of mobility aid products for the elderly
- Installation of energy-saving products permanently installed in residential accommodation

Standard rate 20%
Taxable supplies that are not exempt from VAT or charged at reduced VAT rates are liable at the standard rate of VAT, currently 20% .

VAT invoices

What information should be detailed on VAT invoices or VAT receipts?

Detailed below is a list of contents to be considered in relation to VAT invoices:
- **Name of your business**
- **Address of your business**
- **Contact details of your business: phone, email**
- **VAT registration number of your business**
- **Customer name and address**
- **Date and tax point of invoice**
- **Description of the supply of service and/or product(s)**
- **Sequential invoice number**
- **Value of services rendered or goods supplied excluding VAT**
- **VAT rates charged**
- **Total value of VAT relating to the supply of services or goods supplied**
- **Total value of services rendered or price of goods supplied including VAT**

Detailed below is a list of contents to be considered in relation to VAT receipts for a supply that does not exceed £250:
- **Name of your business**
- **Address of your business**
- **VAT registration number of your business**
- **Contact details of your business: phone, email**
- **Date of receipt, tax point**
- **Description of the supply of services and/or products**
- **VAT rates charged**
- **Total fee for services rendered or price of goods supplied including VAT**

VAT records

A VAT-registered business is obligated to maintain records that will verify and validate VAT returns submitted to the tax authorities. Records relating to VAT transactions should be held for six years. VAT records would include copies of sales invoices issued to customers, purchase invoices received from suppliers and the records used to produce the figures submitted on VAT returns. The information required to complete a VAT return will be recorded in the financial records as part of the bookkeeping system of the business.

VAT calculations

How is VAT calculated on the sale of a product/service?

VAT adds a percentage onto the selling price of a service or a product that is liable to VAT.

If the selling price of a chair is £100 excluding VAT and VAT is to be charged at the standard rate, then the calculation is as follows: £100 x 20% (VAT) = £20 of VAT.

Selling price £100 + VAT £20 = VAT-inclusive selling price of £120. A customer buying the chair will pay £120. The shopkeeper will be liable to pay the tax authorities £20 worth of VAT less any VAT incurred during the period.

How is VAT calculated?

In essence, VAT is the difference between the VAT charged to customers by a business and the VAT charged by suppliers of a business.

- **If the level of VAT charged to customers by a business is greater than the level of VAT charged by suppliers for a given period, then a VAT liability exists**
- **If the level of VAT charged to customers by a business is less than the level of VAT charged by suppliers for a given period, then a VAT refund exists**

The amount of VAT due for payment can be calculated in a number of ways, such as:

- **The standard VAT calculation method (also referred to as the invoice basis or accruals basis, of VAT accounting)**
- **The cash-accounting VAT calculation method**
- **The flat-rate scheme VAT calculation method**
- **The margin scheme for second-hand goods**
- **Various retail schemes of VAT calculation**

The method used to calculate VAT depends on the circumstance of the business and whether a business is eligible to use a particular VAT accounting scheme.

VAT schemes

How is VAT calculated using the standard VAT calculation method?

Standard VAT accounting involves:

- **Paying the tax authorities VAT charged to customers on sales, for a given period, even if payment has not yet been received from customers**
- **Reclaiming VAT charged by suppliers from the tax authorities, for a given period, even if payment has not been issued to the suppliers**

VAT calculated using standard VAT accounting involves a number of basic calculations:

Calculation 1
Calculate the value of sales VAT, also known as output VAT, charged by the business to customers for the period.

Calculation 2
Calculate the value of purchase VAT, also known as input VAT, charged by suppliers for goods and services during the period.

Calculation 3
Deduct purchase VAT (input VAT) from sales VAT (output VAT) to identify if VAT is due to be paid to the tax authorities or due to be repaid by the tax authorities to your business.

Example
Tina buys and sells tables and is VAT registered. In the first quarter of the year she records the following transactions:

SALES

Date	Invoice	Details
1 Jan 2014	S111	Executive table £1,500 + VAT 20% £300 = £1,800 including VAT
1 Feb 2014	S222	Executive table £1,500 + VAT 20% £300 = £1,800 including VAT
1 Mar 2014	S333	Executive table £1,500 + VAT 20% £300 = £1,800 including VAT
TOTAL		Net sales £4,500 Output VAT £900

PURCHASES

Date	Invoice	Details
1 Jan 2014	P111	Executive table £1,000 + VAT 20% £200 = £1,200 including VAT
1 Feb 2014	P222	Executive table £1,000 + VAT 20% £200 = £1,200 including VAT
1 Mar 2014	P333	Executive table £1,000 + VAT 20% £200 = £1,200 including VAT
TOTAL		Net purchases £3,000 Input VAT £600

During April, Tina calculates the VAT using the standard VAT accounting method.

Calculation 1
Output VAT, i.e., sales VAT charged on the three sales invoices issued to customers for the period, amounted to £300 x 3 = £900.

Calculation 2

Input VAT, i.e., purchase VAT charged on the three purchase invoices received from suppliers for the period, amounted to £200 x 3 = £600.

Calculation 3

Output VAT, i.e., sales VAT: £900
Less input VAT, i.e., purchase VAT: £600
VAT due to be paid: £300

Tina is due to pay VAT to the tax authorities of £300 for the period January, February, March.

How is VAT calculated using the cash VAT calculation method?

Cash-accounting VAT involves:
- **Paying the tax authorities VAT charged to customers on sales, for a given period, when payment has been received from customers relating to the sales**
- **Reclaiming VAT charged by suppliers from the tax authorities, for a given period, when payment has been issued to the suppliers**

Eligibility criteria:
- **Taxable turnover is not expected to exceed £1,350,000 during the next year and turnover is currently less that £1,350,000**
- **Current VAT returns must be filed up to date and VAT payments must be up to date**
- **Within the previous twelve months the person has not been subject to a penalty for VAT evasion or has not been convicted of a VAT offence**
- **Eligibility withdrawn if taxable turnover exceeds £1.6 million for twelve months**

> **NOTE: Cash accounting must not be used under certain circumstances, such as:**
> - **Invoices are issued with credit terms exceeding six months**
> - **Invoices are issued in advance of the supply of goods and/or services**

Application process

There is no formal application process to join or leave the cash-accounting scheme. If you are eligible you can start using the cash-accounting scheme. If you are already registered for VAT then you can start using the scheme at the start of any VAT period. If you have just registered for VAT you can start using the scheme from the date your VAT registration commences. If you want to stop using the cash-accounting scheme then you can stop using the scheme at the end of any VAT accounting period.

VAT calculated using cash VAT accounting involves a number of basic calculations:

Calculation 1
Calculate the value of sales VAT, also known as output VAT, charged by the business to customers for which payment has been received from customers during the period.

Calculation 2
Calculate the value of purchase VAT, also known as input VAT, charged by suppliers for goods and services for which payment has been issued to suppliers during the period.

Calculation 3
Deduct purchase VAT (input VAT) paid from sales VAT (output VAT) received to identify if VAT is due to be paid to the tax authorities or due to be repaid by the tax authorities to your business.

Example:
Tina buys and sells tables and is VAT registered. In the first quarter of the year she records the following transactions:

SALES

Date	Invoice	Details
1 Jan 2014	S111	Executive table £1,500 + VAT 20% £300 = £1,800 including VAT
1 Feb 2014	S222	Executive table £1,500 + VAT 20% £300 = £1,800 including VAT
1 Mar 2014	S333	Executive table £1,500 + VAT 20% £300 = £1,800 including VAT
TOTAL		Net sales £4,500 Output VAT £900

PURCHASES

Date	Invoice	Details
1 Jan 2014	P111	Executive table £1,000 + VAT 20% £200 = £1,200 including VAT
1 Feb 2014	P222	Executive table £1,000 + VAT 20% £200 = £1,200 including VAT
1 Mar 2014	P333	Executive table £1,000 + VAT 20% £200 = £1,200 including VAT
TOTAL		Net purchases £3,000 Input VAT £600

Calculation 1

When Tina reviews her receipts, detailed in the bank receipts book, she identifies the following:

Receipts from customers during the period January to March 2014
2 Jan 2014: Payment received from customer for invoice S111 of £1,800
2 Feb 2014: Payment received from customer for invoice S222 of £1,800
Total value of receipts from customers £1,800 x 2 = £3,600
The total value of VAT contained within the receipts is calculated as follows:
£3,600 / 120 x 20 = £600
£600 is the total of output VAT/sales VAT due to the tax authorities.

Calculation 2

When Tina reviews her payments, detailed in the bank payments book, she identifies the following:

Payments to suppliers during the period January to March 2014
2 Jan 2014: Payment issued to supplier for invoice P111 of £1,200
2 Feb 2014: Payment issued to supplier for invoice P222 of £1,200
Total value of payments issued to suppliers £1,200 x 2 = £2,400
The total value of VAT contained within the payments is calculated as follows:
£2,400 / 120 x 20 = £400
£400 is the total of input VAT/purchase VAT to be reclaimed from the tax authorities.

Calculation 3

Output VAT, i.e., sales VAT: £600
Less input VAT, i.e., purchase VAT: £400
VAT due to paid: £200

Based on calculation 3 Tina is due to pay £200 of VAT to the tax authorities.

How is VAT calculated using the flat-rate scheme?

The VAT flat-rate scheme involves:
- **Paying the tax authorities a percentage of the VAT-inclusive value of sales for a period**
- **The percentage used to calculate the VAT varies depending on the type of business you run**
- **The flat-rate percentage used to calculate VAT currently ranges from 4% to 14.5%**
- **In general, input VAT, i.e., VAT on purchases, is not reclaimed**

Eligibility criteria include the following:

- **Taxable turnover is not expected to exceed £150,000 in the next twelve months**
- **Eligibility withdrawn if VAT-inclusive income exceeds £230,000 in twelve months**

Application process

It is necessary to apply to the tax authorities to avail one's business of the flat-rate scheme for VAT. An application can be made by completing a VAT600FRS form. You must notify the tax authorities if you want to leave the flat-rate scheme.

How is VAT calculated using the flat-rate scheme for VAT?

- **Identify the appropriate flat rate relating to your business; see www.hmrc.gov.uk**
- **Avail yourself of the 1% discount off the flat-rate percentage for the first year. NOTE: the twelve-month period for which the discount is available starts from the date of VAT registration, not the date of joining the flat-rate scheme**
- **Apply the flat rate to the VAT-inclusive turnover figure for the period to calculate the VAT due. The VAT-inclusive turnover refers to all supplies, including sales for standard rate, zero rate, reduced rate and exempt**

Example

Alice is an architect and is registered for VAT. She logs onto www.hmrc.gov.uk and identifies the flat rate for her business type is 14.5%. During the three-month trading period January to March she issues the following sales invoices:

SALES

Date	Invoice	Details		
1 Jan 2014	S01	Drawing plans	£2,000 + VAT 20% £400	
		= £2,400 including VAT		
1 Feb 2014	S02	Drawing plans	£2,000 + VAT 20% £400	
		= £2,400 including VAT		
1 Mar 2014	S03	Drawing plans	£2,000 + VAT 20% £400	
		= £2,400 including VAT		
TOTAL		Net sales £6,000	Output VAT £1,200	
		Gross sales £7,200		

During the three-month period January to March she receives supplier invoices. Using the flat-rate scheme, Alice can ignore the purchase VAT (input VAT) she has been charged by her suppliers for the purposes of calculating VAT due. The reason purchase VAT is not relevant is that it has already been accounted for in the calculation of the flat-rate percentage.

However, if Alice had incurred capital goods expenditure during the period she may be allowed to reclaim purchase VAT (input VAT) in relation to same. Examples of capital goods expenditure would be: computer equipment, van, machinery. Certain rules apply to reclaim VAT on capital goods expenditure using the flat-rate scheme; the main issue is the value of the capital expenditure. To qualify it must be greater than £2,000 including VAT. For full details of reclaiming VAT using the flat-rate scheme see www.hmrc.gov.uk, 'Notice 733 Flat-Rate Scheme for Small Businesses'.

In April, Alice identifies that the sales invoices for January and February have been paid, and the March sales invoice remains unpaid. She now needs to establish her flat-rate turnover.

Flat-rate turnover can be calculated in three ways:

- **Basic turnover – this is sales based on invoices issued during the period**
- **Cash-based turnover – this is sales based on payments received from customers during the period**
- **Retailer's turnover – this is sales based on sales receipts from customers via the cash register and any other sales receipts outside the retail environment**

Whichever method is selected to calculate flat-rate turnover, it must be used for at least twelve months.

> **NOTE: Careful consideration needs to be given before signing up to the flat-rate scheme. The benefits of reduced VAT processing might be negated by exposure to higher VAT payments as a result of not reclaiming input VAT.**

VAT flat rate calculated on the basic turnover method:
During the three-month period the total VAT-inclusive turnover of the business was £7,200.
The VAT-inclusive turnover for the period of £7,200 is used to calculate the VAT liability as follows:
£7,200 x 14.5% = £1,044 VAT due.

VAT flat rate calculated on cash-based turnover method:
During the three-month period the total VAT-inclusive turnover payments received was £4,800. This figure is the value of the payments received from clients for the January and February sales invoices.

This figure of £4,800 is used to calculate the VAT liability as follows:
£4,800 x 14.5% = £696 VAT due.

VAT flat rate calculated on retailer's turnover:
This option is not applicable to Alice as she is not a retailer.

How is VAT calculated using the VAT-margin scheme?

The margin scheme for second-hand goods enables VAT to be calculated on the profit margin attained. So if your business involves the sale of second-hand goods this scheme needs consideration. Examples of second-hand goods would be cars, works of art, antiques.

For example, a table is purchased second-hand, from a member of the public who is not VAT registered, by a VAT-registered antiques business for £500. The table is subsequently sold for £750 to a customer of the business. The amount of VAT based on the margin scheme would be as follows:

Selling price: £750
Less cost price: £500
Margin : £250

The £250 margin is used to calculate the sales VAT (output VAT) as follows:
£250 / 120 x 20 = £41.67

In general, to avail oneself of the margin scheme:
- **The goods must be second-hand**
- **No VAT was charged when goods were purchased**

Further details of the scheme can be found at www.hmrc.gov.uk, 'Notice 718 The VAT-Margin Scheme'.

What are the features of retail VAT schemes?

Retail VAT schemes allow retailers to calculate VAT in a manner which can reduce the burden of dealing with VAT calculations. However, with advances in technology it has become considerably easier for retailers to account for VAT, resulting in the retail schemes being less relevant to modern-day retailers. There are a number of retail schemes to choose from; comprehensive details of these schemes can be found at www.hmrc.gov.uk, see 'Notice 727 Retail Schemes'.

What is the annual accounting scheme?

The annual accounting scheme reduces the filing requirement of VAT returns and allows you to file one VAT return each year. The main eligibility criteria is that taxable turnover is not expected to exceed £1,350,000 in the next twelve months.

The payment of VAT during the period is a choice between two options.
- **Option 1 payment intervals – nine individual monthly payments, each payment based on 10% of the VAT liability for the previous year**
- **Option 2 payment intervals – three individual interim payments, based on 25% of the VAT liability for the previous year**

How is VAT calculated using the annual accounting scheme for VAT?

VAT is calculated using the most appropriate VAT calculation method based on eligibility and establishing the most advantageous from the options available.

Application process

It is necessary to apply to the tax authorities to avail one's business of the annual accounting scheme for VAT. An application can be made by completing a VAT600AA form/VAT600AA&FRS form. For full details of the scheme see www.hmrc.gov.uk, 'Notice 732 Annual Accounting'.

VAT returns

How is a VAT return completed?

A VAT return is a form detailing the total value of sales VAT (output VAT), the total value of purchase VAT (input VAT) and the total value of VAT to be paid or VAT to be refunded. In addition, certain other information is recorded, such as details of sales and purchases excluding VAT. Other information may be required if relevant, such as details of supplies or acquisitions to and from other EU member states.

> **NOTE: A fully worked example of how to transfer the figures from the bookkeeping records to the VAT return is detailed in the financial information chapter of this book.**

The VAT return requires certain information to be input into a number of boxes. The information to be detailed on the VAT return can be affected by the various VAT schemes available to a VAT-registered trader. For details of how the information recorded on the VAT return is affected by various VAT schemes it is necessary to refer to www.hmrc.gov.uk and review the relevant notices:
- **Standard VAT accounting – Notice 700/12 filling in your VAT return**
- **Cash-accounting scheme – Notice 731 Cash-Accounting Scheme**
- **Flat-rate scheme – Notice 733 Flat-Rate Scheme For Small Businesses**
- **VAT-margin scheme – Notice 718 The VAT-Margin Scheme**
- **Retail schemes – Notice 727 Retail Schemes**

The information referred to in the section below, Box 1 to Box 9, relates to standard VAT accounting for a business that does not trade with EU member states. It also refers to the DIY Bookkeeping system records to obtain relevant data.

Box 1 – VAT due in this period on sales and other outputs
The figure to be inserted in this box is the VAT charged by your business to its customers in the period. Refer to the sales daybook to identify this figure.

In addition, there can be adjustments to this sales VAT (output VAT) to account for items such as:
- **Supplies to the staff of the business**
- **Fuel used for private motoring when using the fuel scale charge**
- **Goods taken by the business owner for their own private use**
- **Gifts of goods that cost more than £50 excluding VAT**

The sales VAT (output VAT) would need to be reduced by the value of VAT relating to any credit notes or refunds issued to customers during the period.

Box 2 – VAT due in this period on acquisitions from other EU member states
If your business does not trade with EU member states then no acquisitions will be transacted, therefore this box will have a nil value.

Box 3 – Total VAT due (the sum of boxes 1 and 2)
Information source – Box 1 + Box 2
This is a calculated value. It is the value of the addition of Box 1 and Box 2.

Box 4 – VAT reclaimed in this period on purchases and other inputs (including acquisitions from the EU)
The figure to be inserted in this box is the value of all VAT your business has been charged in relation to supplies concerning the business, i.e., purchase VAT (input VAT) for the period. Refer to the purchases daybook and petty cash book to calculate the purchase VAT (input VAT).

Box 5 – Net VAT to be paid to the HMRC or reclaimed by you (difference between Box 3 and Box 4)
Information source: Box 3 and Box 4
This is a calculated value. It is the value of VAT due to be paid or reclaimed.

Box 6 – Total value of sales and all other outputs excluding any VAT. Include your Box 8 figure
Insert the figure for the total value of all sales and other outputs excluding VAT.

Refer to the sales daybook to identify the value of sales excluding VAT.

Box 7 – Total value of purchases and all other inputs excluding any VAT.
Include your Box 9 figure
Insert the figure for the total value of all purchases and other inputs excluding VAT. Refer to the purchases daybook and petty cash book to identify the value purchases excluding VAT.

Box 8 – Total value of all supplies of goods and related costs excluding any VAT, to other EU member states
If your business does not trade with EU member states then no supplies will be transacted, therefore this box will have a nil value.

Box 9 – Total value of all acquisitions of goods and related costs excluding any VAT, from other EU member states
If your business does not trade with EU member states then no acquisitions will be transacted, therefore this box will have a nil value.

How is a VAT return filed?

Practically all businesses must file their VAT returns online. There are extremely limited exemptions from this requirement. In order to file online it is necessary to register for VAT online services. Instructions concerning registration can be found at www.hmrc.gov.uk.

When must a VAT return be filed and paid?

The standard VAT period for VAT returns is quarterly, i.e., every three months. The deadline for VAT returns submitted online is detailed on the online return. The deadline filing date is normally one calendar month and seven days after the end of the VAT period. The payment deadline date for online payments is normally the same as the filing date of the VAT return.

> NOTE: If you are using the annual accounting scheme for VAT, special payment scheduling rules apply.

VAT pitfalls

What type of pitfalls exist concerning VAT?

Using VAT as a source of finance
VAT collected from customers can be consumed by the business as part of day-to-day operating expenditure. This can result in the inability of a business to pay VAT liabilities as they fall due for payment.

Using the wrong VAT rate

It is possible to inadvertently use an incorrect VAT rate for the supply of services and/or products. If a mistake is made and the wrong VAT rate is used it can lead to an incorrect VAT return being submitted. If you are in any doubt concerning the VAT rate applicable, seek professional advice or confirmation from the tax authorities.

Incorrect VAT returns can result in penalties

If a business submits a VAT return that is incorrect it can be exposed to a variety of penalties, such as surcharges and interest.

Not being aware of specialist VAT rules relating to your business sector

Due to the wide variety of business sectors and special VAT rules that exist, it can happen that a business breaches some VAT regulations and is not even aware of same. VAT legislation is frequently changed and it is important to stay up to date concerning VAT issues affecting your business.

Not being aware of VAT rules pertaining to certain types of transactions

Certain types of transactions have to be dealt with in a particular manner to comply with VAT legislation. It is possible not to be aware of what is required. Examples of such transactions would be:

- *Fuel scale charge* – an adjustment is required if fuel for motor vehicles has an element of private use and the fuel scale charge is one method that can be used to make such an adjustment
- *Partial exemption* – there are special VAT rules to comply with if your supplies comprise a mix of exempt and non-exempt
- *Pre-registration input VAT* – it is possible to reclaim purchase VAT (input VAT) incurred prior to VAT registration subject to certain rules

MICRO QUIZ

Q1: Taxable supplies are a supply of goods or services that are liable to VAT, i.e., any supplies that are not exempt from VAT.

True or False?

Q2: There are never any benefits arising from voluntary VAT registration.

True or False?

Q3: If a business is below the VAT threshold it is possible for the business to voluntarily register for VAT.

True or False?

Q4: The VAT registration threshold effective from 1 April 2014 is £89,000 of taxable turnover.

True or False?

Q5: The VAT registration threshold always remains the same.

True or False?

Q6: The standard rate of VAT is currently 5%.

True or False?

Q7: Another name for the standard VAT method of calculation is the invoice basis.

True or False?

Q8: The cash-accounting scheme for VAT is available to all VAT-registered businesses.

True or False?

Q9: The annual accounting scheme means only one payment of VAT is issued per annum.

True or False?

Q10: There is only one flat rate of VAT applicable to all businesses.

True or False?

Micro quiz – solutions

Q1: True

Q2: False

Q3: True

Q4: False

Q5: False

Q6: False

Q7: True

Q8: False

Q9: False

Q10: False

Financial information – how to produce financial information

CHAPTER 19

How to produce financial information from bookkeeping records

Figure 19.1
Financial information overview

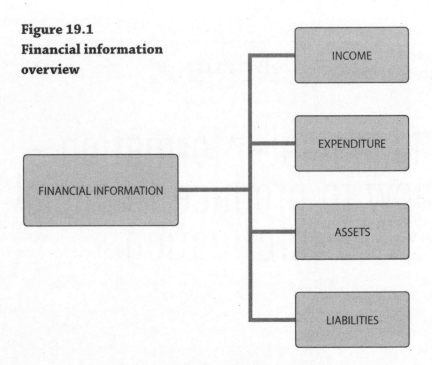

FINANCIAL INFORMATION – OVERVIEW

The set-up and operation of bookkeeping records have been covered in detail in previous chapters. Each bookkeeping record deals with a specific aspect of income or expenditure. Using the data contained in the bookkeeping records and basic techniques it is possible to generate certain financial information that can give an insight into the performance of a business. When reviewing the finances of a business it is necessary to review income, expenditure, assets and liabilities.

The best way to demonstrate how financial information can be derived from bookkeeping records is to review the bookkeeping records of a business for a period and produce financial information from the data presented. This chapter contains a detailed illustrative example explaining the process to produce financial information from bookkeeping records. See Figure 19.1 for an overview of financial information.

Income

DIY Bookkeeping records income of a business as sales income or non-sales income.

Sales income – income relating to the sale of products and/or services. If a business is VAT registered then it is the sales value excluding VAT. This figure can be identified from reviewing transactions recorded in the sales daybook for a given period.

Non-sales income – income not relating to the sale of products and/or services. For example, a loan from a bank or funds from an investor. The figure can be identified from reviewing the bank receipts book for a given period.

Expenditure

DIY Bookkeeping records expenditure in a variety of records depending on how the transaction originated. The records used to identify expenditure are as follows:

- **Purchases daybook**
- **Petty cash book**
- **Bank payments book**
- **Credit card book**
- **Payroll records book**

For the purposes of producing financial information it is important to have a clear understanding of each type of expenditure. In addition, it is necessary to be aware of certain complications relating to expenditure that may require adjustment.

Expenditure may need to be adjusted to account for various complications, such as:

Prepayments – items of expenditure that relate to the following period. For example, an insurance invoice received in March and dated in March that covers a period of twelve months, valued at £1,200. If this expense is recorded in March as £1,200 then the costs for March are overstated. The cost relating to March is £1,200/12 months, i.e., £100. The balance of £1,100 is a prepayment relating to the period April to the following February.

Accruals – items of expenditure that have been incurred in the period but have not been charged for by a supplier must be accrued for. For example, if a business has engaged the services of a solicitor for an agreed fee of £500 in May and by the end of May no invoice has been received, then the business needs to accrue for the £500 cost in the accounts of the business for the period to May.

Capital expenditure – relates to expenditure such as the purchase or acquisition of fixed assets or adding value to fixed assets. This is usually high-value expenditure on assets that will last for more than one year. For example, if a business buys a vehicle for £20,000 it would not be correct to charge the full £20,000 to the current financial trading year as a cost, as it is an asset of the business that will last for several years. The cost of this type of expenditure does not relate entirely to the period the expenditure is incurred and would need to be spread out over the useful economic life of the asset.

Depreciation – the method by which the cost of the wear and tear of an asset is accounted for over its useful economic life. Regarding the vehicle mentioned above that cost £20,000, assume its useful economic life is five years, then the charge for depreciation would be £4,000 each year for five years. The depreciation charge of £4,000 is calculated by dividing the cost of the asset by its useful economic life, £20,000/5 years = £4,000.

The complications noted above concerning expenditure can be dealt with after all expenditure transactions have been recorded in the bookkeeping system. The process involves producing financial information and then establishing if any adjustments are required.

Assets

Assets represent resources invested into the business and comprise of resources owned by the business or monies owed to the business. For the purposes of producing financial information it is important to have a clear understanding of the various types of assets a business may have. Listed below are examples of assets.

Trade debtors – the value of monies due, at the end of the period, from customers who have received goods and/or services during the period and have not yet paid for same.

VAT refund – if the value of purchase VAT exceeds the value of sales VAT then a VAT refund will be due for the period. A VAT refund is an asset of the business. See Section 5 for full details of VAT.

Bank balance – if the opening bank balance plus the value of all bank receipts for a period is greater than the total value of bank payments issued during the period, then the bank account balance will reflect cash available to spend.

Stock – if the business has stock in its storerooms at the end of the period, then this stock represents an asset of the business. To calculate the value of stock held at the end of the period it is necessary to physically count the stock held and value such stock at the cost of purchase. If the stock is considered to be worth less than was paid for it, then the reduced value should be used to value the stock.

Prepayments – expenditure that has been charged for that relates to future periods is effectively an advance payment and as such is an asset of the business.

Liabilities

Liabilities are debts due to third parties. For the purposes of producing financial information it is important to have a clear understanding of the various types of liabilities a business may have. Listed below are examples of liabilities.

Trade creditors – the value of monies due at the end of the period to suppliers for goods and services received during the period but not yet paid for.

VAT liability – the value of VAT due at the end of the period. A VAT liability exists if the value of sales VAT (output VAT) exceeds the value of purchase VAT (input VAT).

NOTE: The VAT liability represents the total value of VAT owed. The amount of the VAT liability due to be paid at any given time depends on the method of calculation for VAT, e.g., standard method, cash method. See Section 5 for full details of VAT.

Bank balance – if the opening bank balance plus the value of all bank receipts for a period is less than the total value of bank payments issued during the period, then the bank account balance will be overdrawn. An overdrawn bank account represents a liability of the business.

Loans – any monies borrowed and still owing at the end of a period represent a liability of the business.

Credit card balance due – if there is a balance outstanding on a credit card account at the end of a period, then the balance represents a liability of the business.

Accruals – items of expenditure that have been incurred in the period but have not been charged for by a supplier must be accrued to identify monies due to the supplier of the goods and/or services received.

Illustrative example – business details

The following example will be used to illustrate how financial information can be produced from bookkeeping records.

- Charlie sells chairs and is registered for VAT (see Section 5 for full details of VAT)
- Charlie buys goods on credit, i.e., he obtains products from his suppliers and pays his suppliers at a later date.
- Charlie sells goods to his customers on credit, i.e., Charlie supplies goods to customers and the customers are given a number of weeks' credit to pay
- Charlie seeks to maintain the most simple system for maintaining records of the income and expenditure of his business
- Charlie has one member of staff
- The example covers a three-month period from January to March

Charlie needs to engage in a step-by-step process in order to record the financial transactions of his business as follows:

Step 1 – Select the appropriate bookkeeping records to maintain.
Step 2 – Record the income of the business in the bookkeeping records.
Step 3 – Record the expenditure of the business in the bookkeeping records.
Step 4 – Calculate VAT.
Step 5 – Produce financial information based on the bookkeeping records.

Step 1 – bookkeeping records selection

Charlie needs to identify what bookkeeping records he needs to maintain so that all relevant financial transactions are recorded. Based on the circumstances of Charlie's business he will need to operate the following bookkeeping records:

Sales daybook – this is a record of all sales invoices of goods and/or services sold for a given period.

Bank receipts book – this is a record of all monies received into the bank account of the business. Monies received will relate to customers' remittances and other funds received.

Purchases daybook – this is a record of all purchase invoices relating to goods and services obtained for a given period.

Petty cash book – this is a record of miscellaneous cash payments and receipts of cash to pay for the same.

Bank payments book – this is a record of all payments issued from the business bank account.

Credit card book – this is a record of all transactions relating to a credit card.

Payroll records book – Charlie employs staff, therefore he does need to maintain payroll records. If a business employs staff, it is highly recommended that they use payroll software to process payroll and calculate tax liabilities. Charlie uses payroll software to calculate payroll and files the appropriate reports in a lever arch file, which is in essence his payroll records book.

Step 2 – recording income

During the period Charlie needs to record sales income and non-sales income.

Sales daybook

During the months of January, February and March Charlie sells a variety of chairs to his customers. Charlie inputs the relevant details of his sales invoices onto his sales daybook software-based spreadsheet as shown in Figure 19.2.

Figure 19.2
Sales Daybook

SALES DAYBOOK					
DATE	CUSTOMER	INVOICE NO.	NET	VAT	GROSS
				20%	
10-Jan-14	Mr Philips	1001	6,250.00	1,250.00	7,500.00
11-Jan-14	Fanfare Ltd	1002	3,750.00	750.00	4,500.00
12-Jan-14	Aztec Ltd	1003	2,500.00	500.00	3,000.00
10-Feb-14	Zero Ltd	1004	5,000.00	1,000.00	6,000.00
11-Feb-14	John Smith	1005	1,500.00	300.00	1,800.00
12-Feb-14	Hitz Ltd	1006	1,000.00	200.00	1,200.00
10-Mar-14	Hire All Ltd	1007	3,750.00	750.00	4,500.00
11-Mar-14	Ms Anne Jones	1008	250.00	50.00	300.00
12-Mar-14	Seats Ltd	1009	750.00	150.00	900.00
			24,750.00	4,950.00	29,700.00

Based on the information contained in the sales daybook Charlie can ascertain the following:
- The sales value for the period can be readily identified as £24,750 excluding VAT
- The amount of VAT charged to customers for the period was £4,950
- The total value of sales including VAT was £29,700

Bank receipts book

During the months January to March Charlie receives monies into the business bank account. Charlie records the details of monies received into the bank account in the bank receipts book as shown in Figure 19.3.

Figure 19.3
Bank Receipts Book

BANK RECEIPTS BOOK					
DATE	NAME CUSTOMER / THIRD PARTY	PAYMENT TYPE	AMOUNT	SALES RECEIPT	OTHER RECEIPTS
03-Jan-14	Loan from relative	Draft	6,500.00		6,500.00
10-Feb-14	Mr Philips	EFT	7,500.00	7,500.00	
11-Feb-14	Fanfare Ltd	EFT	4,500.00	4,500.00	
12-Feb-14	Aztec Ltd	EFT	3,000.00	3,000.00	
10-Mar-14	Zero Ltd	EFT	6,000.00	6,000.00	
11-Mar-14	John Smith	EFT	1,800.00	1,800.00	
12-Mar-14	Hitz Ltd	EFT	1,200.00	1,200.00	
Total			30,500.00	24,000.00	6,500.00

Based on the information contained in the bank receipts book Charlie can ascertain the following:

- The total amount of all monies received for the period was £30,500
- The total amount of monies received from customers was £24,000
- The total amount of monies received from other sources was £6,500, which was a loan from a relative. This figure of £6,500 is non-sales income

Step 3 – recording expenditure

Charlie needs to record expenditure relating to his business for the period and he uses the following bookkeeping records to do so:

- Purchases daybook
- Petty cash book
- Bank payments book
- Credit card book
- Payroll records book

Purchases daybook

During the months of January to March Charlie purchases a variety of goods and services from his suppliers. Based on the information detailed on the purchase invoices Charlie records the relevant details into his purchases daybook as shown in Figure 19.4.

Figure 19.4
Purchases Daybook

PURCHASES DAYBOOK										
Date	Supplier	Invoice Number	Description	Gross Amount	VAT	Net Amount	Goods for Resale	Insurance	Stationery	Rent
05-Jan-14	Leather Chairs Ltd	LC111	Leather Chairs	6,000.00	1,000.00	5,000.00	5,000.00			
15-Jan-14	Property Lets Ltd	PLL123	Rent	3,000.00	500.00	2,500.00				2,500.00
05-Feb-14	Dining Chairs Ltd	DC222	Dining Chairs	4,500.00	750.00	3,750.00	3,750.00			
15-Feb-14	Bits & Bobs Ltd	BB123	Stationery	600.00	100.00	500.00			500.00	
05-Mar-14	Wooden Stools Ltd	WS333	Wooden Stools	3,600.00	600.00	3,000.00	3,000.00			
15-Mar-14	Insurance Ltd	INS123	Insurance	1,200.00	0.00	1,200.00		1,200.00		
Total				18,900.00	2,950.00	15,950.00	11,750.00	1,200.00	500.00	2,500.00

Based on the information contained in the purchases daybook Charlie can ascertain the following:
- **Total expenditure recorded for the period including VAT was £18,900**
- **Total VAT charged by suppliers for the period was £2,950**
- **Total expenditure recorded for the period excluding VAT was £15,950**
- **Expenditure of £11,750 excluding VAT was incurred relating to goods for resale**
- **Expenditure of £1,200 was incurred relating to insurance**
- **Expenditure of £500 excluding VAT was incurred relating to stationery**
- **Expenditure of £2,500 excluding VAT was incurred relating to rent**

Petty cash book
During the months January to March Charlie purchases a variety of goods and services for minor cash amounts. Based on the information detailed on the invoices/receipts Charlie records the relevant information into his petty cash book as shown in Figure 19.5.

Based on the information contained in the petty cash book Charlie can ascertain the following:
- **A sum of £300 was lodged into petty cash at the beginning of January from Charlie's own money**
- **A total of £280.11 was spent on miscellaneous items**
- **A total of £21.02 of VAT was incurred on petty cash expenditure**
- **A total of £259.09 excluding VAT was spent on miscellaneous items**

Figure 19.5 Petty Cash Book

PETTY CASH BOOK

DATE	PAYEE	DESCRIPTION	MONEY IN	GROSS AMOUNT	VAT	Net Amount	Tea/coffee	Fuel	Stamps	Window Cleaning	BALANCE
01-Jan-14	N/A	Cash in from owner	300.00								300.00
10-Jan-14	Spar shop	Tea bags for canteen		4.00	0.00	4.00	4.00				296.00
18-Feb-14	Post Office	Stamps & post		60.00	0.00	60.00			60.00		236.00
20-Feb-14	Joe Bloggs	Window cleaning		45.00	0.00	45.00				45.00	191.00
25-Feb-14	Esso	Fuel		65.66	10.94	54.72		54.72			125.34
10-Mar-14	Joe Bloggs	Window cleaning		45.00	0.00	45.00				45.00	80.34
25-Mar-14	Esso	Fuel		60.45	10.08	50.38		50.38			19.89
			300.00	280.11	21.02	259.09	4.00	105.09	60.00	90.00	19.89

- **A total of £4 was spent on tea bags for the canteen**
- **A total of £105.09 excluding VAT was spent on fuel. The fuel expense is 100% business related**
- **A total of £60 was spent on stamps and postage**
- **A total of £90 was spent on window cleaning**

At the end of the three-month period there was cash remaining of £19.89, which is the difference between the £300 lodged into petty cash and the £280.11 spent.

Bank payments book

During the months January to March Charlie issues payments from the business bank account. Charlie records the details of payments from the business bank account in the bank payments book as shown in Figure 19.6.

Figure 19.6
Bank Payments Book

BANK PAYMENTS BOOK

DATE	PAYEE	PAYMENT TYPE	PAYMENT REFERENCE	GROSS AMOUNT	PURCHASE DAYBOOK PAYMENTS	Drawings	Wages	Bank Charges	Credit Card	Other
05-Jan-14	Leather Chairs Ltd	EFT	LC111	6,000.00	6,000.00					
15-Jan-14	Property Lets Ltd	EFT	PLL123	3,000.00	3,000.00					
31-Jan-14	Joe Soap - staff	EFT	Payroll	1,571.00			1,571.00			
05-Feb-14	Dining Chairs Ltd	EFT	DC222	4,500.00	4,500.00					
15-Feb-14	Bits & Bobs Ltd	EFT	BB123	600.00	600.00					
25-Feb-14	Credit Card Ltd	DD	Jan-14	800.00					800.00	
28-Feb-14	Joe Soap - staff	EFT	Payroll	1,571.00			1,571.00			
05-Mar-14	Proprietor	ATM	Private exp.	450.00		450.00				
10-Mar-14	Bank Allied plc	DD	Bank charges	35.00				35.00		
25-Mar-14	Credit Card Ltd	DD	Feb-14	80.00					80.00	
31-Mar-14	Loan repayment	EFT	J Fick	2,000.00						2,000.00
31-Mar-14	Joe Soap - staff	EFT	Payroll	1,571.00			1,571.00			
				22,178.00	14,100.00	450.00	4,713.00	35.00	880.00	2,000.00

Based on the information contained in the bank payments book Charlie can ascertain the following:
- **The total amount of all payments for the period was £22,178**
- **The total amount of payments for the period relating to the purchases daybook was £14,100**
- **The total amount paid from the bank account relating to drawings was £450. Note: drawings are monies withdrawn from the business for private use by a business owner**
- **The total amount paid from the bank account relating to wages was £4,713**

- The total amount paid from the bank account relating to bank charges was £35
- The total amount spent paying off the debt of the business credit card was £880
- The total amount allocated to Other was £2,000. This relates to a part repayment of a loan Charlie received from his relative at the beginning of the period

Credit card book

During the months January to March Charlie issues payments by credit card. Charlie records the details of payments in the credit card book as shown in Figure 19.7.

Based on the information contained in the credit card book Charlie can ascertain the following:

Figure 19.7
Credit Card Book

CREDIT CARD BOOK

DATE	PAYEE/RECEIPT DETAILS	PAYMENT/RECEIPT REFERENCE	GROSS AMOUNT	PURCHASE DAYBOOK PAYMENTS	Drawings	Credit Card Fees	Credit Card Interest	Payments	Balance
01-Jan-14	Opening Balance		0						0
15-Jan-14	Sun Tours Ltd	Private Holiday	800.00		800.00				800.00
20-Feb-14	Clothes Shop Ltd	Private expenditure	80.00		80.00				880.00
25-Feb-14	Payment		-800.00					-800.00	80.00
15-Mar-14	Insurance Ltd	Invoice INS123	1,200.00	1,200.00					1,280.00
18-Mar-14	Credit Card Ltd	account fee	22.00			22.00			1,302.00
25-Mar-14	Payment		-80.00					-80.00	1,222.00
			1,222.00	1,200.00	880.00	22.00	0.00	-880.00	1,222.00

- The total amount of all payments by credit card for the three-month period was £2,102, comprising purchases daybook payments, drawings and credit card fees, i.e., £1,200+£880+£22 = £2,102
- The total amount of payments for the period relating to the purchases daybook was £1,200
- The total amount of payments for the period relating to drawings was £880
- The total amount of payments for the period relating to credit card fees was £22
- The total amount paid to the credit card company to reduce the balance owed was £880
- The balance owing on the credit card account at the end of the period is £1,222

Payroll records book

During the months January to March Charlie processes the payroll using payroll software.

Charlie prints off a payroll summary report for the period and the data, as shown in Figure 19.8.

Figure 19.8
Payroll Report

PAYROLL RECORDS BOOK					
Month	Employee		Net Pay		Total PAYE/NI
Jan-14	Joe Soap		1,571.00		619.00
Feb-14	Joe Soap		1,571.00		619.00
Mar-14	Joe Soap		1,571.00		619.00
			4,713.00		1,857.00

From the record above the following can be ascertained:
- **The staff member Joe Soap has earned net pay of £1,571 each month. The payment of this wage can be identified in the bank payments book**
- **In total, the business owes taxes to the tax authorities of £1,857 for the three-month period**

Step 4 – VAT Calculation

Now that Charlie has completed steps 1 to 3, he is in a position to deal with VAT. Charlie can ascertain the VAT liability and the VAT due for payment from the bookkeeping records. See Section 5 for full details of VAT.
- **Charlie calculates the VAT using the standard VAT method, to calculate how much VAT he owes in total**
- **Charlie calculates the VAT using the cash-basis method, to calculate how much VAT must be paid, as he avails himself of this payment option**

VAT calculation – standard VAT method

(See Section 5 for detailed explanation.)

VAT liability

Based on the information contained in the following records Charlie can calculate the VAT due for the period January to March using the standard VAT calculation method:

- **Sales daybook**
- **Purchases daybook**
- **Petty cash book**

Charlie reviews his sales daybook and identifies the sales VAT of £4,950.00. (See the above sales daybook and ensure you can identify this figure.)

Charlie reviews his purchases daybook and identifies purchase VAT of £2,950.00. (See the above purchases daybook and ensure you can identify this figure.)

Charlie reviews his petty cash book and identifies purchase VAT of £21.02. (See the above petty cash book and ensure you can identify this figure.)
Total of all purchase VAT: £2,971.02

Based on the above Charlie can calculate the total VAT liability as follows:
Sales VAT for January to March: £4,950.00
Less purchase VAT for January to March: £2,971.02
VAT liability: £1,978.98

The VAT liability figure of £1,978.98, calculated using the standard VAT method, is the total value of VAT that Charlie owes.

If Charlie wanted to file his VAT return based on the standard VAT calculation method then his VAT return would look similar to the VAT return in Figure 19.9 (Note: VAT return wording simplified):

NOTE: It is important that you can trace all the figures shown on the VAT return above, boxes 1 to 9, back to the various bookkeeping records, you should check you can do this.

Box 1 – see sales daybook
Box 2 – not applicable to Charlie's business
Box 3 – calculated value Box 1 plus Box 2
Box 4 – see purchases daybook and petty cash book
Box 5 – calculated value Box 3 minus Box 4
Box 6 – see sales daybook
Box 7 – see purchases daybook and petty cash book
Box 8 – not applicable to Charlie's business
Box 9 – not applicable to Charlie's business

Figure 19.9

VAT Return – Standard VAT Calculation

Standard VAT basis calculation				
VAT Return - Jan Feb Mar				
Value of VAT on sales (output VAT)			Box 1	4,950.00
Value of VAT on acquisitions from member states			Box 2	0.00
Calculated value	Box 1 + Box 2		Box 3	4,950.00
Value of VAT on purchases (input VAT)			Box 4	2,971.02
Calculated value Box 3 minus Box 4			Box 5	1,978.98
Value of sales excluding VAT			Box 6	24,750.00
Value of purchases excluding VAT			Box 7	16,209.09
Value of supplies to EC member states excluding VAT			Box 8	0.00
Value of acquistions from EC member states excluding VAT			Box 9	0.00

VAT calculation – cash basis

(See Section 5 for detailed explanation.)

Based on the information contained in the following records Charlie can calculate the VAT due for payment for the period January to March using the cash basis of VAT calculation method:

- **Sales daybook extended or bank receipts book**
- **Purchases daybook**
- **Petty cash book**

Sales VAT (output VAT) as per the sales daybook extended:
Charlie can track sales VAT actually paid by adding additional columns to the sales daybook to record payments made by customers as shown in Figure 19.10.

The value of VAT due for the period on the cash basis is £4,000, as noted in the final column of the sales daybook.

Sales VAT (output VAT) as per the bank receipts book:
Charlie can also identify the sales VAT paid from the data contained in the bank receipts book. Charlie reviews his bank receipts book and identifies that his

Figure 19.10

Sales Daybook Extended – Noting Invoices Paid

SALES DAYBOOK							
DATE	CUSTOMER	INVOICE NO.	NET	VAT 20%	GROSS	Paid	VAT Due
10-Jan-14	Mr Philips	1001	6,250.00	1,250.00	7,500.00	10-Feb-14	1,250.00
11-Jan-14	Fanfare Ltd	1002	3,750.00	750.00	4,500.00	11-Feb-14	750.00
12-Jan-14	Aztec Ltd	1003	2,500.00	500.00	3,000.00	12-Feb-14	500.00
10-Feb-14	Zero Ltd	1004	5,000.00	1,000.00	6,000.00	10-Mar-14	1,000.00
11-Feb-14	John Smith	1005	1,500.00	300.00	1,800.00	11-Mar-14	300.00
12-Feb-14	Hitz Ltd	1006	1,000.00	200.00	1,200.00	12-Mar-14	200.00
10-Mar-14	Hire All Ltd	1007	3,750.00	750.00	4,500.00		
11-Mar-14	Ms Anne Jones	1008	250.00	50.00	300.00		
12-Mar-14	Seats Ltd	1009	750.00	150.00	900.00		
			24,750.00	4,950.00	29,700.00		4,000.00

customers paid him in total for January to March £24,000 (see Figure 19.3 and ensure you can identify this figure). The figure of £24,000 is the total of payments made by his customers and includes VAT charged. Charlie needs to calculate how much of the £24,000 relates to VAT. To calculate the VAT amount Charlie does the following calculation:

£24,000 = 120%, i.e., it includes VAT, therefore £24,000 divided by 120 = 1%, i.e., £200.

£200 is 1%, therefore to get the VAT at 20% it is necessary to multiply £200 x 20 = £4,000.

Therefore, of the £24,000 received £4,000 is sales VAT (output VAT), the same figure shown in the extended sales daybook.

Purchases VAT (input VAT)

Using the VAT cash-basis calculation, Charlie can only claim VAT on paid purchases. Charlie reviews his purchases daybook to identify the purchase invoices that have been paid in the period January to March. He reviews payments made from the bank payments book and notes the payments in additional columns of the purchases daybook as shown in Figure 19.11.

From the purchases daybook (Figure 19.11), it can be identified that the value of the purchase VAT (input VAT) is £2,350. This £2,350 relates to VAT charged by suppliers and paid by Charlie during the period. The composition of the figure £2,350 can be identified by reviewing the last column in the purchases daybook.

Figure 19.11 Purchases Daybook Extended – Noting Paid Invoices

PURCHASES DAYBOOK												
Date	Supplier	Invoice Number	Description	Gross Amount	VAT	Net Amount	Goods for Resale	Insurance	Stationery	Rent	Paid	VAT Reclaimable
05-Jan-14	Leather Chairs Ltd	LC111	Leather Chairs	6,000.00	1,000.00	5,000.00	5,000.00				05-Jan-14	1,000.00
15-Jan-14	Property Lets Ltd	PLL123	Rent	3,000.00	500.00	2,500.00				2,500.00	15-Jan-14	500.00
05-Feb-14	Dining Chairs Ltd	DC222	Dining Chairs	4,500.00	750.00	3,750.00	3,750.00				05-Feb-14	750.00
15-Feb-14	Bits & Bobs Ltd	BB123	Stationery	600.00	100.00	500.00			500.00		15-Feb-14	100.00
05-Mar-14	Wooden Stools Ltd	WS333	Wooden Stools	3,600.00	600.00	3,000.00	3,000.00					
15-Mar-14	Insurance Ltd	INS123	Insurance	1,200.00	0.00	1,200.00		1,200.00			15-Mar-14	0.00
Total				18,900.00	2,950.00	15,950.00	11,750.00	1,200.00	500.00	2,500.00		2,350.00

Charlie now needs to review the petty cash book (see Figure 19.12) to identify the value of VAT incurred during the period January to March. The petty cash expenditure is money that is actually spent during the period, therefore all the VAT is reclaimable.

Figure 19.12
Petty Cash Book

PETTY CASH BOOK											
DATE	PAYEE	DESCRIPTION	MONEY IN	GROSS AMOUNT	VAT	Net Amount	Tea/coffee	Fuel	Stamps	Window Cleaning	BALANCE
01-Jan-14	N/A	Cash in from owner	300.00								300.00
10-Jan-14	Spar shop	Tea bags for canteen		4.00	0.00	4.00	4.00				296.00
18-Feb-14	Post Office	Stamps & post		60.00	0.00	60.00			60.00		236.00
20-Feb-14	Joe Bloggs	Window cleaning		45.00	0.00	45.00				45.00	191.00
25-Feb-14	Esso	Fuel		65.66	10.94	54.72		54.72			125.34
10-Mar-14	Joe Bloggs	Window cleaning		45.00	0.00	45.00				45.00	80.34
25-Mar-14	Esso	Fuel		60.45	10.08	50.38		50.38			19.89
			300.00	280.11	21.02	259.09	4.00	105.09	60.00	90.00	19.89

Charlie reviews his purchases daybook extended and identifies purchase VAT of £2,350.00.
(See above to ensure you can verify this figure.)
Charlie reviews his petty cash book and identifies purchase VAT of £21.02.
(See above to ensure you can verify this figure.)

Total of purchase VAT actually paid during the period: £2,371.02.

Based on the above, Charlie can calculate the total VAT due for payment as follows:

Sales VAT for January to March: £4,000.00
Purchase VAT for January to March: £2,371.02
VAT due for payment for period January to March: £1,628.98

Based on the calculation of VAT on the cash basis, Charlie establishes he needs to pay £1,628.98 of VAT from a total VAT liability of £1,978.98.
If Charlie wants to file his VAT return based on the cash-basis VAT calculation method, then his VAT return would look similar to the VAT return in Figure 19.13 (Note: VAT return wording simplified):

Figure 19.13

VAT Return – Cash-Basis Calculation

Cash Basis VAT Calculation					
VAT Return - Jan Feb Mar					
Value of VAT on sales (output VAT)				Box 1	4,000.00
Value of VAT on acquisitions from member states				Box 2	0.00
Calculated value	Box 1 + Box 2			Box 3	4,000.00
Value of VAT on purchases (input VAT)				Box 4	2,371.02
Calculated value	Box 3 minus Box 4			Box 5	1,628.98
Value of sales excluding VAT				Box 6	20,000.00
Value of purchases excluding VAT				Box 7	13,209.09
Value of supplies to EC member states excluding VAT				Box 8	0.00
Value of acquisitions from EC member states excluding VAT				Box 9	0.00

NOTE: It is important that you can trace all the figures shown on the VAT return above, boxes 1 to 9, back to the various bookkeeping records; you should check you can do this.

Box 1 – see extended sales daybook or calculate based on customer receipts in bank receipts book

Box 2 – not applicable to Charlie's business

Box 3 – calculated value Box 1 plus Box 2

Box 4 – see extended purchases daybook and petty cash book

Box 5 – calculated value Box 3 minus Box 4

Box 6 – see extended sales daybook or calculate based on customer receipts in bank receipts book

Box 7 – see extended purchases daybook and petty cash book

Box 8 – not applicable to Charlie's business

Box 9 – not applicable to Charlie's business

> NOTE: The figure for Box 6 is the net value of sales for which payment has been received. The extended sales daybook notes that sales invoices 1001 to 1006 have been paid. The net value of these sales invoices is £20,000.
>
> The figure for Box 7 is the net value of purchase invoices for which payment has been issued during the period and the net value of petty cash for the period. The 'Purchase Invoices Paid' as per the extended purchases daybook is all the purchase invoices except for Wooden Stools Ltd. Therefore £15,950 excluding VAT less £3,000 excluding VAT is £12,950. The petty cash figure of £259.09 excluding VAT for the period needs to be added to the £12,950 to give the figure of £13,209.09 to be included in Box 7.

Step 5 – producing financial information

> NOTE: The financial information to be produced in the example below does not use double-entry accounting as it is beyond the scope of this book to illustrate this. Double-entry accounting records financial transactions using a system of debits and credits.
>
> When producing information based on the example below it is imperative that all assets and liabilities are identified and valued correctly.
>
> When the assets and liabilities have been identified, it may be necessary to adjust the figures to account for such items as accruals, prepayments, capital expenditure, depreciation. See above section, financial overview, for explanations.
>
> The example below accounts for all assets and liabilities, and ensures they are valued correctly. It also ensures relevant adjustments are reviewed and accounted for appropriately.

Now that Charlie has recorded income and expenditure for the period in the bookkeeping records, and calculated VAT, he is in a position to produce some financial information concerning his business. The financial information that Charlie can produce will relate to key financial figures (KFFs) relating to his business.

Charlie needs to ascertain the following for the period:
- **ASSETS: the value of business assets at the end of the period**
- **LIABILITIES: the value of business liabilities at the end of the period**

Assets

Assets are resources invested in the business or monies owed to the business. Charlie needs to review his bookkeeping records to ascertain what assets exist as at the 31st of March 2014. In addition, Charlie needs to consider if there are any other assets relating to the business not disclosed in the bookkeeping records.

Charlie reviews his bookkeeping records and considers any other assets of the business and produces the following list:

Debtors

Debtors are monies owed by customers to a business at the end of a period. In order to calculate debtors, it is necessary to establish/review the following:

1. **Identify if there are any debtors' balances due at the beginning of the period**
2. **Identify the total value of sales invoices inclusive of VAT for the period as shown in the sales daybook**
3. **Identify the total value of sales receipts from customers for the period as shown in the bank receipts book**

Charlie needs to slot the numbers into the following and process the calculation:

Opening debtors: Nil
Add – Sales including VAT for January to March: £29,700 (see sales daybook)
Less – Sales receipts January to March: £24,000 (see bank receipts book)
Debtors as at 31 March 2014: £5,700

This figure can be verified by reviewing the sales daybook with additional columns used to identify debtors outstanding, see Figure 19.14. Debtors is the

Figure 19.14
Sales Daybook – Debtors Balance

SALES DAYBOOK

DATE	CUSTOMER	INVOICE NO.	NET	VAT 20%	GROSS	Amount Paid	Paid	VAT Due	Balance Due
10-Jan-14	Mr Philips	1001	6,250.00	1,250.00	7,500.00	7,500.00	10-Feb-14	1,250.00	0.00
11-Jan-14	Fanfare Ltd	1002	3,750.00	750.00	4,500.00	4,500.00	11-Feb-14	750.00	0.00
12-Jan-14	Aztec Ltd	1003	2,500.00	500.00	3,000.00	3,000.00	12-Feb-14	500.00	0.00
10-Feb-14	Zero Ltd	1004	5,000.00	1,000.00	6,000.00	6,000.00	10-Mar-14	1,000.00	0.00
11-Feb-14	John Smith	1005	1,500.00	300.00	1,800.00	1,800.00	11-Mar-14	300.00	0.00
12-Feb-14	Hitz Ltd	1006	1,000.00	200.00	1,200.00	1,200.00	12-Mar-14	200.00	0.00
10-Mar-14	Hire All Ltd	1007	3,750.00	750.00	4,500.00				4,500.00
11-Mar-14	Ms Anne Jones	1008	250.00	50.00	300.00				300.00
12-Mar-14	Seats Ltd	1009	750.00	150.00	900.00				900.00
			24,750.00	4,950.00	29,700.00			4,000.00	5,700.00

value, including VAT, of the three invoices: 1007, 1008 and 1009, total £5,700.

The sales daybook above has been extended to record debtor payments and also calculate the outstanding balance due to Charlie's business. The final column, balance due, shows monies outstanding from customers of £5,700.

Petty Cash

Cash held at the end of the period in the petty cash tin is an asset of the business and must be recorded. According to the petty cash book (see Figure 19.15), the value of cash at the end of the period is £19.89. In total £300 of cash was put into the petty cash tin during the period, and £280.11 was spent during the period, leaving a balance of £19.89. This figure of £19.89 needs to be verified by Charlie, who will count the cash in the petty cash tin to ensure it equals £19.89. If £19.89 is not in the petty cash tin Charlie would need to establish the reason.

Figure 19.15
Petty Cash Book

PETTY CASH BOOK

DATE	PAYEE	DESCRIPTION	MONEY IN	GROSS AMOUNT	VAT	Net Amount	Tea/coffee	Fuel	Stamps	Window Cleaning	BALANCE
01-Jan-14	N/A	Cash in from owner	300.00								300.00
10-Jan-14	Spar shop	Tea bags for canteen		4.00	0.00	4.00	4.00				296.00
18-Feb-14	Post Office	Stamps & post		60.00	0.00	60.00			60.00		236.00
20-Feb-14	Joe Bloggs	Window cleaning		45.00	0.00	45.00				45.00	191.00
25-Feb-14	Esso	Fuel		65.66	10.94	54.72		54.72			125.34
10-Mar-14	Joe Bloggs	Window cleaning		45.00	0.00	45.00				45.00	80.34
25-Mar-14	Esso	Fuel		60.45	10.08	50.38		50.38			19.89
			300.00	280.11	21.02	259.09	4.00	105.09	60.00	90.00	19.89

Bank balance

In order to calculate the closing bank balance, i.e., the amount of monies available to spend in the bank account or the amount by which the bank account is overdrawn at the end of the period, it is necessary to establish/review the following:

1. Identify if there is an opening bank balance at the beginning of the period
2. Identify the total value of all monies received into the bank account as per the bank receipts book for the period
3. Identify the total value of all payments issued from the bank account as per the bank payments book for the period

Charlie needs to slot the numbers into the following and process the calculation:

Opening bank balance: Nil
Add – Bank receipts January to March: £30,500 (see bank receipts book)
Less – Bank payments January to March: £22,178 (see bank payments book)
Bank balance as at 31 March 2014: £8,322

Drawings
Monies that Charlie has taken from the business for his own private use are technically an asset of the business, as Charlie owes this money back to the business. Charlie identifies from the following records the level of drawings he has taken:

Bank payments book: £450
Credit card book: £880
Total drawings: £1,330

Charlie uses the information calculated above concerning the assets of the business and creates a list of the assets. Based on his workings so far he has ascertained the total value of assets is £15,371.89 (see Figure 19.16).

Figure 19.16
Assets

ASSETS AS AT 31 MARCH 2014			
Debtors			5,700.00
Petty cash			19.89
Bank			8,322.00
Drawings			1,330.00
Total Assets			15,371.89

Liabilities
Liabilities are debts due to third parties. Charlie needs to review his bookkeeping records to ascertain what liabilities exist as at 31 March 2014. In addition,

Charlie needs to consider if there are any other liabilities relating to the business not disclosed in the bookkeeping records.

Charlie reviews his bookkeeping records and considers any other liabilities of the business and produces the following list:

Trade Creditors

In order to calculate trade creditors, i.e., the amount of monies owed to suppliers at the end of the period, it is necessary to establish/review the following:

1. **Identify if there are any trade creditors' balances due at the beginning of the period**
2. **Identify the total value of purchase invoices, inclusive of VAT, for the period as shown in the purchases daybook**
3. **Identify the total value of purchases daybook payments to suppliers for the period as shown in the bank payments book and/or the credit card book**

Charlie needs to slot the numbers into the following and process the calculation:

Opening creditors: Nil
Add – Purchases for January to March: £18,900 (see purchases daybook)
Less – Purchases daybook payments January to March
      Issued from bank account: £14,100 (see bank payments book)
      Issued by credit card: £1,200 (see credit card book)
Trade creditors as at 31 March 2014: £3,600

In order to verify this figure Charlie should obtain statements from his creditors

Figure 19.17
Purchases Daybook – Extended

PURCHASES DAYBOOK														
Date	Supplier	Invoice Number	Description	Gross Amount	VAT	Net Amount	Goods for Resale	Insurance	Stationery	Rent	Paid	VAT Reclaimable	Paid Invoices	Balance Due
05-Jan-14	Leather Chairs Ltd	LC111	Leather Chairs	6,000.00	1,000.00	5,000.00	5,000.00				05-Jan-14	1,000.00	6,000.00	0.00
15-Jan-14	Property Lets Ltd	PLL123	Rent	3,000.00	500.00	2,500.00				2,500.00	15-Jan-14	500.00	3,000.00	0.00
05-Feb-14	Dining Chairs Ltd	DC222	Dining Chairs	4,500.00	750.00	3,750.00	3,750.00				05-Feb-14	750.00	4,500.00	0.00
15-Feb-14	Bits & Bobs Ltd	BB123	Stationery	600.00	100.00	500.00			500.00		15-Feb-14	100.00	600.00	0.00
05-Mar-14	Wooden Stools Ltd	WS333	Wooden Stools	3,600.00	600.00	3,000.00	3,000.00							3,600.00
15-Mar-14	Insurance Ltd	INS123	Insurance	1,200.00	0.00	1,200.00		1,200.00			15-Mar-14	0.00	1,200.00	0.00
Total				18,900.00	2,950.00	15,950.00	11,750.00	1,200.00	500.00	2,500.00		2,350.00	15,300.00	3,600.00

that identify how much money is owed by his business to his suppliers/trade creditors at the period end.

The figure for trade creditors can also be verified by adding additional columns on the purchases daybook to record payments issued to suppliers as noted in Figure 19.17.

The purchases daybook identifies that all invoices have been paid for the period except the invoice for £3,600 due to Wooden Stools Ltd.

VAT
See Step 4 – VAT calculation above for detailed explanation of the VAT liability of £1,978.98 and its calculation.

PAYE/NI
Charlie reviews his payroll records book and notes that the business owes the tax authorities £1,857 worth of payroll taxes as at 31 March 2014 (see Figure 19.18).

Figure 19.18
Payroll Records Book

PAYROLL RECORDS BOOK						
Month	Employee			Net Pay		Total PAYE/NI
Jan-14	Joe Soap			1,571.00		619.00
Feb-14	Joe Soap			1,571.00		619.00
Mar-14	Joe Soap			1,571.00		619.00
				4,713.00		1,857.00

Loan
In order to calculate the value of the loan outstanding at the end of the period, it is necessary to establish/review the following:
1. **Identify the value of the outstanding loan at the beginning of the period**
2. **Identify the total value of loans advanced in the period, as detailed in the bank receipts book**
3. **Identify the total value of repayments issued against the loan during the period, as detailed in the bank payments book**

Charlie needs to slot the numbers into the following and process the calculation:

Opening loan balance: Nil
Add – Loan(s) received January to March: £6,500 (see bank receipt book)
Less – Loan repayments January to March: £2,000 (see bank payments book)
Loan balance as at 31 March 2014: £4,500

Credit card account

In order to calculate the value of monies due on the credit card account at the end of the period, it is necessary to establish/review the following:

1. **Identify if there is an opening credit card balance due at the beginning of the period**
2. **Identify the total value of all payments made by credit card to pay for goods and services as per the credit card book for the period**
3. **Identify the total value of all payments receipts issued to the credit card account by the account holder to reduce the value of monies owed, as per the credit card book for the period**

Charlie needs to slot the numbers into the following and process the calculation:

Opening credit card balance: Nil
Add – Credit card payments January to March: £2,102 (see credit card book)
Less – Credit card payment receipts January to March: £880 (see credit card book)
Credit card balance as at 31 March 2014: £1,222

Charlie reviews the credit card book and identifies payments issued by credit card for the period of £1,200 to the purchases daybook, £880 to drawings, £22 to credit card fees, total £2,102. He also identifies £880 was paid to the credit card company during the period. The credit card book shows £1,222 is owed as at 31 March 2014 as noted in the final column; see Figure 19.19.

Figure 19.19
Credit Card Book

CREDIT CARD BOOK

DATE	PAYEE/RECEIPT DETAILS	PAYMENT/RECEIPT REFERENCE	GROSS AMOUNT	PURCHASE DAYBOOK PAYMENTS	Drawings	Credit Card Fees	Credit Card Interest	Payments	Balance
01-Jan-14	Opening Balance		0						0
15-Jan-14	Sun Tours Ltd	Private Holiday	800.00		800.00				800.00
20-Feb-14	Clothes Shop Ltd	Private expenditure	80.00		80.00				880.00
25-Feb-14	Payment		-800.00					-800.00	80.00
15-Mar-14	Insurance Ltd	Invoice INS123	1,200.00	1,200.00					1,280.00
18-Mar-14	Credit Card Ltd	account fee	22.00			22.00			1,302.00
25-Mar-14	Payment		-80.00					-80.00	1,222.00
			1,222.00	1,200.00	880.00	22.00	0.00	-880.00	1,222.00

Cash injection by Charlie

Charlie recorded in the petty cash book that he personally put £300 of his own money in the petty cash tin during the period. Technically, the business owes this £300 to Charlie, therefore Charlie records the £300 as a liability of the business. Alternatively, the £300 cash injected could be used to reduce Charlie's level of drawings from the business for the period.

Charlie uses the information calculated above concerning the liabilities of the business and creates a list of the liabilities (see Figure 19.20). Based on his workings so far he has ascertained the total value of liabilities is £13,457.98.

Figure 19.20
Liabilities

LIABILITIES AS AT 31 MARCH 2014		
Creditors		3,600.00
VAT		1,978.98
PAYE/NI		1,857.00
Loan		4,500.00
Credit card account		1,222.00
Charlie - petty cash lodgement		300.00
Total Liabilities		13,457.98

Charlie reviews his assets and liabilities by placing the lists side by side (see Figure 19.21). He notes that his assets of £15,371.89 are £1,913.91 higher than his liabilities of £13,457.98.

Figure 19.21
Assets and Liabilities

ASSETS AS AT 31 MARCH 2014				LIABILITIES AS AT 31 MARCH 2014			
Debtors			5,700.00	Creditors			3,600.00
Petty cash			19.89	VAT			1,978.98
Bank			8,322.00	PAYE/NI			1,857.00
Drawings			1,330.00	Loan			4,500.00
				Credit card account			1,222.00
				Charlie - petty cash lodgement			300.00
Total Assets			15,371.89	Total Liabilities			13,457.98

Figure 19.22
Assets and liabilities Balanced

ASSETS AS AT 31 MARCH 2014				LIABILITIES AS AT 31 MARCH 2014			
Debtors			5,700.00	Creditors			3,600.00
Petty cash			19.89	VAT			1,978.98
Bank			8,322.00	PAYE/NI			1,857.00
Drawings			1,330.00	Loan			4,500.00
				Credit card account			1,222.00
				Charlie - petty cash lodgement			300.00
				Profit - January to March (balancing figure)			1,913.91
Total Assets			15,371.89	Total Liabilities			15,371.89

Charlie understands that the accounting equation states that assets must equal liabilities; see above explanation of the accounting equation. Charlie has calculated that the business assets are £15,371.89 and the business liabilities are £13,457.98, resulting in the difference of £1,913.91. Charlie assumes that the difference of £1,913.91, i.e., the balancing figure, is the profit of the business for the three-month period, until he performs further adjustments to verify the same. The profit figure is a liability of the business and needs to be included with the other liabilities. The reason that the profit is referred to as a liability of the business is because, technically, the money is owed by the business to Charlie.

Charlie now inserts the balancing figure that he assumes is profit into the liability list and draws up a new list of assets and liabilities (see Figure 19.22).

The above list of assets and liabilities needs to be reviewed to identify if any adjustments need to be made to any of the figures. Depending on the circumstances of a business, adjustments may need to be made relating to such matters as:

- **Stock**
- **Fixed assets**
- **Depreciation**
- **Accruals**
- **Prepayments**

Stock

On 31 March 2014 Charlie conducted a stock take. Charlie physically counted all chairs he had in stock. He identified five wooden stools, each valued at £30 cost. The total value of the stock at the period end is therefore £150. This figure of £150 needs to be included in the assets of the business as at 31 March 2014. The effect of including the stock figure will be that assets will increase by £150 and profits will also increase by £150 (see Figure 19.23).

Fixed Assets

Fixed assets are resources invested in the business over the long term, i.e., for more than one year. Charlie had been using a computer to record the financial transactions of the business. The computer was purchased in late December, the month before the business started to trade. The computer cost him £1,500. He purchased the computer second-hand from a private individual and therefore

Figure 19.23
Assets and Liabilities – Adjusted for Stock

ASSETS AS AT 31 MARCH 2014			LIABILITIES AS AT 31 MARCH 2014	
Debtors		5,700.00	Creditors	3,600.00
Petty cash		19.89	VAT	1,978.98
Bank		8,322.00	PAYE/NI	1,857.00
Drawings		1,330.00	Loan	4,500.00
Stock		150.00	Credit card account	1,222.00
			Charlie - petty cash lodgement	300.00
			Profit - January to March (balancing figure)	2,063.91
Total Assets		15,521.89	Total Liabilities	15,521.89

was not charged VAT. Charlie uses the computer exclusively for business. The computer is capital introduced by the owner of the business and needs to be included in the list of assets and liabilities of the business (see Figure 19.24).

Figure 19.24
Assets and Liabilities – Adjusted for Assets

ASSETS AS AT 31 MARCH 2014			LIABILITIES AS AT 31 MARCH 2014		
Debtors		5,700.00	Creditors		3,600.00
Petty cash		19.89	VAT		1,978.98
Bank		8,322.00	PAYE/NI		1,857.00
Drawings		1,330.00	Loan		4,500.00
Stock		150.00	Credit card account		1,222.00
Fixed Asset - computer		1,500.00	Charlie - petty cash lodgement		300.00
			Capital Introduced - (Computer)		1,500.00
			Profit - January to March (balancing figure)		2,063.91
Total Assets		17,021.89	Total Liabilities		17,021.89

Depreciation

Fixed assets, such as motor vehicles, equipment, machinery and computers, reduce in value as time progresses. Such assets are subject to wear and tear and eventually need to be replaced. The wear and tear of an asset is recorded as depreciation in the records of a business. Depreciation can be calculated in a number of different ways.

One of the most straightforward methods of depreciation is referred to as straight-line depreciation. To calculate straight-line depreciation the cost of the asset is divided by its useful economic life, i.e., how long it will last. Charlie estimates that the computer he purchased for £1,500 will last for three years. This means the useful economic life of the computer is three years. The straight-line depreciation calculation for the computer would be £1,500 divided by 3 = £500 worth of depreciation each year. The period of financial transactions that Charlie is covering is for three months. The depreciation charge is £500 divided by 12 months = £41.67 for a month. Each month the computer is depreciating at £41.67. Therefore three months' depreciation is £41.67 x 3 months = £125 rounded to the nearest pound value.

The depreciation needs to be included in the assets and liabilities listing. Its inclusion will result in the profit figure reducing by the amount of depreciation charged and the value of assets reducing by the depreciation charged. The assets and liabilities of the business will then reflect what is shown in Figure 19.25.

Figure 19.25
Assets and Liabilities – Adjusted for Depreciation

ASSETS AS AT 31 MARCH 2014			LIABILITIES AS AT 31 MARCH 2014	
Debtors		5,700.00	Creditors	3,600.00
Petty cash		19.89	VAT	1,978.98
Bank		8,322.00	PAYE/NI	1,857.00
Drawings		1,330.00	Loan	4,500.00
Stock		150.00	Credit card account	1,222.00
Fixed Asset - computer		1,500.00	Charlie - petty cash lodgement	300.00
			Capital Introduced - (Computer)	1,500.00
			Depreciation	125.00
			Profit - January to March (balancing figure)	1,938.91
Total Assets		17,021.89	Total Liabilities	17,021.89

Accruals

An accrual is the process of recording a financial transaction for an expense incurred during a period, for which no invoice has been received at the period end. Charlie had engaged the services of a web developer to produce a digital brochure in March. Charlie has received the digital brochure but has not received an invoice relating to the service. Charlie had agreed a fee of £175 with the service provider, who was not registered for VAT. Charlie needs to account for this expense as an accrual. The accrual will reduce profits by £175 and increase the liabilities of the business by £175 as the money is owed to a third party. The transaction will result in the assets and liabilities shown in Figure 19.26.

Prepayments

Prepayments are payments made in advance of an expense being due for payment or billed for in advance of the expense being due for payment. Charlie noticed that the insurance invoice recorded in the purchases daybook from Insurance Ltd for £1,200 relates to a twelve-month period. The insurance

Figure 19.26

Assets and Liabilities – Adjusted for Accruals

ASSETS AS AT 31 MARCH 2014				LIABILITIES AS AT 31 MARCH 2014		
Debtors		5,700.00		Creditors		3,600.00
Petty cash		19.89		VAT		1,978.98
Bank		8,322.00		PAYE/NI		1,857.00
Drawings		1,330.00		Loan		4,500.00
Stock		150.00		Credit card account		1,222.00
Fixed Asset - computer		1,500.00		Charlie - petty cash lodgement		300.00
				Capital Introduced - (Computer)		1,500.00
				Depreciation		125.00
				Accrual		175.00
				Profit - January to March (balancing figure)		1,763.91
Total Assets		17,021.89		Total Liabilities		17,021.89

invoice covers the period from March 2014 to February 2015. This means that only one month of this invoice relates to the period he is producing the financial information for. Charlie needs to account for the prepayment of the insurance. Charlie calculates the prepayment as follows:

£1,200 relates to twelve months of insurance, therefore one month of insurance is £1,200 divided by 12 months = £100.

This means that only £100 relates to the period ending 31 March 2014 and £1,100 is a prepayment relating to the period April 2014 to February 2015. Charlie needs to record the prepayment as an asset of the business. The effect of the prepayment will be to increase the assets by £1,100 and increase the profits by £1,100. See Figure 19.27.

The information that Charlie has produced concerning assets and liabilities can be displayed in an alternative format, to enable greater insight into the finances of the business. Charlie displays the information in a balance sheet format. A balance sheet is a list of assets and liabilities as at a particular date. Charlie has already calculated the assets and liabilities of the business, so it is merely a matter of putting the figures into a different format, see Figure 19.28.

Figure 19.27

Assets and Liabilities – Adjusted for Prepayments

ASSETS AS AT 31 MARCH 2014			LIABILITIES AS AT 31 MARCH 2014		
Debtors		5,700.00	Creditors		3,600.00
Petty cash		19.89	VAT		1,978.98
Bank		8,322.00	PAYE/NI		1,857.00
Drawings		1,330.00	Loan		4,500.00
Stock		150.00	Credit card account		1,222.00
Fixed Asset - computer		1,500.00	Charlie - petty cash lodgement		300.00
Prepayment		1,100.00	Capital Introduced - (Computer)		1,500.00
			Depreciation		125.00
			Accrual		175.00
			Profit - January to March (balancing figure)		2,863.91
Total Assets		18,121.89	Total Liabilities		18,121.89

Fixed Assets

Fixed assets are resources invested in the business for the long term. Examples would be such items as a premises, motor vehicles, machinery, equipment, computers, fixtures and fittings. Charlie has only one fixed asset, a computer that cost £1,500. Charlie has calculated the depreciation for the three-month period to be £125. The net book value of the computer at 31 March 2014 is the cost less the depreciation.

Current Assets

Current assets are resources invested in the business for the short term, up to twelve months. Charlie's business has a variety of current assets such as stock, debtors, prepayments, bank and petty cash.

Creditors < 1 year

Creditors < 1 year are current liabilities of the business representing monies due to third parties that are payable within twelve months. Charlie's business has a number of liabilities due within twelve months: trade creditors, VAT, PAYE/NI, credit card account and accruals.

Creditors > 1 year

Creditors > 1 year are debts due to third parties due for payment in more than

Figure 19.28
Balance Sheet

BALANCE SHEET	as at 31 March 2014			
Fixed Assets				
Computer	Cost		1,500.00	
Computer	Less depreciation		125.00	
Net Book Value			1,375.00	A
Current Assets				
Stock			150.00	
Debtors			5,700.00	
Prepayments			1,100.00	
Bank			8,322.00	
Petty Cash			19.89	
			15,291.89	B
Creditors < 1 Year				
Trade Creditors			3,600.00	
VAT			1,978.98	
PAYE/NI			1,857.00	
Credit Card Account			1,222.00	
Accruals			175.00	
			8,832.98	C
Creditors > 1 Year				
Loan			4,500.00	D
Total Assets Less Liabilities	(A+B-C-D)		3,333.91	
Capital Account				
Capital - (value of computer asset introduced into business)			1,500.00	
Capital - cash introduced re petty cash			300.00	
Profit for the period			2,863.91	
Drawings			-1,330.00	
			3,333.91	

twelve months. Instalment repayments may be made during the period to reduce part of the liability but the overall liability is not due for repayment for more than twelve months. Charlie owes money to a relative at the end of the period. At the period end date 31 March 2014 the monies due to his relative was £4,500.

Capital Account

The capital account represents the amount of money invested in the business by the business owner. Money invested can comprise a variety of items such as:

- **Cash lodged into the business by the owners of the business**
- **Profits of the business not yet paid out to the owners of the business**
- **The value of assets introduced into the business for use by the business**

The capital account is reduced by drawings or the payment of profits to the owners of the business.

The business produced a profit of £2,863.91 for the three-month period. The profit of £2,863.91 is money due to Charlie as he is the owner of the business.

Charlie lodged £300 into petty cash but also took drawings of £1,330, resulting in a net withdrawal of monies from the business of £1,030. Essentially this £1,030 is a part payment of the profits due to Charlie, therefore the accumulated profits available for appropriation are reduced by this amount.

Although Charlie understands the accounting equation, he is aware that it is necessary to use double-entry bookkeeping to produce financial statements. Financial statements comprise a profit and loss account (income statement) and a balance sheet. Charlie has managed to produce the balance sheet himself but would like it verified. Charlie brings his bookkeeping records to his accountant Anne. He asks Anne to verify his figures. Anne uses double-entry bookkeeping to generate a profit and loss account and a balance sheet to verify Charlie's figures. A profit and loss account details the income for a period less expenditure for a period. Anne gives Charlie a profit and loss account containing explanations so he can identify the source of the figures she has calculated. See Figure 19.29.

NOTE: PDB = Purchases daybook, PCB = Petty Cash Book, BPB = Bank Payments Book, CCB = Credit Card Book, PRB = Payroll Records Book

---

The net profit noted on the profit and loss account is £2,863.91, which is the same profit figure as calculated by Charlie in the balance sheet.

Figure 19.29
Profit and Loss Account

Profit & Loss Account / Income Statement for period ending 31 March 2014					
		Info. source			Note
Sales				24,750.00	A
Opening Stock			0.00		
Purchases (goods for resale)		PDB*	11,750.00		
Less closing Stock		Stock take	-150.00		
Cost of sales		Calculated value	11,600.00	11,600.00	B
Gross Profit		Calculated value		13,150.00	(A - B)
Less Expenditure					
Insurance		PDB*	1,200.00		
Stationery		PDB	500.00		
Rent		PDB	2,500.00		
Tea		PCB*	4.00		
Fuel		PCB	105.09		
Stamps		PCB	60.00		
Window cleaning		PCB	90.00		
Wages		BPB*	4,713.00		
Bank charges		BPB	35.00		
Credit card fees		CCB*	22.00		
Payroll Taxes		PRB*	1,857.00		
Adjustments:					
Accruals		Digital brochure	175.00		Increases costs
Prepayments		Insurance invoice	-1,100.00		Reduces costs
Depreciation		Computer asset	125.00		Increases costs
Total expenditure		Calculated value	10,286.09	10,286.09	(C)
Net Profit		Calculated value		2,863.91	(A - B - C)

MICRO QUIZ

Q1: A prepayment is an amount of money due to a third party.
    True or False?

Q2: To calculate the closing bank balance for a period, it is necessary to add the opening bank balance to the bank receipts for the period and deduct the bank payments for the period.
    True or False?

Q3: To calculate the closing debtors balance for a period, it is necessary to add the opening debtors balance to all the sales for the period including VAT, less the total value of all remittances received from customers for the period.
    True or False?

Q4: To calculate the closing balance of creditors for a period, it is necessary to deduct the total value of payments to suppliers for the period from the total value of purchase invoices.
    True or False?

Q5: If a business has received the benefit of goods or services from a supplier for a given period and the supplier has not issued an invoice then it is necessary to record an accrual for the period.
    True or False?

Q6: Drawings are monies taken from the business by the owner for private use.
    True or False?

Q7: The amount noted as owed to trade creditors on the balance sheet can be verified by reconciling creditor statements.
    True or False?

Q8: Trade debtors reflect monies owed to the business by customers who have purchased on credit and who have not yet paid at the end of the period.
    True or False?

Q9: Trade creditors reflect monies owed to third parties by the business for goods and services purchased on credit and who have not yet paid at the date of the balance sheet.
    True or False?

Q10: Stock shown on the balance sheet represents goods physically located in the stores at the period end valued at selling price.
    True or False?

Micro quiz – solutions

Q1: False   Q6: True
Q2: True   Q7: True
Q3: True   Q8: True
Q4: False   Q9: True
Q5: True   Q10: False

Appendix A: Value Added Tax – Ireland

VALUE ADDED TAX (VAT) – OVERVIEW

> **NOTE: This section deals specifically with Irish VAT. All the examples use Irish VAT rates and are denoted in the euro currency in all examples except Figure A.2.**

The examples presented in this book have been denoted in sterling. The examples concerning VAT-registered businesses have been shown with UK VAT rates. In order to adjust the examples presented using UK VAT to represent Irish VAT rates, it is a simple matter of calculating the VAT at Irish rates and denoting the currency in euro. The standard rate of VAT in the UK is 20% and the standard rate of VAT in Ireland is 23%. Therefore an example previously noted in chapter 8 of a sales daybook is reproduced below as Figure A.2 and is adjusted to Irish VAT as shown in Figure A.3.

The process to convert any of the daybooks denoting VAT from UK status to Irish status involves the following:

- **Replace the '£' symbol with the '€' symbol**
- **Replace the UK VAT rate with the appropriate Irish VAT rate**
- **Recalculate the figures**

All examples in this book can be converted from UK examples to Irish examples by following the explanation above.

A business can be obliged to register for VAT depending on the types of products and/or services it supplies and based on the level of sales the business generates. Value added tax adds a percentage tax to the cost of the supply of certain goods or services. The percentage of VAT charged depends upon the type of goods or services supplied. For the majority of businesses VAT is relatively straightforward. In essence, VAT is charged on the supply of goods and services by a business to its customers and this sales VAT is owed to the tax authorities. The amount of sales VAT due can be reduced by deducting VAT the business has been charged for goods and services it has purchased. See Figure A.1 for an overview of VAT.

VAT relates to charging tax on taxable supplies. The question that you need to answer in relation to your business is as follows:

Figure A.1
VAT Overview

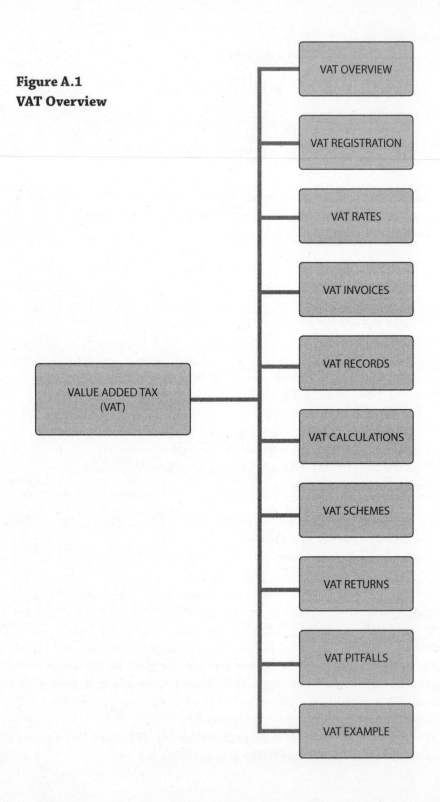

Figure A.2
Sales Daybook – VAT (UK VAT)

SALES DAYBOOK					
DATE	CUSTOMER DETAILS	INVOICE NUMBER	£ GROSS AMOUNT	VAT 20%	Net
03-Jan-14	ABC Ltd	1001	1,200	200	1,000
04-Jan-14	XYZ Ltd	1002	240	40	200
11-Jan-14	PPP Ltd	1003	120	20	100
15-Jan-14	LOL Ltd	1004	6,000	1,000	5,000
Total			7,560	1,260	6,300

Figure A.3
Sales Daybook – VAT (Ireland)

SALES DAYBOOK					
DATE	CUSTOMER DETAILS	INVOICE NUMBER	€ GROSS AMOUNT	VAT 23%	Net
03-Jan-14	ABC Ltd	1001	1,230	230	1,000
04-Jan-14	XYZ Ltd	1002	246	46	200
11-Jan-14	PPP Ltd	1003	123	23	100
15-Jan-14	LOL Ltd	1004	6,150	1,150	5,000
Total			7,749	1,449	6,300

Are the goods and/or services your business supplies to customers a taxable supply, i.e., liable to a VAT charge? If the answer is yes, then you need to address the following:
- When is there an obligation to register for VAT?
- Is there a benefit to voluntary registration for VAT, prior to being obligated to register for VAT?

- What is the procedure for VAT registration?
- What rate of VAT needs to be charged?
- What information should be detailed on VAT invoices?
- What VAT records need to be maintained?
- How is VAT charged on the sale of a product/service?
- How is VAT calculated?
- How is VAT calculated using the standard VAT calculation method?
- How is VAT calculated using the cash-accounting scheme?
- How is VAT calculated using the margin scheme for second-hand goods?
- What type of special VAT schemes exist?
- Can a VAT return be filed on an annual basis?
- How is a VAT return form completed?
- How is a VAT return filed?
- When must a VAT return be filed and paid?
- What is a return of trading details form?
- What type of pitfalls exist concerning VAT?

VAT registration

When is there an obligation to register for VAT?

If the goods and/or services your business supplies are liable to VAT then you will be obligated to register for VAT if your sales breach certain thresholds. The thresholds differ depending on the business offering. The main thresholds concerning a business trading in the domestic market are as follows:

- **Sales of services only: sales > €37,500 in a continuous twelve-month period**
- **Sales of goods only: sales > €75,000 in a continuous twelve-month period**

Other conditions apply whereby there is an obligation to register for VAT concerning matters such as distance sales and acquisitions. See www.revenue.ie for full details concerning VAT registration.

Is there a benefit to voluntary registration for VAT, prior to being obligated to register for VAT?

If the goods and/or services your business supplies are liable to VAT then you will be obligated to register for VAT if your sales breach certain thresholds. However, if your business has not breached the VAT registration thresholds then you may still register for VAT.

The issues you need to consider prior to voluntary VAT registration are as follows:

- **Fixed-asset purchases**

- **Image**
- **VAT-registered customers**
- **Non-VAT-registered customers**

Fixed-asset purchases

If the business will incur VAT on the purchases of fixed assets during the set-up phase, then the business can benefit from reclaiming VAT. This is particularly the case if the business is buying fixed assets such as computer equipment or machinery.

Image

If your business is not registered for VAT and is selling taxable supplies then customers and suppliers will be aware that your sales are below the VAT threshold. This may hinder your business as your business could be classed as insignificant in the marketplace, especially if you are dealing with large companies.

VAT-registered customers

If the business sells services and/or products to VAT-registered individuals or businesses then the VAT can be reclaimed by such customers. Customers who are VAT-registered are less concerned with being charged VAT, as they can claim it back.

Non-VAT-registered customers

If the customers of the business are not VAT registered, then these customers will not be able to reclaim the VAT charged and it may make your service or goods more expensive for them to buy. If your business is competing with VAT-registered businesses, then you may be in a position to undercut the competitors' prices if your business remains non-VAT registered.

What is the procedure for VAT registration?

If you decide to voluntarily register for VAT or your business is obligated to register, then it is necessary to notify the tax authorities. You can register online at www.revenue.ie using the revenue online service (ROS).

> **NOTE: If you are in any doubt concerning the VAT status of the goods and/or services your business supplies, then you should request written confirmation from the tax authorities to clarify this.**

VAT rates

What rate of VAT needs to be charged?

VAT is charged at different rates depending on the goods or services supplied. VAT rates are noted below:

- **Exempt – VAT not applicable**
- **Zero rate**
- **4.8% rate**
- **5% rate**
- **9% rate**
- **13.5% rate**
- **23% rate**

It is important to ensure you charge VAT at the appropriate rate. The website www.revenue.ie contains listings of hundreds of examples of goods and services and the rate of VAT such goods and services are liable at. If you remain unsure what VAT rate applies to your business you should seek clarification from the tax authorities.

VAT invoices

What information should be detailed on VAT invoices?

Detailed below is a non-exhaustive list for you to consider in relation to VAT invoices:

- **Name of your business**
- **Address of your business**
- **Contact details of your business: phone, email, website**
- **Customer name and address**
- **Date of invoice and supply of service and/or products**
- **Sequential invoice number**
- **Details of services rendered or goods supplied excluding VAT**
- **VAT rates charged**
- **Total VAT relating to the supply of services or goods supplied**
- **Total fee for services rendered or price of goods supplied including VAT**
- **The VAT number of your business**
- **The VAT number of the customer if supplying to an EU VAT-registered customer and details of the same**
- **The VAT number of the customer if a reverse charge* applies and details of the same**

> ***NOTE: A reverse charge of VAT means the recipient of the goods or services is obliged to account for the VAT, not the supplier.**

VAT records

What VAT records need to be maintained?

A VAT-registered business is obligated to maintain records that will verify and validate VAT returns submitted to the tax authorities. Records relating to VAT transactions should be held for six years. VAT records would include copies of sales invoices issued to customers, purchase invoices received from suppliers and the records used to produce the figures submitted on VAT returns. The information required to complete a VAT return form will be recorded in the financial records of the business.

VAT calculations

How is VAT charged on the sale of a product/service?

VAT adds a percentage to the selling price of a service or a product that is liable to VAT.

If the selling price of a chair is €100 excluding VAT and VAT is to be charged, then the calculation is as follows:

€100 x 23% = €23 of VAT
Selling price €100 + VAT €23 = VAT-inclusive selling price of €123

A customer who purchases the chair from a shop will pay €123. The shopkeeper will be liable to pay the tax authorities €23 worth of sales VAT less any VAT incurred during the period.

How is VAT calculated?

In essence, VAT is the difference between the VAT charged to customers by a business and the VAT charged by suppliers of a business.
- **If the level of VAT charged to customers by a business is greater than the level of VAT charged by suppliers for a given period, then VAT liability exists**
- **If the level of VAT charged to customers by a business is less than the level of VAT charged by suppliers for a given period, then a VAT refund exists**

The amount of VAT due for payment can be calculated in a number of ways, such as:
- **The standard VAT calculation method (also referred to as the invoice basis or accruals basis of VAT accounting calculation)**
- **The cash-accounting VAT calculation method**
- **The margin scheme for second-hand goods**
- **Various retail schemes of VAT calculation**

The method used to calculate VAT depends on the circumstance of the business and if a business is eligible to use a particular VAT accounting scheme.

How is VAT calculated using standard VAT accounting?

VAT calculated using standard VAT accounting involves a number of basic calculations:

Calculation 1

Calculate the value of sales VAT, also known as output VAT, charged by the business to customers for the period.

Calculation 2

Calculate the value of purchase VAT, also known as input VAT, charged by suppliers for goods and services during the period.

Calculation 3

Deduct purchase VAT (input VAT) from sales VAT (output VAT) to identify if VAT is due to be paid to the tax authorities or due to be repaid by the tax authorities to your business.

Example

Tina buys and sells tables and is VAT registered. She records the following transactions:

SALES

Date	Invoice	Details			
1 Jan 2014	S111	Executive table	3,000 + VAT 23%	690 =	3,690 including VAT
1 Feb 2014	S222	Executive table	3,000 + VAT 23%	690 =	3,690 including VAT
TOTAL			Net sales 6,000	Output VAT 1,380	

PURCHASES

Date	Invoice	Details			
1 Jan 2014	P111	Executive table	1,000 + VAT 23%	230 =	1,230 including VAT
1 Feb 2014	P222	Executive table	1,000 + VAT 23%	230 =	1,230 including VAT
TOTAL			Net purchases 2,000	Input VAT 460	

During March, Tina calculates the VAT using the standard VAT accounting method.

Calculation 1

Output VAT, i.e., sales VAT charged on the two sales invoices issued to customers for the period, amounted to €690 x 2 = €1,380.

Calculation 2
Input VAT, i.e., purchase VAT charged on the two purchase invoices received from suppliers for the period, amounted to €230 x 2 = €460.

Calculation 3
Output VAT, i.e., sales VAT: €1,380
Less input VAT, i.e., purchase VAT: €460
VAT due to be paid: €920

Tina is due to pay VAT to the tax authorities of €920 for the period January to February.

How is VAT calculated using the cash-accounting scheme?

VAT can be calculated on the cash basis (money received basis) based on the following:
- **VAT-registered traders whose supplies of goods or services are almost exclusively (at least 90%) made to unregistered persons**
- **VAT-registered traders whose annual turnover (exclusive of VAT) does not exceed or is not likely to exceed €2 million (with effect from 1 January 2014)**

VAT calculated using cash VAT accounting involves a number of basic calculations:

Calculation 1
Calculate the value of sales VAT, also known as output VAT, charged by the business to customers, for which payment has been received from customers during the period.

Calculation 2
Calculate the value of purchase VAT, also known as input VAT, charged by suppliers for goods and services during the period.

Calculation 3
Deduct purchase VAT (input VAT) charged from sales VAT (output VAT) received to identify if VAT is due to be paid to the tax authorities or due to be repaid by the tax authorities to your business.

Example
Tina buys and sells tables and is VAT registered. She records the following transactions:

SALES

Date	Invoice	Details			
1 Jan 2014	S111	Executive table	3,000 + VAT 23%	690 =	3,690 including VAT
1 Feb 2014	S222	Executive table	3,000 + VAT 23%	690 =	3,690 including VAT
TOTAL			Net sales 6,000	Output VAT 1,380	

PURCHASES

Date	Invoice	Details			
1 Jan 2014	P111	Executive table	1,000 + VAT 23%	230 =	1,230 including VAT
1 Feb 2014	P222	Executive table	1,000 + VAT 23%	230 =	1,230 including VAT
TOTAL			Net purchases 2,000	Input VAT 460	

Calculation 1

When Tina reviews her receipts, detailed in the bank receipts book, she identifies the following:

Receipts from customers during the period January to February 2014
January: No payments received from customers
February: Payment received from a customer for invoice S111 of €3,690

Total value of receipts from customers is €3,690. The total value of VAT contained within the receipts is calculated as follows:

€3,690 / 123 x 23 = €690 of VAT
€690 is the total of output VAT/sales VAT due to the tax authorities.

Calculation 2

When Tina reviews her purchases, detailed in the purchases daybook, she identifies the following:

Purchases during the period January to February 2014.

Date	Invoice	Details
1 Jan 2014	P111	1,230 including VAT
1 Feb 2014	P222	1,230 including VAT

The total VAT-inclusive value of the above purchase invoices is €2,460. The value of the VAT included can be calculated as follows:
€2,460 / 123 x 23 = €460

€460 is the total of input VAT/purchase VAT to be reclaimed from the tax authorities.

Calculation 3
Output VAT, i.e., sales VAT: €690
Less input VAT, i.e., purchase VAT: €460
VAT due to be paid: €230

Based on calculation 3, Tina is due to pay VAT of €230 to the tax authorities.

How is VAT calculated using the margin scheme for second-hand goods?

The margin scheme for second-hand goods enables VAT to be calculated on the profit margin attained. So if your business involves the sale of second-hand goods this scheme needs consideration. Examples of second-hand goods would be cars, works of art, antiques, certain precious metals and stones.

For example, a table is purchased second-hand from a member of the public who is not VAT registered by a VAT-registered antiques business for €500. The table is subsequently sold for €750.

The amount of VAT based on the margin scheme would be as follows:

Selling price: €750
Less cost price: €500
Margin: €250

The €250 margin is used to calculate the sales VAT (output VAT) as follows:
€250 / 123 x 23 = €46.74
Sales VAT (output VAT) = €46.74

In general, to avail of the margin scheme:
- **The goods must be second-hand**
- **No VAT was charged when goods were purchased**

What type of special VAT schemes exist?

- **Travel agents' margin scheme**
- **Retailers' schemes**
- **Flat-rate farmer scheme**

Can a VAT return be filed on an annual basis?

It is possible to file an annual VAT return based on certain conditions. It is necessary to make an application to the Revenue Commissioners to avail oneself of the option.

VAT returns

How is a VAT return completed?

A VAT return is a form detailing the total value of sales VAT (output VAT), the total value of purchase VAT (input VAT) and the total value of VAT to be paid or VAT to be refunded. Certain other information may also be required if you trade with businesses in other EU member states.

VAT is calculated as follows:
- Identify sales VAT for the period from the financial records. This is the figure that is entered into the 'T1' box on the VAT return
- Identify purchase VAT for the period from the financial records. This is the figure that is entered into the 'T2' box on the VAT return
- Subtract purchase VAT from sales VAT. This is done by clicking on the 'calculate' box on the ROS VAT screen

If the sales VAT figure is greater than the purchase VAT figure then a VAT liability exists. This is the figure that is entered into the 'T3' box on the VAT return.

If the purchases VAT figure is higher than the sales VAT figure then a VAT refund exists. This is the figure that is entered into the 'T4' box on the VAT return.

A business that trades with customers in other EU member states needs to complete details concerning such transactions on the VAT return in the following sections:
- E1: Total value of goods to other EU countries
- E2: Total value of goods from other EU countries
- ES1: Total value of services to other EU countries
- ES2: Total value of services from other EU countries

NOTE: A fully illustrated example of how to use the financial records of a business to calculate VAT is detailed at the end of this appendix.

How is a VAT return filed?

VAT returns can be filed online. In order to file online it is necessary to be registered on ROS for online services. Instructions concerning registration can be found at www.revenue.ie.

When must a VAT return be filed and paid?

The standard VAT period for VAT returns is bimonthly. The tax authorities can authorize VAT returns to be for different time periods based on the VAT liabilities/circumstances of the VAT-registered business.

Monthly VAT returns

Where a business is in a permanent VAT-repayment position the tax authorities may authorize the filing of monthly VAT returns.

Biannual VAT returns

If the annual VAT liability of the business is less than €3,000 then two biannual returns may be filed each year.

VAT returns – four-month period

If the annual VAT liability of the business is between €3,000 and €14,000 then returns may be filed every four months.

Annual VAT returns

A VAT-registered business may apply to the tax authorities to file a single annual VAT return. If the request is granted, the VAT-registered business will need to set up a monthly VAT payment on account.

VAT payment due dates

VAT returns that are filed and paid online are subject to a deadline of the 23rd day following the end of the VAT period. For example, a VAT return relating to the period January to February must be filed and paid online on or before 23 March.

What is a return of trading details form?

The return of trading details form currently needs to be completed once a year. The form requires information concerning the value excluding VAT of goods and services purchased and sold during the period.

VAT pitfalls

What type of pitfalls exist concerning VAT?

Using VAT as a source of finance

VAT collected from customers can be consumed by the business as part of day-to-day operating expenditure. This can result in the inability of a business to pay VAT liabilities as they fall due for payment.

VAT late payment leads to interest charges

If a business does not pay its VAT when it falls due for payment it is liable for late interest charges imposed by the tax authorities.

VAT late payment can lead to potential VAT inspections

If a business is consistently late paying VAT due, it can be identified as a potential candidate for a VAT inspection.

Using the wrong VAT rate

It is possible to use an incorrect VAT rate for the supply of services and/or products. If a mistake is made and the wrong VAT rate is used, the VAT-registered trader is liable for any shortfall. If you are in any doubt concerning the VAT rate applicable, seek professional advice or confirmation from the tax authorities.

Not being aware of specialist VAT rules relating to your business sector

Due to the wide variety of business sectors and special VAT rules that exist, it can happen that a business breaches some VAT regulations and is not even aware of doing so. VAT legislation is frequently changed and it is important to stay up to date concerning VAT issues affecting your business.

Not being aware of VAT rules pertaining to certain types of transactions

Certain types of transactions have to be dealt with in a particular manner to comply with VAT legislation. It is possible not to be aware of what is required. Examples of such transactions would be:

- *Partial exemption* – there are special VAT rules to comply with if your business supplies comprise a mix of exempt and non-exempt
- *Non-deductible VAT* – there are certain restrictions concerning the reclaiming of input VAT for certain items, such as petrol not used as stock in trade

VAT return – illustrative example

The following worked example regarding the completion of a VAT return is based on the DIY Bookkeeping system described in this book and on the Irish VAT system.

Charlie sells chairs and is registered for VAT. He only trades within the state. He does not have a business credit card. He engages in a variety of business transactions for the period January to February that he controls using his bookkeeping system as follows:

- Step 1: Record all income for the period
- Step 2: Record all expenditure for the period
- Step 3: Calculate VAT liability and calculate the VAT due for payment

Step 1 – Record income for the period

Sales daybook

During the months of January and February Charlie sells a variety of chairs to his customers. Charlie inputs relevant details of his sales invoices into his sales daybook software-based spreadsheet. See Figure A.4.

Figure A.4
Sales Daybook

SALES DAYBOOK						
DATE	CUSTOMER	INVOICE NO.	NET	VAT 23%	GROSS	
03-Jan-14	Mr Philips	1001	3,000.00	690.00	3,690.00	
04-Jan-14	Fanfare Ltd	1002	7,500.00	1,725.00	9,225.00	
11-Jan-14	Aztec Ltd	1003	3,300.00	759.00	4,059.00	
15-Jan-14	Zero Ltd	1004	900.00	207.00	1,107.00	
02-Feb-14	John Smith	1005	600.00	138.00	738.00	
20-Feb-14	Hitz Ltd	1006	3,250.00	747.50	3,997.50	
22-Feb-14	Hire All Ltd	1007	1,400.00	322.00	1,722.00	
25-Feb-14	Ms Anne Jones	1008	450.00	103.50	553.50	
			20,400.00	4,692.00	25,092.00	

SALES – Based on the sales daybook, the sales value for the period can be readily identified as €20,400 excluding VAT.

> **NOTE: Charlie could add additional columns to the sales daybook to record payment of sales invoices from customers. These additional columns could then be used to calculate VAT on a cash receipts basis. Alternatively, Charlie can use the bank receipt book to calculate VAT on a cash receipts basis as shown below.**

Bank receipts book

During the months of January and February Charlie receives monies into the business bank account. Charlie records the details of monies received into the bank account in the bank receipts book as shown in Figure A.5.

Based on the information contained in the bank receipts book Charlie can ascertain the following:

- **The total amount of all monies received for the period January to February was €24,581**
- **The total amount of monies received from customers was €18,081**
- **The total amount of monies received from other sources was €6,500, which was a loan from a relative**

Figure A.5
Bank Receipts Book

BANK RECEIPT BOOK					
DATE	NAME CUSTOMER/THIRD PARTY	PAYMENT TYPE	AMOUNT €	SALES RECEIPT	OTHER RECEIPTS
03-Jan-14	Loan from relative	cheque	6,500.00		6,500.00
02-Feb-14	Mr Philips	cheque	3,690.00	3,690.00	
02-Feb-14	Fanfare Ltd	EFT	9,225.00	9,225.00	
20-Feb-14	Aztec Ltd	cheque	4,059.00	4,059.00	
22-Feb-14	Zero Ltd	cash	1,107.00	1,107.00	
Total			24,581.00	18,081.00	6,500.00

Step 2 – Record expenditure for the period

Purchases daybook

During the months of January and February Charlie purchases a variety of goods and services from his suppliers on credit. Based on the information detailed on the purchase invoices Charlie records the relevant data into his purchases daybook as shown in Figure A.6.

Figure A.6
Purchases Daybook

PURCHASES DAYBOOK										
Date	Invoice No.	Supplier	Description	Gross Amount	VAT	Net Amount	Goods for Resale	Light & Heat	Stationery	Rent
02-Jan-14	4596	Super Chairs Ltd	Leather Chairs	1,230.00	230.00	1,000.00	1,000.00			
03-Jan-14	99856	Wooden Chairs Ltd	Wooden Stools	3,075.00	575.00	2,500.00	2,500.00			
10-Jan-14	A01	Big Chairs Ltd	Executive Chairs	1,353.00	253.00	1,100.00	1,100.00			
15-Jan-14	145	Office Supplies	20 Boxes of A4	123.00	23.00	100.00			100.00	
01-Feb-14	LH442	Utilities Ltd	Electricity	158.90	18.90	140.00		140.00		
15-Feb-14	LL01	Joe Biggs	Rent Jan/Feb	1,845.00	345.00	1,500.00				1,500.00
16-Feb-14	4610	Super Chairs Ltd	Leather Chairs	615.00	115.00	500.00	500.00			
Total				8,399.90	1,559.90	6,840.00	5,100.00	140.00	100.00	1,500.00

Based on the information contained in the purchases daybook Charlie can ascertain the following:
- Total expenditure recorded for the period including VAT was €8,399.90
- Total VAT charged by suppliers was €1,559.90 at various VAT rates
- Total expenditure recorded for the period excluding VAT was €6,840.00
- Expenditure of €5,100 excluding VAT was incurred relating to goods for resale
- Expenditure of €140 excluding VAT was incurred relating to light and heat
- Expenditure of €100 excluding VAT was incurred relating to stationery
- Expenditure of €1,500 excluding VAT was incurred relating to rent

Petty cash book
During the months of January and February Charlie purchases a variety of goods and services for minor cash amounts. Based on the information detailed on the invoices/receipts Charlie records the relevant details into his petty cash book as shown in Figure A.7.

Figure A.7
Petty cash book

PETTY CASH BOOK

DATE	PAYEE	DESCRIPTION	MONEY IN	GROSS AMOUNT	VAT	Net Amount	Tea/coffee	Stationery	Stamps	Window Cleaning	BALANCE
01-Jan-14		Cash in from owner	300.00								300.00
10-Jan-14	Spar shop	Tea bags for canteen		4.00	0.00	4.00	4.00				296.00
18-Jan-14	Post Office	Stamps & post		55.00	0.00	55.00			55.00		241.00
18-Feb-14	Joe Bloggs	Window cleaning		95.00	0.00	95.00				95.00	146.00
25-Feb-14	Spar shop	note books + other		104.55	19.55	85.00		85.00			41.45
			300.00	258.55	19.55	239.00	4.00	85.00	55.00	95.00	41.45

Based on the information contained in the petty cash book Charlie can ascertain the following:
- Monies lodged into petty cash for the period was €300
- Total expenditure from petty cash for the period was €258.55 including VAT
- Total VAT charged for the period was €19.55
- Total expenditure from petty cash for the period was €239 excluding VAT
- The amount of cash left in petty cash at the end of the period was €41.45

Bank payments book

During the months of January and February Charlie issues payments from the business bank account. Charlie records the details of payments from the business bank account in the bank payments book as shown in Figure A.8.

Based on the information contained in the bank payments book Charlie can ascertain the following:

- **The total amount of all payments for the period January to February was €7,003**
- **The total amount paid towards the purchases daybook, i.e., supplier payments, was €5,781**
- **The total amount paid from the bank account relating to wages was €800**
- **The total amount paid from the bank account relating to drawings was €380**
- **The total amount paid from the bank account relating to bank charges was €42**

Step 3 – Calculate VAT liability

Now that Charlie has completed Step 1 and Step 2 he is in a position to deal with VAT. Charlie can ascertain the VAT liability from the bookkeeping records. The VAT liability is the total value of VAT that is due by the business to the tax authorities. This figure is ascertained by calculating VAT on the standard VAT calculation basis.

VAT liability

Based on the information contained in the sales daybook, purchases daybook, petty cash book and bank payments book, Charlie can calculate the VAT liability for the period January to February.

Calculation – standard VAT calculation method (see above for detailed explanation)

Charlie reviews his sales daybook and identifies the sales VAT of €4,692.00 (see above sales daybook and ensure you can identify this figure).

Charlie reviews his purchases daybook and identifies purchase VAT of €1,559.90

Charlie reviews his petty cash book and identifies purchase VAT of €19.55 (see above and ensure you can identify these figures).

Total of purchase VAT: €1,579.45

Figure A.8 Bank Payments Book

BANK PAYMENTS BOOK

DATE	PAYEE	PAYMENT TYPE	PAYMENT REFERENCE	GROSS AMOUNT	PURCHASE DAYBOOK PAYMENTS	Wages	Drawings	Bank Charges
05-Jan-14	Charlie	ATM	Cash	80.00			80.00	
10-Jan-14	Bank charges	DD	Ref December	42.00				42.00
15-Jan-14	Charlie	ATM	Cash	300.00			300.00	
22-Jan-14	Joe Soap	EFT	Wages	800.00		800.00		
02-Feb-14	Super Chairs Ltd	Chq 9663	Invoice 4596	1,230.00	1,230.00			
03-Feb-14	Wooden Chairs Ltd	Chq 9664	Invoice 99856	3,075.00	3,075.00			
14-Feb-14	Big Chairs Ltd	EFT	Invoice A01	1,353.00	1,353.00			
15-Feb-14	Office Supplies	EFT	Ref 145	123.00	123.00			
				7,003.00	5,781.00	800.00	380.00	42.00

Based on the above Charlie can calculate the total VAT liability as follows:

Sales VAT for January to February: €4,692.00
Purchase VAT for January to February: €1,579.45
VAT liability: €3,112.55

The VAT liability figure of €3,112.55 is the total value of VAT that Charlie owes. If Charlie is calculating and paying VAT on the standard VAT calculation basis then the VAT liability is the same as the VAT due for payment. Charlie would complete the VAT return online and it would look similar to that shown in Figure A.9.

Figure A.9
VAT Return – Standard VAT Calculation

VAT Return - Jan Feb			
VAT on Sales		T1	4,692.00
VAT on Purchases		T2	1,579.45
VAT	Net payable	T3	3,112.55
VAT	Net repayable	T4	0.00
Total goods to other EU countries		E1	0.00
Total goods from other EU countries		E2	0.00

NOTE: ROS (revenue online service), does not require the cent values to be input.

If Charlie is paying VAT based on the cash basis of VAT calculation then the VAT due for payment will be as detailed below:

Calculation – cash basis (see above for detailed explanation)
Charlie can track sales VAT actually paid by adding additional columns to the sales daybook to record payments from customers received, see Figure A.10.

Charlie can identify from the extended sales daybook that he has received €3,381.00 worth of VAT from his customers during the VAT period. He can also identify that he is still due €7,011 from his customers at the end of February.

Figure A.10   Sales Daybook Extended to Record Customer Payments

SALES DAYBOOK

DATE	CUSTOMER	INVOICE NO.	NET	VAT 23%	GROSS	Total Amount Paid	Paid	VAT Due	Balance due
03-Jan-14	Mr Philips	1001	3,000.00	690.00	3,690.00	3,690.00	02-Feb-14	690.00	0.00
04-Jan-14	Fanfare Ltd	1002	7,500.00	1,725.00	9,225.00	9,225.00	02-Feb-14	1,725.00	0.00
11-Jan-14	Aztec Ltd	1003	3,300.00	759.00	4,059.00	4,059.00	20-Feb-14	759.00	0.00
15-Jan-14	Zero Ltd	1004	900.00	207.00	1,107.00	1,107.00	22-Feb-14	207.00	0.00
02-Feb-14	John Smith	1005	600.00	138.00	738.00				738.00
20-Feb-14	Hitz Ltd	1006	3,250.00	747.50	3,997.50				3,997.50
22-Feb-14	Hire All Ltd	1007	1,400.00	322.00	1,722.00				1,722.00
25-Feb-14	Ms Anne Jones	1008	450.00	103.50	553.50				553.50
			20,400.00	4,692.00	25,092.00	18,081.00		3,381.00	7,011.00

Charlie can also identify the sales VAT paid from the data contained in the bank receipts book.

Charlie reviews his bank receipts book and identifies that his customers paid him in total for January and February €18,081 (see above bank receipts book and ensure you can identify this figure). The figure of €18,081 is the total of payments made by his customers and includes VAT charged by Charlie. Charlie needs to calculate how much of the €18,081 relates to VAT. To calculate the VAT amount Charlie does the following calculation:

€18,081 = 123%, therefore €18,081 divided by 123 = 1%, i.e., €147.
€147 is 1%, therefore to get the VAT at 23% it is necessary to multiply €147 x 23 = €3,381.00
Of the €18,081 received €3,381 is sales VAT.

Charlie reviews his purchases daybook and identifies purchase VAT of €1,559.90
Charlie reviews his petty cash book and identifies purchase VAT of €19.55 (see above daybooks and ensure you can identify these figures).

Total of purchase VAT: €1,579.45

Based on the above Charlie can calculate the total VAT due for payment as follows:

Sales VAT for January to February: €3,381.00
Less purchase VAT for January to February: €1,579.45
VAT due for payment for period January to February: €1,801.55

Based on the calculation of VAT on the cash basis; Charlie establishes he needs to pay €1,801.55 of VAT from a total VAT liability of €3,112.55.

Charlie would complete the VAT return online and it would look similar to that shown in Figure A.11.

> NOTE: ROS (revenue online service), does not require the cent values to be input.

MICRO QUIZ

Q1: The VAT registration threshold is the same for a service business and a product-based business.
>   True or False?

Q2: There are never any benefits arising from voluntary VAT registration.
>   True or False?

Q3: If a business is below the VAT threshold it is possible for the business

Figure A.11
VAT Return – Cash Basis VAT Calculation

VAT Return - Jan Feb					
VAT on Sales				T1	3,381.00
VAT on Purchases				T2	1,579.45
VAT	Net payable			T3	1,801.55
VAT	Net repayable			T4	0.00
Total goods to other EU countries				E1	0.00
Total goods from other EU countries				E2	0.00

to voluntarily register for VAT.

    True or False?

Q4: The standard rate of VAT is currently 13.5%.

    True or False?

Q5: Another name for the standard VAT method of calculation is the invoice basis.

    True or False?

Q6: A VAT trading return is due to be filed every month.

    True or False?

Q7: Records and documents detailing the composition of VAT returns must be maintained by the business.

    True or False?

Q8: VAT calculated using the cash basis can give a cash-flow advantage over VAT calculated using the invoice basis.

    True or False?

Q9: There are no financial penalties for late payment of VAT.

    True or False?

Q10: VAT records need to be retained for a three-year period.

    True or False?

Micro quiz – solutions

Q1: False	Q6: False
Q2: False	Q7: True
Q3: True	Q8: True
Q4: False	Q9: False
Q5: True	Q10: False

FURTHER INFORMATION

There is a wealth of information available on the Internet concerning bookkeeping, tax and accounting. Here is a list of some of the more useful websites available at the time of going to press.

Association of Accounting Technicians – www.aat.org.uk
Association of Chartered Certified Accountants – www.accaglobal.com
Chartered Institute of Management Accountants – www.cimaglobal.com
The Institute of Chartered Accountants in England and Wales – www.icaew.com
The Association of Taxation Technicians – www.att.org.uk
HM Revenue & Customs – www.hmrc.gov.uk
Government information – www.gov.uk/business
Federation of Small Businesses – www.fsb.org.uk
Institute of Certified Bookkeepers – www.bookkeepers.org.uk
How to books – www.howtobooks.co.uk
Revenue Commissioners – www.revenue.ie
Irish Small and Medium Enterprises - www.isme.ie
Enterprise Boards – www.enterpriseboards.ie
Small Firms Association – www.sfa.ie
Irish Tax Institute – www.taxinstitute.ie
Accounts Direct – www.accountsdirect.ie

Index